UNCOMMON SENSE

THE REAL AMERICAN MANIFESTO

WRITTEN BY A REAL-AMERICAN

Library of Congress Cataloging-in-Publication Data

Murray, William James, 1942-1992.
    Uncommon Sense: The Real American
    Manifesto by William James Murray.
    p.   cm.
    ISBN 0-922356-95-5 : $6.95
    1. United States–History–Revolution, 1775-
    1783–Causes. 2. United States–History
    –Revolution, 1775-1783–Influence. 3. United
    States–Politics and government–Philosophy.
    4.National characteristics, American.
    5. United States–Civilization.
    I. Title.
E209.M88 1994   94-27822
973.3'11"–dc20   CIP

Published by
AMERICA WEST PUBLISHERS
P.O. Box 3300
Bozeman, MT 59772

Printed in the United States of America
10 9 8 7 6 5 4 3 2 1

DEDICATION
To the Creator of the Real-American spirit

Contents

Introduction

What kind of American are you?

Does this question confuse you? It should. Americans are experiencing an identity crisis. They don't understand who they are. Worse yet, they don't understand who they are supposed to be.

You love our great country, are proud to be an American, and consider yourself patriotic, right? But could you give anyone a good definition of the words "patriotism" or "Americanism" if your life depended on it? And, believe it or not, it does. And there's only one accurate definition for each word.

Basically you feel patriotic by instinct, coming from your heart, not from your brain, because NOT to feel patriotic about your country is simply unthinkable, isn't it?

You outwardly manifest your patriotism only when you stand up for the Star Spangled Banner at ballgames because everyone else does, or when you attend Fourth of July fireworks, or when you fly the flag occasionally, or when you vote occasionally, or when you join the military service. It's doubtful whether you can think of one more time. Granted, this doesn't mean that you are a bad American, but it doesn't mean that you are a good American either.

Can you recite the only accurate definition, in a political sense, of the world "freedom," which requires that you NOT use the word "free" or "freedom" in the definition?

As a so-called American, you take your freedom for granted because you inherited it. Who ever appreciates what they haven't earned? Others earned freedom for you, starting at Lexington and Concord, paying for it in lead and blood. Those heroic revolutionaries are tossing in their hallowed graves because you are squandering away what cost them their lives. Ever wonder if you would have stood to fire the shots heard 'round the world?

What kind of American are you?

There exists an identity crisis in these United States. This book intends to help so-called Americans resolve it by helping them to answer two personal questions: what kind of American am I now, and what kind of American do I really want to be?

You will have only three choices: a Real-American, a Pseudo-American, or a Socialist-American. That's all. There are no other choices. Never will be, ever.

Real-Americans are philosophical descendants of revolutionaries like George Washington, Thomas Jefferson, Patrick Henry, Molly Pitcher, and Tom Paine, who all loved freedom enough to fight for it.

Pseudo-Americans are philosophical descendants of the cowardly colonial neutrals, who all refused to take a stand for either side during our entire Revolution.

Socialist-Americans are philosophical descendants of English King George, the colonial Tories or Loyalists, and traitor Benedict Arnold, who all loved governmental power and who wished to use it to control other people's lives.

Outside of the RA's, PA's, and SA's mentioned above, every other description of our people hides their true identity. Words to identify so-called Americans such as liberal, conservative, Republican, Democrat, leftwinger, rightwinger, union, non-union, and others, are totally useless and should be ignored. Drop them from your vocabulary.

This could be the most challenging and disturbing book that you could ever read in your lifetime. After reading it, you could possibly consider it an unforgivable sin to refer to yourself or any fellow citizen using the stand-alone title of "American," because you could see the point of using the revealing titles of Real-American, Pseudo-American, or Socialist-American.

What kind of American are you? What is your true identity? You can't hide any more. It's time to take sides. The Second American Revolution is starting. You will be part of the problem or part of the solution.

Part I
THE REVOLUTION

Chapter 1

The Cause

> *There is nothing so powerful as truth, and*
> *often nothing so strange.*
> —*Daniel Webster*

What really caused the American Revolution, our War for Independence? Do you remember?

Have you ever had a serious argument, or disagreement, or verbal fight with someone? Have you ever almost had a physical fist fight? Have you ever participated in an actual fist fight? It was all pretty scary, wasn't it? Dry mouth, sick stomach, trembling, disbelief, the fear of actual pain of physical injury or disfigurement, etc.

Fights of any kind are usually caused by a bully who is trying somehow to take advantage of you—a bully who is mentally or physically pushing you around.

A fight usually occurs between a bully and a bully's victim. The bully could be a total stranger, or someone you know, like a friend, neighbor, boss, partner, fellow worker, or a relative.

When confronted by a bully, normal people have three options: give in, argue, or fight. Said another way: submit, resist, or fight. Said another way: surrender, negotiate, or fight.

Decent people fight as a last resort.

The basic principles involved in an individual physical fight are exactly the same as those involved in the bigger physical fight called war. War is simply a physical fight on a larger scale between a bully country and its victim country, and for the exact same reason: one is trying to take advantage of the other. And the victim finally decides to fight.

No matter what phony excuses for war are offered by the bully country to its own people who have to fight it, greed is usually the underlying cause of war. Whose greed? Obviously the greed of the bullies who control the stooges who run the government.

Greed is defined as an excessive desire for anything, but is commonly thought of as an excessive desire for the identical twins of wealth and power. The key word here is "excessive." Greed is excessive desire, not normal desire. Greed is not a sin of the "have nots," but a sin common among the "haves." If you have little, and want more, you have normal desire. If you have a lot, and want a lot more, you have excessive desire and are greedy.

Alexander the Great had conquered the then known world and wept when there was no more territory for him to conquer. Think his desire was excessive?

Also, forget all of the cover-up explanations peddled by historians, sociologists, journalists, and psychologists about insane madmen causing wars. These so-called madmen, as leaders of their countries living high on the hog, are not insane. In fact, they're very sane. They've tasted wealth and power and like it so much so that they want a lot more of it. They're just greedy and willing tools of the greedy. They're just bullies and willing tools of bullies.

Why all this talk about greed and bullies? Because greed and bullies cause all wars. They caused the

American War for Independence—our Revolution.

Old England was taking advantage of her thirteen colonies situated across the Atlantic Ocean in the new England. The English colonists of the new England first submitted, then argued, then fought. The colonists submitted as Englishmen, argued as Englishmen, fought FIRST as Englishmen, but then as Americans.

How was the old England taking advantage of the new England in North America? Here is the story in brief, and the main culprits were the big businessmen of the old England, organized into groups then called Trading Companies. These companies carried on foreign trade, shipping, and export-import businesses. Today we'd call them giant conglomerates or multinational companies, or simply big business.

Big businessmen are always so wealthy and powerful. They like to have things their own way, and always try to get it that way. Most big businessmen tend to be greedy, and most big businessmen tend to be bullies. Does this fact surprise you? Welcome to the real world. You probably never got real familiar with someone who rides in a chauffeur-driven Rolls Royce and lives in a mansion located on a thousand acres with servants.

Greedy bullies don't like competition. They like monopolies which they control. The big English businessmen operating the trading companies got rich for a hundred years by keeping the English colonists as captive customers and docile employees. They had a monopoly. Trading company profits began to drop when the English colonists began to produce goods for themselves, and to sell those goods among themselves, and to sell those goods to foreign markets, in essence, when the English colonists became competitors with the trading companies. The bottom line was this: rivalry in trade provoked the long quarrel which resulted in the American Revolution.

Man had always dreamed for centuries of discovering a promised land dripping with free-for-the-taking milk and honey, and gold and silver. But the flat earth theory deterred Europeans from sailing the uncharted ocean to find it. Then the voyage of Christopher Columbus proved the round earth theory. His stories of red-skinned natives adorned with gold and fabulous wealth excited the imaginations of others to go and do likewise.

English big businessmen dreamed of planting colonies of people in the new land for two reasons. First, the English colonists in the new land would be their employees who would produce raw materials, like timber, furs, foods, and precious metals and minerals, which the big businessmen could import into old England to there be converted into finished products for sale to domestic customers in the old England and around the world. Second, their employees in the new land would also become captive foreign customers to whom the English big businessmen could export and sell finished products like wood, furniture, clothing, jewelry, tools, ships, etc. The English big businessmen in the trading companies expected the English colonists to remain two things: employees and customers buying from the company store.

English big businessmen were lured by the idea of fabulous profits which they felt lay in the foreign trading business. To accomplish their goals, they realized that they had to build more and more ships, and master control of the seas. And they looked to the new England across the ocean to supply the shipbuilding products, especially lumber for shipbottoms and poles for ship masts.

The English kings and queens encouraged the English big businessmen to form trading companies to exploit foreign markets, so these businessmen could be able to supply the old England with so many new products in abundance to increase the standard of living of themselves and their subjects. Monarchs in other countries also followed similar patterns for the same reasons.

So the crowns granted charters to the trading companies to stimulate their trading activities. Granted that some charters were given to religious sects apparently for the purpose of religious liberty, but most were granted to big businessmen in trading companies for the purposes of trade. Some of the trading companies which participated in the founding of the English colonies in the new England in the 1600's were the London Company, the Plymouth Company, and the Massachusetts Bay Company.

The trading company big businessmen had a monopolistic mentality. These big businessmen required that their new world employees produce everything for the trading company, and nothing for themselves. They desired the exclusive monopoly to control all of the raw material gathering, manufacturing, trading, and selling functions. They also fixed all prices, wages, and trading policies.

The bottom line was this: the English big businessmen trading companies expected their English colonists to work exclusively for the prosperity of the old English big businessmen, in particular, and the mother country in general, and never for their own prosperity. Never.

Adventurers who risk disease and horribly excruciating death by drowning to travel cooped-up like sardines across 3,000 miles of an unpredictable ocean on a sailboat for a few months, are not exactly the type of people you should expect to control for life. These early settlers were willing to face extreme hardships, painful freezing, belly-swelling starvation, and head-splitting tomahawks once they reached their destination. These were brave people who scorned fear, had a self-reliant and courageous attitude, and who thought they could make it. Not the type of people you should expect to remain your loyal employees for life. You just can't keep good people down for very long.

These early English settlers, these English colonists, loyally continued to fulfill their rightful obligation to the trading company businessmen who sent them to the new land, but for their own survival and to improve their own living conditions, most sooner or later saw the personal benefits to moonlighting or going into business for themselves. They started to grow their own food, to hunt and trap wild game for themselves, and to manufacture their own clothing, furniture and tools, instead of buying every essential from the trading company businessmen who imported these items from the old England. Each family tried hard to become a self-sufficient unit, indeed a family factory. If they produced extra, they sold the extra to their neighbors. They even began to build their own ships to transport the extras to sell these goods to their neighbors in other colonies.

The more self-sufficient in goods the settlers became, they naturally bought less goods from the trading company businessmen. The businessmen running the trading companies were losing customers and profits.

And once the settlers began to sell their extras to their neighbors, former trading company employees and customers were becoming trading company competitors. Big businessmen everywhere hate competition and will do anything necessary to destroy it to maintain their monopoly.

The northern colonies had rocky soil and long, cold winters; the southern colonies had richer soil and warmer climate. The early settlers in the northern colonies consequently specialized in fishing, manufacturing, and shipbuilding, while their neighbors in the southern colonies specialized in farming, ranching and raising tobacco, cotton and rice.

During the icy winters, when fishing drops off, northern colonists loaded their ships with salt, molasses, cloth, hats, stockings, iron kettles, wooden bowls, and rugs made in their homes and little shops and sailed to the southern colonies to trade these items for southern products like pork, corn, rice, tobacco, tar for shipbuilding, and leather. Colonists in Massachusetts used the leather to manufacture saddles and shoes which they then sold back to southern colonists. Domestic trading gradually evolved into a booming business, and every colonist's standard of living rose.

English big businessmen in the trading companies complained loudly that the colonists were not buying enough of their exports from the mother country, but were trading among themselves. Trouble was brewing.

Then ambitious colonists had the further audacity to act like free men by initiating foreign trade and began to sell their tobacco, cotton, sugar, and other goods to Spain and other foreign countries, thus further cutting into the trading company businessmen's pockets. These colonists delivered their goods to their foreign customers in ships they built themselves, not in ships bought or leased from trading company business-men. The colonists engaged in foreign trade were able to price their goods more competitively than trading company businessmen since they delivered their goods directly to the foreign country without ever docking in old England's ports where they would be forced to pay taxes and customs duties on all their merchan-dise, which would result in higher price tags on those goods for foreign customers.

English big businessmen became so incensed at this colonial competition and their subsequent loss of prof-its, that they published their official position that colo-nial traders must be stopped, and that these new English colonists must be forced somehow to work exclusively for the prosperity of the old English big businessmen, and the mother country.

The book explaining this English big businessmen's official position was entitled, "A New Discourse of Trade," written by Sir Josiah Child, chairman of the East India Company, and published in London in 1694. One paragraph in his book just about told the whole story. He wrote:

> *"Many of our American commodities, espe-cially tobacco and sugar, are transported directly in NEW ENGLISH shipping to Spain and other foreign countries without being landed in En-gland, or paying duty to His Majesty. This is a loss to the King, to the navigation of OLD EN-GLAND, and to the English merchant in those ports where NEW ENGLISH vessels trade. Since no custom dues are paid in NEW ENGLAND, and great custom paid in OLD ENGLAND, the NEW*

ENGLISH merchant will be able to sell cheaper than the OLD ENGLISH merchant. And those who sell cheaper will get the whole trade sooner or later.''

Big businessmen everywhere are monopoly lovers. They want it all, and hate competition. If they can't beat the competition fair and square, their bully nature surfaces and they become willing to play dirty to get the job done.

Playing dirty means using their great power and wealth to buy control of the people who run their government, and make the laws. Once they buy the people who run the government, these big businessmen instruct their government lackeys to pass laws to hurt their competitors badly. This is standard operating procedure for all big businessmen for the last 2,000 years, and is commonly referred to as ''The Big Business Trick.'' Big businessmen always control the governments in their respective countries. It is never the other way around, no matter how it ever looks. That's why it's called a trick.

No business monopoly can exist for very long without government being an accomplice. Government is the only culprit which can keep a monopoly alive. Think about that.

The rich English big businessmen in the trading companies of the mother country decided to play dirty. They were greedy, and decided to act like bullies. They decided to use The Big Business Trick. They bought control of the people running Parliament, and had their lackeys in Parliament pass restrictive laws governing all colonial shipping and trade. These laws became known as the Navigation Acts, whose purpose was to make old English big businessmen richer at the expense of the colonists.

The Scrooges of this world are very real people. Few of these bastards ever get miraculously converted.

The Navigation Acts and other laws passed by the big businessmen-controlled Parliament were designed to destroy the shipping and manufacturing capabilities of the colonies, and to thereby force the colonists to buy everything from the old English big businessmen, and to sell everything to them also. These oppressive laws were designed to make the colonists again dependent on the old English big businessmen.

The Navigation Acts passed by the big-business-bought Parliament made it illegal for foreign vessels to bring goods directly to the colonies. These laws stipulated that all European goods bound for the colonies had to be shipped to old England first, where duty had to be paid before the goods could be re-shipped to the colonies. These laws stipulated that all goods going to the colonies had to be shipped only in old English vessels, manned by old English subjects. These laws forbid the colonists to trade with foreign countries except under impossible restrictions. These laws forbid the colonists to ship tobacco, cotton, and other items to any other country but old England. These laws forbid the colonists to import sheep, so they would lack wool to manufacture clothing. Other laws forbid the colonists to manufacture any items which the old English big businessmen were exporting and selling to the colonists. All raw materials for such items which the colonists produced had to be sold to old English big businessmen. And any colonial vessel caught in "illegal" trade on the high seas would be confiscated along with its cargo, and its crew would be arrested.

The old English big businessmen-controlled Parliament had passed laws creating a legal monopoly for old English big businessmen.

The King's officers in the colonies began armed searches of the colonists' homes looking for ''smuggled goods,'' meaning anything not imported legally from old England. They would confiscate any ''contraband'' they found, and then proceed to arrest the owner, who would have to await trial by judges sent to the colonies from old England. The match was lit and moving closer to the fuse.

Throughout all of human history, there has always been two types of prostitutes. You are familiar with the existence of sexually promiscuous men and women who sell their bodies for pay. This is the relatively harmless type, at least before herpes and AIDS. Compared to the other type, these sexual prostitutes are kittens, who are not bullies trying to push you around.

The other type of prostitute is as dangerous as a tiger, and is a bully who DOES try to push you around. This life-threatening prostitute is a government bureaucrat. This type of prostitute sells its body, AND its mind and soul for pay.

Sexual prostitutes deliver a service of perceived value. Bureaucrat prostitutes deliver nothing of value.

Bureaucrat prostitutes love for the government to pass new laws and regulations which need enforcing because these new rules create paying jobs for these whores. This deadly type of prostitute is an inferior creature who cannot ''make it'' in the real world. Without the government, these parasites might starve. These weaklings worship their one, true god of perpetual job security with the government. These bureaucrat prostitutes are either stupid, lazy bums or sadists who love to persecute their victims. And the most dedicated sadists get promoted.

Bureaucrat prostitutes are bullies and cowards who need the authority of government to operate. They never concern themselves with concepts of right or wrong, truth or justice, because they sold their consciences to the government. They rationalize that they are "just doing their jobs" and that "they don't make the rules." Bureaucrats can put human beings in gas chambers and sleep well at night because they are "just doing their jobs." Without bureaucrats, there could never be tyrants. Think about that.

If you've never had a bad personal experience with government bureaucrats, it might be difficult for you to understand their mentality. Comparing government bureaucrats with their next of kin, their kissing cousins, the corporate bureaucrats, might be helpful.

Corporate bureaucrats have much in common with government bureaucrats. Corporate bureaucrats sell their bodies, minds, and souls to the corporation, and if you work for them, they are also dangerous to your health, security, and freedom. They are company men and women, organization people. They sell out for a bigger paycheck, and make a career of dodging bullets by directing them at you. They are also bullies who worship at the shrine of job security. When they persecute you, they also rationalize that they are "just doing their jobs" and that "they don't make the rules." Like government bureaucrats, corporate bureaucrats have no hearts, and are as warm as penguins. In modern times, these types often tend to gravitate towards the data processing areas, or the human resources departments, among others. They work hardest at justifying their existence, and scoring brownie points with their superiors. Back then, corporate bureaucrats in the old English trading companies worked closely with their cousins, the government bureaucrats, in the old English government to enforce the obnoxious new laws on the colonists.

Government bureaucrats and corporate bureaucrats of the world have given human beings a bad name, and have largely been responsible for swelling the ranks of animal lovers. Soldiers and policemen are a slightly different story and present a unique dilemma. They are really the only legitimate government employees, and should not technically be classified as government bureaucrats.

Soldiers and policemen have a valid purpose for their existence: to protect the God-given rights of the people. But unfortunately, soldiers and policemen do possess some of the undesirable traits of the bureaucrats, with the worst being the mindless execution of orders. Government bureaucrats deserve no respect, but soldiers and policemen do because they are not cowards. On the contrary, they are brave. They literally risk their lives everyday they wear their uniforms. They hate the bad guys, love the good guys, and wish to protect the good people from the bad people. Their motivation is purer than the motivation of bureaucrats, and their purpose is perverted by their bosses, and when this occurs, soldiers and policemen themselves become front-line victims of government legislators and bureaucrats.

It is a sad fact to contemplate how soldiers and policemen become tools in the hands of big-business-men-bought legislators and government bureaucrats when they are ordered to enforce unjust laws on the good guys, instead of just laws on the bad guys. Such unjust law enforcement tragically gets them injured or killed. Such was the fate of the Redcoats who were eventually to die unknowingly for the prosperity of the old English big businessmen.

As the colonists attempted to comply with the obnoxious new laws, or shucked, jived, and boogied to stay in business without getting caught in violations, it became expensive for the old English to enforce all of the rules. More law enforcement officers and bureaucrats were needed by the old English to watch, chase, and harass the naughty colonists, because targeted victims invent ingenious methods of evasion, and a moving target is harder to hit. And guile is a virtue when necessity knows no law.

Do you think the old English big businessmen were stupid enough to absorb this increased cost of enforcement? No way. So who was supposed to pay? Guess. The victims, of course.

There are always two parts to the Big Business Trick, like a double barreled shotgun. The first barrel is to buy the lawmakers into passing the laws to destroy big business's competition. The second barrel is to have the lawmakers tax the intended victims so the controlled government can generate enough money to afford to pay the salaries of the army of soldiers, police, and bureaucrats needed for the enforcement of the victims' destruction.

So the controlled Parliament began levying taxes on the colonial victims to pay for their own subjugation, taxes on imported glass, paper, paints, magazines, newspapers, and tea.

The taxes, the Boston Massacre, and the Boston

Tea Party lit the fuse. The explosion occurred at Lexington and Concord and our revolution for freedom had begun.

At sunrise at Lexington on Wednesday, April 19, 1775, about a hundred colonists stood firm with loaded muskets, facing over 400 Redcoats. Major Pitcairn, the Redcoat officer in charge, yelled out, "Disperse, you villians! Lay down your arms!" The colonists did not budge. When Pitcairn gave the order for the Redcoats to surround the rebels, the shots heard 'round the world were fired. Three Redcoats lay wounded, but eight rebels were killed.

This was the first battle of our Revolution. Why did it happen? Burn this answer into your soul: the English came to get our guns. That's right. The English came to disarm their victims to destroy their potential to resist the growing tyranny. Never forget this. Whenever a government sends its agents to disarm you, it is the Universal Signal to shoot with a clear conscience, needing no one's permission but your own. The example of Lexington and Concord perfectly illustrates a fundamental principle of Americanism, which is: NEVER GIVE UP YOUR GUNS. NEVER.

Your gun is the Great Bully Equalizer. Better to have one and not need it, than to need one and not have it. With your gun, you are seven feet tall, and weigh 300 pounds. Without your gun, you are a pansy pushover. Every bully wants you to be disarmed in order to be able to freely take advantage of you, whether that bully is a common criminal, or a bully agent sent by your own government.

Would you try to push someone around if you thought that they were carrying a gun? Our founders understood this vital connection between firearms and human freedom and security. They knew that you could not have the one without the other. To guarantee each American's freedom and security from being oppressed by his own government for all times, our founders passed the Second Amendment to our Constitution which affirms that "the right of the people to keep and BEAR arms shall not be infringed." Our founders obviously meant that no American would ever need anyone's permission to carry a gun whenever and wherever he or she pleased. A fundamental principle of Americanism is this: all gun laws against non-criminals are un-American.

Our founders understood that the only realistic antidote to the government's potentially oppressive army and police was an armed citizenry. This is the main purpose of the Second Amendment.

Returning to our story, the English had learned that our rebels had stockpiled their guns and ammunition in the town of Concord. English General Gage dispatched some of his Redcoats from Boston around midnight on Tuesday, April 18th, to march on Concord to capture the rebels' military supplies. But our rebels were alerted to the Redcoats' purpose for coming by Paul Revere's famous ride, shouting "the British are coming," and decided that "disarmament" was the straw that always breaks the camel's back. The resistance our rebels offered at Lexington bought them the time they needed to hide their military supplies in the woods at Concord.

After the skirmish at Lexington, the Redcoats marched on Concord, destroyed what they could find as our rebels resisted, and then Pitcairn ordered a retreat back to Boston. All along the retreat, our rebels fired on the Redcoats. That day, April 19, 1775, the Redcoats lost 65 killed, 183 wounded, with 28 taken as prisoners. Our rebels lost 49 killed, 39 wounded, with 5 missing. The War had begun.

Chapter 2

Reformers and Revolutionaries

> *A coward dies a thousand deaths.*
> *A brave person dies but one.*
> —*Chinese proverb*

Reformers and revolutionaries are similar types of people because both attempt to change the system of government that they live under.

Reformers and revolutionaries are dedicated people, motivated people, activist people. They are agents of change, and change agents are willing to pay a price to achieve their goals. That price is time, energy, money, or their lives. The degree of their intelligence and the degree of their courage eventually determines how much of their time, energy, money, and lives they are willing to spend and risk in the pursuit of their objectives. In other words, the degree of their conviction and commitment is directly dependent upon the degree of their intelligence and courage.

Every reformer and every revolutionary claims to be working for the good of the people. Every reformer and every revolutionary claims nothing but good intentions. But you can never trust their rhetoric and propaganda.

Forget intentions. Results count more than intentions. People may intend to help you, but they may actually hurt you. People may intend to hurt you, but they may actually help you. Intentions are academic, debatable, uncertain, irrelevant, unprovable, and often forever undiscoverable. So who cares? Whereas results are what you live with. Good intentions do not change bad results. The results remain. Intentions are subjective. Results are objective. The results are the bottom line. Results count more than intentions.

The important question in this connection is this: if the reformers or revolutionaries win, and if the reformations or revolutions succeed in changing the form of the existing government, are the new living conditions for the people better or worse than before the change? Results count more than intentions.

Reformers and revolutionaries are similar types of people because both attempt to change their existing system of government. But reformers and revolutionaries differ in their use of methods.

Reformers use the peaceful method of voting to achieve a change in their government. Revolutionaries use the violent method of shooting to achieve a change in their government. Reformers are patient and believe in the ballot box. Revolutionaries have lost their patience and believe in the cartridge box. Reformers use ballots. Revolutionaries use bullets.

Reformers maintain a respectable image with the people because of their non-violent approach, while people usually consider revolutionaries to be fanatics because they are willing to kill their enemies if necessary. People usually consider reformers as the loyal opposition or moderates, and usually consider revolutionaries to be radicals and extremists.

Legislative bodies make the laws, while executive branches enforce the laws. When the big business-controlled Parliament began making oppressive laws for the colonists, the executive leader, King George, in complete agreement with Parliament, enforced these oppressive laws against the colonists. King George especially approved of the obnoxious new tax laws so that he would be able to afford to pay his new law enforcement agents.

To their credit, America's founders first resisted the old English tyranny as reformers. They pleaded and petitioned the King and Parliament for reasonableness and mercy for endless years. But their cries were basically falling on deaf ears.

The colonists had no representation in the big business-controlled Parliament. The straw that broke the proverbial camel's back, converting our reformers into revolutionaries, was the gradual realization that they would never be able to vote themselves out of their mess. The colonists had long sought legislative representation in the old English Parliament in order to be able to defend their rights by voting, and to be able to eventually control their own destiny. But to gain a seat in Parliament, the rules required that you must reside in old England, and King George and Parliament adamantly refused to change the rules. Consequently, the colonists were left with the choices to surrender and suffer, or to fight by shooting.

Had the King and Parliament granted the colonists' desire for representation to be able to eventually have a beneficial effect on their own destiny, the American Revolution may never have occurred. But the King and the big business-controlled Parliament remained bullies. A leopard doesn't change its spots. Bullies taking advantage have two mottos for their victims: never give a victim an even break, and I dare you to fight.

And fight the colonist did. They were pushed into becoming revolutionaries, fanatics, radicals, and extremists in their rightful attempt to restore their lost freedoms.

Is it difficult for you to consider George Washington a revolutionary, a fanatic, a radical, and an extremist? Well, he was. All revolutionaries are. Have you ever thought of George Washington as a revolutionary? Or all of our founders as revolutionaries? Well, they all were. Think about that.

Our founders shot and were shot at. They killed and were killed — for 8 years. Eight years of a shooting war! Can you believe it? Eight years of bloody revolution. Incredible. America was founded on red-running blood in 308 battles. Think about that.

Forget intentions. What were the results produced by these violent American revolutionaries? History proves that the results produced were the most glorious freedom, fantastic material abundance, and phenomenally better living conditions for the American people than man had ever experienced throughout all of recorded human history, because our founders created a true republic.

Non-violent reformers who prefer voting to shooting do NOT become violent revolutionaries overnight. But when reformers finally reach the conclusion that reform will never succeed, revolution is inevitable. Each reformer has a different straw, a different mental Rubicon. Each reformer takes his or her own good time in arriving at such a drastic conclusion. Decent people exhaust every available option before deciding to physically fight.

Perhaps the taxation issue converted reformer John Dickinson into a revolutionary. In a letter he wrote which was published in a Pennsylvania newspaper, he said this in 1768:

"Let these truths be indelibly impressed on your minds—that we cannot be happy without being free—that we cannot be free without being secure in our property—that we cannot be secure in our property, if, without our consent, others may as by right take it away.

Here then, let my countrymen ROUSE themselves, and behold the ruin hanging over their heads. If they ONCE admit, that Great Britain may lay duties upon her exportations to us, FOR THE PURPOSE OF LEVYING MONEY ON US ONLY, she then will have nothing to do, but to lay those duties on the articles which she prohibits us to manufacture—and the tragedy of American liberty is finished."

What straw broke Patrick Henry's back, we may never know for sure. Perhaps it was the obnoxious taxes the English laid on the colonists without allowing colonial representation in the English Parliament. "Taxation without representation is tyranny" had become a widespread revolutionary slogan throughout all of the colonies.

Perhaps the English reaction to the Boston Tea Party was the straw for Patrick Henry. Just before Christmas in 1773, three English ships loaded with tea were docked in Boston Harbor, but the English bureaucrats would not allow the tea to be unloaded until the Boston tea merchants paid all of the taxes on it first. The tea merchants wanted to pay all of the taxes later, after they sold the tea to the colonists, and IF they could sell it. The tea merchants were afraid of assuming the risk of losing money because they feared that the colonists might not buy the tea from them with the taxes attached. The merchants did not want unsalable tea in their inventory on which they would have already paid taxes, which tax money they wouldn't be able to recover from customers.

So now you should understand the principle that businessmen and businesswomen never pay taxes on the products and services that they sell. YOU DO. The customer always pays all of the taxes imposed by government. Whenever the government imposes a tax on any product or service, the businessperson simply passes the tax along to you, the customer. In addition, whenever the government imposes a new rule or regulation on the businessperson which will cost the businessperson money to comply with, the businessperson automatically raises the price on his products and services, and again passes along the new costs to you, the customer. So in essence, the businessperson never pays for any bureaucratic governmental action, but always keeps his or her profit margin intact, while you the customer always pay for all of the additional costs associated with the legislators and bureaucrats imposing new taxes on anything and new rules and regulations on the businessperson. Think about that.

In the particular case under discussion, and in protest of the Parliament tax laws, colonists (dressed like "wild Indians") boldly boarded the three tea ships in Boston Harbor and threw 342 chests of tea overboard, thus ruining the tea. When the English Parliament demanded that the colonists in Boston pay for the tea, the colonists refused. As a severe punishment, Parliament directed their soldiers and bureaucrats to close Boston Harbor to all vessels wishing to enter bringing essential foodstuffs and other critical supplies needed by Bostonians to survive. All Bostonians began to suffer. The English even sent warships to Boston with thousands of Redcoats which they forcibly housed in private homes, in order to enforce the closing edict. How would you like your police chief to visit you tonight to inform you that tomorrow you will have three policemen boarding in your house, OR ELSE. Nice, right?

So perhaps it was the Boston Harbor closing which was the straw that made reformer Patrick Henry a revolutionary. We may never know for sure, but he publicly announced that he had become a revolutionary on March 23, 1775 when he delivered his "We Must Fight" speech, just four weeks before Lexington and Concord. Read it here in its entirety:

"No man thinks more highly than I do of the patriotism, as well as abilities, of the very worthy gentlemen who have just addressed the house. But different men often see the same subject in different lights; and, therefore, I hope it will not be thought disrespectful to those gentlemen, if entertaining, as I do, opinions of a character very opposite to theirs, I shall speak forth my *sentiments freely, and without reserve. This is no time for ceremony. The question before the*

house is one of awful moment to this country. For my own part, I consider it as nothing less than a question of freedom or slavery. And in proportion to the magnitude of the subject, ought to be the freedom of debate. It is only in this way that we can hope to arrive at truth and fulfill the great responsibility which we hold to God and our country. Should I keep back my opinions at such a time through fear of giving offense, I should consider myself guilty of treason toward my country, and of an act of disloyalty toward the majesty of Heaven when I revere above all earthly kings.

Mr. President, it is natural for man to indulge in the illusions of hope. We are apt to shut our eyes against a painful truth — and listen to the song of the siren till she transforms us into beasts. Is this the part of wise men engaged in a great and arduous struggle for liberty? Are we disposed to be of the number of those who, having eyes, see not, and, having ears, hear not, the things which so nearly concern their temporal salvation? For my part, whatever anguish of spirit it might cost, I am willing to know the whole truth; to know the worst and provide for it.

I have but one lamp by which my feet are guided; and that is the lamp of experience. I know of no way of judging the future but by the past. And judging by the past, I wish to know what there has been in the conduct of the British ministry for the last ten years to justify those hopes with which gentlemen have been pleased to solace themselves and the house? Is it that insidious smile with which our petition has been lately received? Trust it not, sir; it will prove a snare to your feet. Suffer not yourselves to be betrayed with a kiss. Ask yourselves how this gracious reception of our petition comports with those warlike preparations which cover our waters and darken our land. Are fleets and armies necessary to a work of love and reconciliation? Have we shown ourselves so unwilling to be reconciled that force must be called in to win back our love? Let us not deceive ourselves, sir. These are the implements of war and subjugation—the last arguments to which kings resort. I ask gentlemen, sir, what means this martial array if its purpose be not to force us to submission? Can gentlemen assign any other possible motive for it? Has Great Britain any enemy in this quarter of the world to call for all this accumulation of navies and armies? No, sir, she has none. They are meant for us: they can be meant for no other. They are sent over to bind and rivet upon us those chains which the British Ministry have been so long forging. And what have we to oppose them? Shall we try argument? Sir, we have been trying that for the last ten years. Have we anything new to offer upon the subject? Nothing. We have held the subject up in every light of which it is capable; but it has been all in vain. Shall we resort to entreaty and humble supplication? What terms shall we find which have not been already exhausted? Let us not, I beseech you, sir, deceive ourselves longer. Sir, we have done everything that could be done to avert the storm which is now coming on. We have petitioned—we have remonstrated—we have supplicated—we have prostrated ourselves before the throne, and have implored its interposition to arrest the tyrannical hands of the ministry and Parliament. Our petitions have been slighted; our remonstrances have produced additional violence and insult; our supplications have been disregarded; and we have been spurned, with contempt, from the foot of the throne. In vain, after these things, may we indulge the fond hope of peace and reconciliation. There is no longer any room for hope. If we wish to be free—if we mean to preserve inviolate those inestimable privileges for which we have been so long contending—if we mean not basely to abandon the noble struggle in which we have been so long engaged, and which we have pledged ourselves never to abandon until the glorious object of our contest shall be obtained—we must fight! I repeat it, sir, we must fight!! An appeal to arms and to the God of Hosts is all that is left us!

They tell us, sir, that we are weak—unable to cope with so formidable an adversary. But when shall we be stronger? Will it be the next week, or the next year? Will it be when we are totally disarmed, and when a British guard shall be stationed in every house? Shall we gather strength by irresolution and inaction? Shall we acquire the means of effectual resistance by lying supinely on our backs, and hugging the delusive phantom of Hope, until our enemies shall have bound us hand and foot? Sir, we are not weak, if we make a proper use of those means which the God of nature hath placed in our power. Three millions

*of people, armed in the holy cause of liberty,
and in such a country as that which we possess,
are invincible by any force which our enemy can
send against us. Besides, sir, we shall not fight
our battles alone. There is a just God who presides
over the destinies of nations, and who will raise
up friends to fight our battles for us. The battle,
sir, is not to the strong alone; it is to the vigilant,
the active, the brave. Besides, sir, we have no
election. If we were base enough to desire it, it
is now too late to retire from the contest. There
is no retreat, but in submission and slavery! Our
chains are forged, their clanking may be heard
on the plains of Boston! The war is inevitable—
and let it come!! I repeat it, sir, let it come!!!*

*It is in vain, sir, to extenuate the matter. Gentle-
men may cry, peace, peace—but there is no peace.
The war is actually begun. The next gale that
sweeps from the North will bring to our ears
the clash of resounding arms! Our brethren are
already in the field! Why stand we here idle?
What is it that gentlemen wish? What would they
have? Is life so dear, or peace so sweet, as to
be purchased at the price of chains and slavery?
Forbid it, Almighty God! I know not what course
others may take; but as for me, give me liberty
or give me death!"*

The idea of reformation was dying quickly, as the
idea of revolution was being born. The idea of peaceful
change was dying, as the idea of violent change was
being born. Lexington and Concord became reform's
mortician and revolution's mid-wife.

When discussing a peaceful change of government

by voting (reformation), or when discussing a violent change of government by shooting (revolution), the key words to remember in this discussion are "political" or "social." There are only these two types of reformations and revolutions and no others.

The purpose of both a political reformation and a political revolution is MAXIMUM freedom for the people. On the contrary, the purpose of both a social reformation and a social revolution is MINIMUM freedom for the people. Freedom for the people is the goal of both a political reformation and a political revolution. Regimentation of the people is the goal of both a social reformation and a social revolution.

Successful political reformations and successful political revolutions both result in the people taking more control of their governments. Successful social reformations and successful social revolutions both result in the government taking more control of their people.

Political reformations and revolutions are the direct opposite of social reformations and revolutions. Social reformations and revolutions are the direct opposite of political reformations and revolutions.

After a successful political reformation or revolution, the people achieve more authority and control over the humans running their government. After a successful social reformation or revolution, the humans running the government achieve more authority and control over the people.

The main issue involved in either a reformation or a revolution is always this: who controls whom? Reformations or revolutions are always waged over the issue of freedom. Reformations or revolutions are always waged by reformers or revolutionaries to determine whether the humans running the government need permission to act from the people, or whether the people need permission to act from the humans running their government.

It is important for you to remember that our founders waged a political reformation, not a social reformation. Our founders waged a political revolution, not a social revolution. So they were trying to take charge of the government.

Our founders lost the political reformation, but won the political revolution. And America's revolution was the first successful political revolution in all of recorded human history.

Lovers or haters.

Political reformers and revolutionaries are lovers. Social reformers and revolutionaries are haters.

Political reformers and revolutionaries truly love mankind, man, and their fellow human beings. Social reformers and revolutionaries truly hate mankind, man, and their fellow human beings.

Political reformers and revolutionaries love people. Their attitude towards people is sympathetic and understanding. They have no desire to control other people's lives. They seek no governmental power to run other people's lives. They are humble, love their own privacy and respect others' privacy, and love freedom. They believe in the concepts of "live and let live" and the Golden Rule, and believe in gentle persuasion as the only legitimate tool to influence others' behavior. And they worship God.

Social reformers and revolutionaries hate people. Their attitude towards people is obnoxious, autocratic, and dictatorial. They desire to control other people's lives. They seek governmental power to run other people's lives in the manner that they think those lives should be run. They have a superiority complex. They think of themselves as smarter than most other people. They hate other people's privacy. They hate other people's freedom. They hate the concept of ''live and let live,'' and believe ONLY in governmental force to control everyone's behavior. They have a god complex, worship themselves, and hate you.

What type of reformer or revolutionary could you see yourself becoming—political or social? Think about that.

Social reformers and social revolutionaries are scum, and are thoroughly un-American.

Chapter 3

The Father of American Independence

*A prophet is never respected in his or her
own land.*   *—From the Bible*

As you know, Virginian Thomas Jefferson wrote
our Declaration of Independence. But most Americans
are unaware of how the doctrine of independence from
England was born, fertilized, and nurtured before the
idea blossomed into a legal reality on July 4, 1776.
This is the true story of the one man who made it
all happen.

There was a baby boy born in 1737 whose parents
gave him the first name of Thomas, and just one document he would later author would permanently change
the course of the world forever.

The beautiful state of Virginia has certainly produced more than its fair share of courageous founding
fathers. Virginian Patrick Henry is rightfully considered to be the VOICE of our Revolution, and Virginian
George Washington is rightfully considered to be the
SWORD. But this Tom born in 1737 must rightfully
be considered to be its PEN.

George Washington earned the title of Father of
our Country, but this Tom earned the title of Father
of American Independence.

For the past 200 years, no other American, except

this Tom, has had such phenomenally logical reasoning powers, combined with such a magnificent command of the English language to express his ideas on paper so simply, clearly, and understandably, and with the intense mental force of a sledgehammer smashing the reader's brains, agitating his blood, upsetting his stomach, piercing his soul, and producing in the reader hot anger leading to cold reserve, dedicated conviction, undying commitment, and finally, courageous action and resistance. How mere words can do this to people, nobody knows, unless the timing is right, expressing an idea whose time has come, to people who are ready to hear it.

No American would ever again write better than this Tom, ever. What this Tom wrote will always and forever represent the classic epitome of the truth of the saying that the pen is truly mightier than the sword. And adding to his glory, Tom had the unbelievable guts to write ideas down on paper which were a crime to express . . . ideas which had only been whispered among more timid souls for centuries.

But remember this: you could be disappointed if you expect Tom's writings to produce the same startling effects in your mind that they did in enough colonial minds. Reading now what Tom wrote back then during our Revolution could not possibly produce the same type of emotional effects in today's readers, because today's readers will naturally find Tom's writings to be "out of context," unless the readers possess super imaginations which enable them to understand and appreciate what it felt like to be alive in 1776. If you can imagine yourself "in the 1776 context," you will better catch the electric of what Tom was saying. In other words, timing is always everything, and Tom's writings were about as prophetically timed as is touching fire to gasoline.

The first shots of our Revolution were fired at Lexington and Concord in April of 1775, but our rebels were NOT fighting for independence from England. Did you realize that? Eight full months later, during our Commander-in-Chief's seige of Boston, George Washington holding a modest Christmas party with all of his officers present, would still raise his glass and offer the customary toast of well wishes to the King of England, which everyone drank to. And, of course, John Adams formally confirmed in his remarks preceding the vote on independence on July 4, 1776 that when our Revolution started, independence was NOT the original goal. And, of course, our independence was not declared until 14 months after Lexington and Concord. Did you realize that?

With war raging, but 6 months before our Declaration of Independence was written, Tom wrote things popularizing the idea of independence from England, and popularizing ideas about freedom, and analyzing why the mind tends to hold onto old ideas, and to resist new ones.

He said: "Perhaps the sentiments contained in the following pages, are not YET sufficiently fashionable to procure them general favor; a long habit of not thinking a thing WRONG, gives it a superficial appearance of being RIGHT, and raises at first a formidable outcry in defense of custom."

He said: "Society in every state is a blessing, but government even in its BEST state is but a necessary evil."

Remember now, at this time, practically everyone

accepted the "divine right of kings" without question, like they used to accept the "flat earth theory" without question.

Tom said: "There is something exceedingly ridiculous in the composition of monarchy; it first excludes a man from the means of information, yet empowers him to act in cases where the highest judgment is required. The state of a king shuts him from the world, yet the business of a king requires him to know it thoroughly; wherefore the different parts, by unnaturally opposing and destroying each other, prove the whole character to be absurd and useless."

He said: "But there is another and greater distinction, for which no truly natural or religious reason can be assigned, and that is, the distinction of men into KINGS and SUBJECTS. Male and female are the distinctions of nature, good and bad are distinctions of heaven; but how a race of men came into the world so exalted above the rest, and distinguished like some new species, is worth inquiring into, and whether they are the means of happiness or of misery to mankind."

He said: "In the early ages of the world, according to the scripture chronology, there were no kings; the consequence of which was, there were no wars; it is the pride of kings which throw mankind into confusion."

He said: "Government by kings was first introduced into the world by the Heathens, from whom the children of Israel copied the custom. It was the most prosperous invention the Devil ever set on foot for the promotion of idolatry. The Heathens paid divine honors to their deceased kings, and the Christian world hath improved on the plan, by doing the same to their living ones. How impious is the title of sacred majesty applied to a worm, who in the midst of his splendor is crumbling into dust!''

Tom's attacking the institution of monarchy (kings and queens) in 1776 was more devastating THEN to the minds of his colonial readers, than if an American writer dared to attack the institution of the Presidency today. For you to feel an emotional disturbance similar to the kind which Tom's attack on monarchy created in the minds and bellies of his readers in 1776, the following questions should be helpful.

If you are a Catholic, how would you feel after you read a Catholic writer's attack on the Pope? If you are a Protestant, how would you feel after you read a Protestant writer's attack on Billy Graham? If you are a Christian fundamentalist, how would you feel after you read a fundamentalist writer's attack on Pat Robertson? If you are a Jew, how would you feel after you read a Jewish writer's attack on your favorite rabbi?

What Tom was saying about monarchy was tantamount to his saying that the earth is round, before Columbus' voyage. Imagine the personal reactions.

Tom continued: ''. . . as no man at first could possess any other public honors than were bestowed upon him, so the givers of those honors could have no power to give away the right of posterity. And though they might say, 'We choose you (the king) for OUR head,' they could not, without manifest injustice to their children, say 'that your children and your children's children shall reign over OURS forever.' Because such an unwise, unjust, unnatural compact might (perhaps) in the next succession put them under the government of a rogue or a fool. Most wise men . . . have ever treated hereditary right with contempt;

yet it is one of those evils, which when once established is not easily removed; many submit from fear, others from superstition, and the more powerful part shares with the king the plunder of the rest (of the population)."

Tom continued: "This is supposing the present race of kings in the world to have had an honorable origin; whereas it is more than probable, that could we take off the dark covering of antiquity, and trace them to their first rise, that we should find the first of them nothing better than the principal ruffian of some restless gang, whose savage manners or pre-eminence in subtlety obtained him the title of chief among plunderers; and who by increasing in power, and extending his depredations, overawed the quiet and defenseless to purchase their safety by frequent contributions. Yet his electors could have no idea of giving hereditary right to his descendants . . . Wherefore, hereditary succession in the early ages of monarchy could not take place as a matter of claim . . . ; but as few or no records were extant in those days, and traditional history stuffed with fables, it was very easy, after the lapse of a few generations, to trump up some superstitious tale, conveniently timed, . . . to cram hereditary right down the throats of the vulgar (common people). Perhaps the disorders which threatened, or seemed to threaten on the decease of a leader and the choice of a new one (for elections among ruffians could not be very orderly) induced many at first to favor hereditary pretentions; by which means it happened, as it hath happened since, that what at first was submitted to as a convenience, was afterwards claimed as a right."

Tom was obviously trying to use plain logic to

undermine his readers' faith in and loyalty to the King as the necessary first step to their opening their minds to consider the idea of independence.

Tom continued: "England, since the conquest, hath known some few good monarchs, but groaned beneath a much larger number of bad ones; yet no man in his senses can say that their claim under William the Conqueror is a very honorable one. A French bastard landing with an armed banditti, and establishing himself king of England against the consent of the natives, is in plain terms a very paltry rascally original. It certainly hath no divinity in it. However, it is needless to spend much time in exposing the folly of hereditary right; if there are any so weak as to believe it, let them promiscuously worship the ass and lion, and welcome. I shall neither copy their humility, nor disturb their devotion."

Tom continued: "Another evil which attends hereditary succession is, that the throne is subject to be possessed by a minor at any age; all which time the regency (bureaucracy), acting under the cover of a king, have every opportunity and inducement to betray their trust."

Tom continued: "The most plausible plea, which hath ever been offered in favour of hereditary succession, is, that it preserves a nation from civil wars; and were this true, it would be weighty; whereas, it is the most barefaced falsity ever imposed upon mankind. The whole history of England disowns the fact. Thirty kings and two minors have reigned in that distracted kingdom since the conquest, in which time there have been (including the Revolution) no less than eight civil wars and nineteen rebellions. Wherefore instead of making for peace, it makes against it, and destroys the very foundation it seems to stand on.''

Tom continued: "The contest for monarchy and succession, between the houses of York and Lancaster, laid England in a scene of blood for many years . . . The Parliament always following the strongest side . . . In short, monarchy and succession have laid but the world in blood and ashes. 'Tis a form of government which the word of God bears testimony against, and blood will attend it.''

Tom continued: "The nearer any government approaches to a republic the less business there is for a king.''

Tom continued: "In England a king hath little more to do than to make war and give away places; which in plain terms, is to impoverish the nation . . . A pretty business indeed for a man to be allowed eight hundred thousand sterling a year for, and worshipped into the bargain! Of more worth is one honest man to society and in the sight of God, than all the crowned ruffians that ever lived.''

After de-mystifying the king, Tom turned directly to the subject of dependence on, versus independence from England.

He said: "By referring the matter from argument to arms, a new era for politics is struck; a new method of thinking hath arisen . . . As much as been said of the advantages of reconciliation . . . it is but right, that we should examine the contrary side of the argument, and inquire into some of the many material injuries which these colonies sustain, and always will sustain, by being connected with, and dependent on

Great-Britain: To examine that connexion and dependence, on the principles of nature and common sense, to see what we have to trust to, if separated, and what we are to expect, if dependent.''

He continued: ''I have heard it asserted by some, that as America hath flourished under her former connexion with Great-Britain, that the same connexion is necessary towards her future happiness, and will always have the same effect. Nothing can be more fallacious than this kind of argument. We may as well assert that because a child has thrived upon milk, that it is never to have meat, or that the first twenty years of our lives is to become a precedent for the next twenty.''

He continued: ''We have boasted the protection of Great-Britain, without considering, that her motive was INTEREST not ATTACHMENT; that she did not protect us from OUR ENEMIES on OUR ACCOUNT, but from HER ENEMIES on HER OWN ACCOUNT, from those who had no quarrel with us on any OTHER ACCOUNT, and who will always be our enemies on the SAME ACCOUNT. Let Britain wave her pretentions to the continent (of America), or the continent throw off the dependence, and we should be at peace with France and Spain were they at war with Britain . . . France and Spain never were, nor perhaps ever will be our enemies as AMERICANS, but as our being the subjects of Great Britain.''

He continued: ''But Britain is the parent country, say some. Then the more shame upon her conduct. Even brutes do not devour their young, nor savages make war upon their families; . . . and the phrase PARENT or MOTHER COUNTRY hath been . . .

adopted by the king and his parasites . . . Europe, and not England, is the parent country of America. This new world hath been the asylum for the persecuted lovers of civil and religious liberty from EVERY PART of Europe. Hither have they fled, not from the tender embraces of the mother, but from the cruelty of the monster; and it is so far true of England, that the same tyranny which drove the first emigrants from home, pursues their descendants still.''

He continued: ''But admitting, that we were all of English descent, what does it amount to? Nothing. Britain, being now an open enemy, extinguishes every other name and title: And to say that reconciliation is our duty, is truly farcical.''

He continued: ''Our plan is commerce . . . I challenge the warmest advocates for reconciliation (with England), to shew, a single advantage that this continent can reap, by being connected with Great-Britain. I repeat the challenge, not a single advantage is derived. Our corn will fetch its price in any market in Europe, and our imported goods must be paid for, buy them where we will . . . But the injuries and disadvantages we sustain by that connexion, are without number; and our duty to mankind at large, as well as to ourselves, instruct us to renounce the alliance: Because, any submission to, or dependence on Great-Britain, tends directly to involve this continent in European wars and quarrels; and sets us at variance with nations, who could otherwise seek our friendship and against whom, we have neither anger nor complaint. As Europe is our market for trade, we ought to form no partial connexion with any part of it. It is the true interest of America to steer clear of European contentions, which she never can do, while by her dependence on Britain, she is made the make-weight in the scale of British politics."

He continued: "Europe is too thickly planted with kingdoms to be long at peace, and whenever a war breaks out between England and any foreign power, the trade of America goes to ruin, BECAUSE OF HER CONNEXION WITH BRITAIN."

He continued: "Every thing that is right or natural pleads for separation. The blood of the slain, the weeping voice of nature cries, 'TIS TIME TO PART. Even the distance at which the Almighty hath placed England and America, is a strong and natural proof, that the authority of the one, over the other, was never the design of Heaven."

He continued: "Though I would carefully avoid giving unnecessary offense, yet I am inclined to believe, that all those who espouse the doctrine of reconciliation (as opposed to independence), may be included within the following descriptions. Interested men, who are not to be trusted; weak men, who CANNOT see; prejudiced men, who WILL NOT see; and a certain set of moderate men, who think better of the European world than it deserves; and this last class, by an ill-judged deliberation, will be the cause of more calamaties to this continent, than all the other three."

The colonists were reading all of this from Tom in January of 1776, while George Washington's seige was trying to free the Bostonians from the Redcoat persecution of them because of the Boston Tea Party and the battles of Lexington and Concord.

Tom continued: "It is good fortune of many to live distant from the scene of sorrow; the evil is not sufficient brought to THEIR doors to make THEM feel the precariousness with which all American property is possessed. But let our imaginations transport us for a few moments to Boston, that seat of wretchedness will teach us wisdom, and instruct us forever to renounce a power in whom we can have no trust. The inhabitants of that unfortunate city, who but a few months ago were in ease and affluence, have now, no other alternative than to stay and starve, or turn out to beg. Endangered by the fire of their friends (Washington's artillery) if they continue within the city, and plundered by the (Redcoat) soldiery if they leave it. In their present condition they are prisoners without the hope of redemption, and in a general attack for their relief, they would be exposed to the fury of both armies.''

Pretty graphic, no? Doesn't Tom make you feel it?

He continued: ''Bring the doctrine of reconciliation to the touchstone of nature, and then tell me, whether you can hereafter love, honor, and faithfully serve the power that hath carried fire and sword into your land? . . . Your future connexion with Britain, whom you can neither love nor honor, will be forced and unnatural . . . But if you say, you can still pass the violations over (meaning forgetting them), then I ask, Hath your house been burned? Hath your property been destroyed before your face? Are your wife and children destitute of a bed to lie on, or bread to live on? Have you lost a parent or child by their hands, and yourself the ruined and wretched survivor? If you have not, then are you not a judge of those who have. But if you have, and still can shake hands with the murderers, then you are unworthy the name of hus-

band, father, friend, or lover, and whatever may be
your rank or title in life, you have the heart of a
coward, and the spirit of a sycophant (a polite, euphemistic way of calling somebody an ass-kisser) . . .
This is not inflaming or exaggerating matters, but trying them by those feelings and affections which nature
justifies . . . I mean not to exhibit horror for the
purpose of provoking revenge, but to awaken us from
fatal and unmanly slumbers, that we may pursue deter-
minately some fixed object (independence).''

Is your blood boiling yet? If not, why not?

He continued: ''It is repugnant to reason, to the
universal order of things, to all examples from former
ages, to suppose, that this continent can longer remain
subject to any external power. The utmost stretch of
human wisdom cannot, at this time, compass a plan
short of separation . . . Reconciliation is NOW a
fallacious dream. Nature hath deserted the connexion,
and Art cannot supply her place. For, as Milton wisely
expresses, 'never can true reconcilement grow, where
wounds of deadly hate have pierc'd so deep.''

He continued: ''I am not induced by motives of
pride, party, or resentment to espouse the doctrine
of separation and independence; I am clearly, positively, and conscientiously persuaded that it is the
true interest of this continent to be so; that every thing
short of THAT is mere patchwork, that it can afford
no lasting felicity, that IT IS LEAVING THE SWORD
TO OUR CHILDREN, and shrinking back at a time,
when, a little more, a little farther, would have rendered this continent the glory of the earth.''

Trying to make the point that there is no going
back to the old system, that independence from the

king and from England should be the only goal, Tom continued.

". . . is he (the king), or is he not, a proper man to say to these colonies, 'You shall make no laws but what I please.' . . . and is there any man so unwise, as not to see, that (considering what has happened) he will suffer no law to be made here, but such as suit HIS purpose . . . To bring the matter to one point. Is the power who is jealous of our prosperity, a proper power to govern us? Whoever says NO to this question, is an INDEPENDENT, for independency means no more, than, whether we shall make our own laws, or whether the king, the greatest enemy this continent hath, or can have, shall tell us 'THERE SHALL BE NO LAWS BUT SUCH AS I LIKE.''

He continued: "America is only a secondary object in the system of British politics. England consults the good of THIS country, no further than it answers her OWN purpose. Wherefore, her own interest leads her to suppress the growth of OURS in every case which doth not promote her advantage, or in the least interferes with it.''

Remember now, that the colonists are reading all of this in January of 1776, six months before the Declaration of Independence, and eight months after Lexington and Concord. Tom continues.

"If there is any true cause of fear respecting independence, it is because NO PLAN IS YET LAID DOWN. Men do not see their way out. Wherefore, as an opening into that business, I offer the following hints; at the same time modestly affirming, that I have no other opinion of them myself, than that they may be the means of giving rise to something better.''

Tom then suggested that we form a constitutional republic, giving us the kernels which later blossomed into our Constitution. What an amazing outline Tom drew then.

Summing up, Tom challenged his readers: "O ye that love mankind! Ye that dare oppose, not only the tyranny, BUT THE TYRANT, stand forth!"

And finally, in this one pamphlet of approximately 40 pages, published in January of 1776, Tom finished up with brilliant arguments explaining why he felt that the Americans would surely win the war with England, but only if they boldly declared INDEPENDENCE as their goal.

And it was these logical arguments in Tom's pamphlet which would finally completely dissolve any remaining doubts in George Washington's mind regarding the wisdom of independence from England AS THE ONLY CORRECT PURPOSE of our Revolution; and Tom's logical arguments in this pamphlet also caused George to see the light that no other objective, other than the objective of independence from England, could possibly inspire and motivate our rebels to continually persevere through the terrible hardships of the battlefield. So because of Tom, George Washington would never again raise his glass in a toast of well wishes to the King of England at Christmas time.

There was a baby boy born in 1737, whose parents gave him the first name of Thomas. He would later become the Father of American Independence, and just one document that he would author would permanently change the course of the world forever.

His full name was Thomas Paine, and the document he wrote, from which everything above was quoted, was called "Common Sense." And on this document's cover page, Tom's name did not appear, nor did his name appear at the end, thus keeping his identity virtually incognito. But on COMMON SENSE's cover page was printed the phrase: WRITTEN BY AN ENGLISH-MAN.

Chapter 4

The Price

> *It is natural to man to indulge in the illusions of hope. We are apt to shut our eyes against a painful truth . . . Is this the part of wise men, engaged in a great and arduous struggle for liberty? Are we disposed to be of the number of those who, having eyes, see not, and having ears, hear not, the things which so nearly concern their temporal salvation? For my part, whatever anguish of spirit it may cost, I am willing to know the whole truth; to know the worst and to provide for it.* —Patrick Henry

It is a principle of logic to favor the opposite of what you oppose, and to oppose the opposite of what you favor. This principle is usually referred to as the two-sided coin. If you favor health, you oppose disease. If you love good, you hate evil.

The political revolutionaries who founded our country were freedom lovers, and therefore, slavery haters. Slavery as a concept means human involuntary servitude, or simply, humans forced by fear of punishment to do something against their will, or humans forced by fear of punishment to ask permission before they act. Slavery as a concept is the direct opposite of freedom as a concept. If you are free, you are not a slave. If you are a slave, you are not free.

Slavery as an institution means the buying, selling,

and keeping of human beings in forced bondage for labor purposes.

Our freedom-loving political revolutionary founders opposed both the concept and the institution of slavery as totally inconsistent with their gradually evolving thinking regarding the God-given rights of man.

Unfortunately, slavery as an institution had existed for countless centuries, and no one even knows when it had begun. It is almost impossible for modern man to fathom how slavery could have existed as a respectable business for so long, nor how it could have been generally accepted without question. But it did, and it was.

Slavery had existed in the new English colonies for over one hundred years before George Washington and Thomas Jefferson were even born. So our founders inherited the awful system as the economy of our agriculturally inclined southern colonies had become quite dependent on it, as well as the shipping industry of our northern colonies.

Why does evil of any kind exist anywhere, or anytime? Because somebody is making MONEY from it. Whatever is not profitable dies a natural death.

Who was making money from the institution of slavery in the new English colonies? Guess. Here we go again. Queen Anne of England owned stock in a company formed to buy Negroes in Africa and to sell them in North and South America. Big business trading companies in old England could make a fortune providing laborers to the colonies, and to their customers in South America. Records show that for the eight year period between 1680 and 1688, the Royal African Company, the chartered old English slave-hunting firm, landed about 47,000 captured Negroes in the

Americas. Incredible. And Washington, Jefferson, and every other future American revolutionary weren't even born yet.

Around 1690, the fathers and mothers of our future political revolutionary founders in the colony of Pennsylvania expressed the first written protest of slavery thusly:

> *"Here (in the colonies) is liberty of conscience, which is right and honorable; here ought to be likewise liberty of body, except of evildoers. But to bring men hither, or to rob and sell them against their will, WE STAND AGAINST."*

By 1732, when Lord Oglethorpe founded the colony of Georgia, he made a law prohibiting slavery in any form, but greedy big businessmen later overturned this law when Oglethorpe passed out of the picture.

The freedom-loving thinking of our founders was definitely headed in one direction: abolish slavery in the colonies forever. In the first draft of the Declaration of Independence, Thomas Jefferson included a revealing paragraph which unfortunately was rescinded from the finished document, but which actually blamed King George for allowing the trading companies to promote the evils of slavery in the colonies.

While we were in the full scale revolt process of becoming a new nation, the majority of the colonies passed legislation forbidding the importation of slaves and permitting slave owners to unconditionally free all of them. From the first shots fired at Lexington and Concord to the writing of our Constitution (between the years of 1775 to 1787), freedom-loving founders in the legislatures of Connecticut, Delaware,

Maryland, Massachusetts, New Hampshire, Pennsylvania, Rhode Island, and Virginia passed such laws in their colonies against the evil institution of slavery.

The direction our founders were headed was clear and consistent with their evolving principles of Americanism and freedom. The break with English practices of greed and bullyism would be total—slavery was to be completely abolished.

But unfortunately for every Negro in the colonies at the time, and also for every other innocent colonist living at that time, and also for every other innocent future American of every race, color, and creed yet to be born, our founders were not perfect men. And as history and hindsight clearly prove, they made the biggest mistake of the Revolution by not keeping the abolition of slavery in our Declaration of Independence and especially not writing it into our Constitution where it clearly belonged. They should have done so. Had they done so then, we could have averted the terrible price of our Civil War 74 years later. Why they didn't has been the subject of thousands of volumes of arguments, mainly concerning the big businessmen's molasses, rum, and slaves triangle, and the time our colonists needed to wean themselves off of it, reminiscent of the doctor's infamous remark, "The operation was a complete success, but the patient died." The bottom line remains: results count more than intentions. There is no good excuse. They blew it. But blowing it at that time can never change the fact that our founders were freedom-lovers.

Our founders loved freedom so much, and hated slavery so much, that they proved it by the extreme price they paid to buy freedom for us all. They not only put their money where their mouths were, but they put their lives there too. What more could be expected from anyone?

All wars cost governments astronomical sums of money to wage. To fight a war, governments must first borrow money from private sources, private individuals, private lenders, in order to buy the necessary supplies to feed, clothe and militarily equip their soldiers. Have you ever thought of it this way? When a government can't borrow enough funds to pay cash for these supplies, they buy from suppliers on credit. When the war is over, the government is in great debt, and because government produces nothing, has nothing, owns nothing until it first takes it from the people, the government must heavily tax its citizens to obtain the money needed to pay back its creditors. Where else could the government obtain its funding? All wars are eventually paid for by the people themselves, always. Did you realize that? Our Revolution cost our founders millions and millions of dollars, estimated to be about $50 million at that time.

War is hell. There is nothing glorious about it. Nothing romantic about it. It is killing and more killing. It is cutting, bleeding, disembowelment, filth, strangulation, suffocating, vomiting, hacking, burning, captivity, thirst, broken bones, disease, starving, slaughter, gangrene, amputations, heart attacks, drowning, shock, murder, insanity, crying, lice, dysentery, melting heat, shivering cold, freezing, hanging, shaking, screaming, blindness, deafness, moaning, explosions, bullet holes, prisoners, missing in action, "we regret to inform you" letters, torture, fear, agony, pain, and death. Man's inhumanity to man. Literally. There is nothing good about it, ever. War is hell. War sucks.

But war is not the worst evil in the world. It is

the second worst. Only one evil is worse than war. Slavery. Slavery is the worst evil in the world. The only legitimate justification for fighting a war is to avoid becoming a slave. Forget about fighting a war to gain territory, to improve your standard of living, to secure lucrative foreign markets for greedy big businessmen, to make the big business military-industrial complex richer by their supplying war material, to make the bankers and money lenders rich on interest, to make the rest of the world safe for democracy, etc., etc., etc. The only legitimate justification for fighting a war is to avoid becoming a slave. This is the American philosophy which gave our founders the courage necessary to risk the ultimate price of death.

When serious trouble started with England, a committee was formed to represent the thirteen colonies as a single entity facing a common enemy, working on the logical principle that in unity there is strength (united we stand, divided we fall). This committee, consisting of concerned citizens from each colony and meeting for the first time in 1774 in Philadelphia, called itself the Continental Congress. The Continental Congress was the nucleus of what would later become the first governmental body of the United States of America.

The Continental Congress appointed George Washington as Commander-in-Chief of all the colonial militias composing the Continental Army soon after Lexington and Concord. Washington and his staff were charged with the responsibility of planning the overall battle strategy in the physical fight for freedom, but the Continental Congress did not declare complete independence from England until July 4, 1776, fourteen months after the shooting had started. So for fourteen months, the war was technically being fought between two opposing factions of Englishmen, old Englishmen and new Englishmen. The colonists had their eggs in two baskets.

The new English political revolutionaries didn't become Americans for the first time until July 4, 1776, when the Continental Congress proclaimed our Declaration of Independence. This date is the actual birthdate of our country, the United States of America. From that date forward, our revolutionaries would never again consider themselves to be Englishmen, but Americans. There was no turning back for them after this day.

Prior to our Declaration, King George insisted that our revolutionaries were simply rebellious Englishmen, or common criminals, with some of the leaders being traitors. But after our Declaration, King George declared that all of the rebels were traitors. The English punishment for the crime of treason was death by hanging.

Why did it take so long for the Continental Congress to declare independence from England after actual physical warfare had been raging for 14 months?

When you break a law, your government's law enforcement authorities, of course, consider you a lawbreaker. The synonym for the word lawbreaker is criminal. How would you personally feel if your government's law enforcement authorities considered you to be a criminal? Hurts, doesn't it? Think about that for a moment. Could you face it? Scary, isn't it?

There are many different categories of criminals. How would you feel if your government's law enforcement authorities considered you to be a thief? Could you psychologically tolerate it? What if someone violently attacked you with deadly force, and in self-defense you killed the attacker, and your government's law enforcement authorities considered you to be a murderer? Could you stand the shame without a mental breakdown?

Could you face your mother, father, boyfriend, girl-friend, husband, wife, children, other relatives, friends, neighbors, and the public in general if you were accused of a serious crime, and everybody knew about it? Think about this question for a moment. If you're not beginning to feel sick in your stomach, you're not thinking about this, or you're a Martian.

How much psychological pain are you capable of tolerating? You might be strong enough to explain to people that you are being falsely accused, and that you are not a thief, and not a murderer. But what would you be able to explain to people if your own government's law enforcement authorities accused you of treason against your own country? How 'bout that one? Heavy, isn't it?

Treason, high treason, is the most heinous crime known to man. Killing an individual is bad enough, but treason is tantamount to country killing. How would you like that charge to be leveled against you? You are a damn traitor! Could you stand that charge? Talk about stress.

Allowing the idea of the charge of treason to be resolved in their minds, hearts, and souls, and in each rebel's mind, heart, and soul is why our founders delayed proclaiming our Declaration of Independence for 14 months after the shooting began at Lexington and Concord.

Even after the fighting began, optimists in all thirteen colonies still clung tenatiously to the hope that the shooting war would convince King George and the big business-controlled Parliament to back down, and to repeal the legislation oppressing the colonists, and to grant them the representation that they desired in the Parliament. In other words, the colonists still wanted to consider themselves LOYAL but ABUSED Englishmen. In fact, even during the shooting, King George considered most of the rebels to be criminals and rebellious Englishmen, but not traitors.

Every colonist understood that King George and Parliament would interpret a declaration of independence to be treason, from which there could be no return. The controversial topic of independence was on everyone's mind, causing the most heated arguments and debates imaginable between neighbors, friends, and family members. Fathers fought with sons, mothers fought with daughters, brothers with brothers, sisters with sisters, husbands fought with wives, neighbors with neighbors, friends with friends. Quarrels concerning independence were intense, dividing every personal relationship. Fistfights broke out everywhere. It was a fornicating mess! Mental torture and agony.

The Continental Congress had agreed to vote on the issue of independence in Philadelphia on July 4, 1776. The entire nation held its breath. Caesar Rodney, one of the delegates from Delaware, with malignant skin cancer covering half of his face, would rather die than miss this opportunity to vote in favor of independence. Rushing from his home in Delaware, he rode several different horses all night long through a blinding thunderstorm to appear inside the Philadelphia hall just seconds before presiding officer, John Hancock, called the session to order.

Every one of the 56 delegates was not as convinced as Rodney was regarding the wisdom of independence. In fact, John Hancock opened the meeting urging moderation, restraint, and caution, pointing out the benefits he perceived if the colonists would remain subjects of England. This, even with war raging for the last 14 months.

Many of the assembled delegates began to nod their heads in apparent agreement with Hancock's remarks, regarding the ideas that they expressed as a safer and more prudent approach to their problematical situation. With Jefferson's document before them which they had been reading and discussing for nearly a week, the vote was seconds away, but John Adams interrupted and asked for the floor. Adams, one of the delegates from Massachusetts, rejected Hancock's appeasing ideas. Pointing a finger at Hancock, he said:

> *"Sink or swim, live or die, survive or perish, I give my hand and my heart to this vote. It is true, indeed, that in the beginning we aimed not at independence. But there's a Divinity which shapes our ends. The injustice of England has driven us to arms; and, blinded to her own interest for our good, she had obstinately persisted, till independence is now within our grasp. We have but to reach forth to it, and it is ours.*
>
> *Why, then, should we defer the Declaration? Is any man so weak as now to hope for a reconciliation with England? . . .*
>
> *You and I, indeed, may rue it. We may not*

live to the time when this Declaration shall be made good. We may die; die Colonists; die slaves; die, it may be, ignominiously and on the scaffold.

Be it so. Be it so.

If it be the pleasure of Heaven that my country shall require the poor offering of my life, the victim shall be ready . . . But while I do live, let me have a country, or at least the hope of a country, and that a free country.

But whatever may be our fate, be assured . . . that this Declaration will stand. It may cost treasure, and it may cost blood; but it will stand, and it will richly compensate for both.

Through the thick gloom of the present, I see the brightness of the future, as the sun in heaven. We shall make this a glorious, an immortal day. When we are in our graves, our children will honor it. They will celebrate it with thanksgiving, with festivity, with bonfires, and illuminations. On its annual return they will shed tears, copious, gushing tears, not of subjection and slavery, not of agony and distress, but of exultation, of gratitude and of joy.

Sir, before God, I believe the hour has come. My judgment approves this measure, and my whole heart is in it. All that I have, and all that I am, and all that I hope, in this life, I am now ready here to stake upon it; and I leave off as I began, that live or die, survive or perish, I am for the Declaration. It is my living sentiment, and by the blessing of God it shall be my dying sentiment. Independence now, and Independence forever.''

Adams sat down. The hall was quiet. The vote was taken. It was unanimous. In favor of Independence.

After 14 months of excruciating soul searching since the war had started, the 56 delegates to the Continental Congress voted unanimously to proclaim our independence from England, knowing full well that they were deliberately committing the heinous crime of treason.

The English penalty for the crime of treason was death by hanging. Every one of the 56 signers of the Declaration realized that they were signing their own death warrant if the Revolution failed, but they still signed. The moment they signed, these 56 men became the first Americans. All of their eggs were now in one basket. They all realized after the signing that there was no turning back, and that you can't unscramble an egg.

Few of our modern countrymen have ever taken the time to read America's birth certificate in its entirety. When you do, you should keep in mind a very important fact. Every single document written prior to the Declaration blamed the big business-controlled Parliament and the King's agents for every abuse they were inflicting on the colonists. The King was never blamed. But the Declaration for the first time focuses ALL of the blame on the King alone. Why?

Our founders were polite gentlemen practitioners of Robert's Rules of Order because so many of them were attorneys. As men schooled in English law, they viewed the Declaration as a legal document, which in fact it was and is. Its author, Thomas Jefferson, was in fact an attorney. Lawyers are very precise and exact when they write legal documents, especially those for public viewing and scrutiny. According to the letter of the law of the then current old English Constitution, the monarch was ultimately responsible for every single act of the English government. Legal technicality dictated that even acts of Parliament were to be considered in legal terminology as acts of the Crown-in-Parliament. This means that the King was technically legally responsible for everything his government did.

These facts explain why all of the abuses endured by the colonists are laid at the door of the King, and why each of the 27 grievances listed in the Declaration begins with the word "He," referring to King George III.

This technique is understandable from a LEGAL point of view, but was another big mistake our founders made during our Revolution because this legal technique hid from future Americans the fact that IT WAS THE BIG BUSINESS CONTROL OF ENOUGH MEMBERS OF PARLIAMENT WHICH MAINLY CAUSED OUR REVOLUTION.

So please keep this legal technicality fact fresh in your mind as you read the entire Declaration, lest you lose sight of the real truth regarding the real culprits:

THE DECLARATION OF INDEPENDENCE
In Congress July 4, 1776
The Unanimous Declaration of the Thirteen United States of America

When in the Course of human events, it becomes necessary for one people to dissolve the political bands which have connected them with another, and to assume among the powers of the earth, the separate and equal station to which the Laws of Nature and of Nature's God entitle them, a decent respect to the opinions of mankind requires that they should declare the causes which impel them to the separation.

We hold these truths to be self-evident, that all men are created equal, that they are endowed by their Creator with certain unalienable Rights, that among these are Life, Liberty and the pursuit of Happiness. That to secure these rights, Governments are instituted among Men, deriving their just powers from the consent of the governed. That whenever any Form of Government becomes destructive of these ends, it is the Right of the People to alter or to abolish it, and to institute new Government, laying its foundation on such principles and organizing its powers in such form, as to them shall seem most likely to effect their Safety and Happiness. Prudence, indeed, will dictate that Governments long established should not be changed for light and transient causes; and accordingly all experience hath shewn, that mankind are more disposed to suffer, while evils are sufferable, than to right themselves by abolishing the forms to which they are accustomed. But when a long train of abuses and usurpations, pursuing invariably the same Object, evinces a design to reduce them under absolute Despotism, it is their right, it is their duty, to throw off such Government, and to provide new Guards for their future security. Such has been the patient sufferance of these Colonies; and such is now the necessity which constrains them to alter their former

Systems of Government. The history of the present King of Great Britain is a history of repeated injuries and usurpations, all having in direct object the establishment of an absolute Tyranny over these States. To prove this, let Facts be submitted to a candid world.

He has refused his Assent to Laws, the most wholesome and necessary for the public good.

He has forbidden his Governors to pass Laws of immediate and pressing importance, unless suspended in their operation till his Assent should be obtained; and when so suspended, he has utterly neglected to attend to them.

He has refused to pass other laws for the accommodation of large districts of people, unless those people would relinquish the right of Representation in the Legislature, a right inestimable to them and formidable to tyrants only.

He has called together legislative bodies at places unusual, uncomfortable, and distant from the depository of their public Records, for the sole purpose of fatiguing them into compliance with his measures.

He has dissolved Representative Houses repeatedly, for opposing with manly firmness his invasions on the rights of the people.

He has refused for a long time, after such dissolutions, to cause others to be elected; whereby the Legislative powers, incapable of Annihilation, have returned to the People at large for their exercise; the State remaining in the meantime exposed to all the dangers of invasion from without, and convulsions within.

He has endeavored to prevent the population

of these States; for that purpose obstructing the Laws for Naturalization of Foreigners; refusing to pass others to encourage their migrations hither, and raising the conditions of new Appropriations of Lands.

He has obstructed the Administration of Justice, by refusing his Assent to Laws for establishing Judiciary powers.

He has made Judges dependent on his Will alone, for the tenure of their offices, and the amount and payment of their salaries.

He has erected a multitude of New Offices, and sent hither swarms of Officers to harass our people, and eat out their substance.

He has kept among us, in times of peace, Standing Armies without the Consent of our legislatures.

He has affected to render the Military independent of and superior to the Civil power.

He has combined with others to subject us to a jurisdiction foreign to our constitution, and unacknowledged by our laws; giving his Assent to their Acts of pretended Legislation:

For quartering large bodies of armed troops among us:

For protecting them, by a mock Trial, from punishment for any Murders which they should commit on the Inhabitants of these States:

For cutting off our Trade with all parts of the world:

For imposing Taxes on us without our Consent:

For depriving us in many cases of the benefits of Trial by Jury:

For transporting us beyond Seas to be tried for pretended offenses:

For abolishing the free System of English Laws in a neighbouring Province, establishing therein an Arbitrary government, and enlarging its Boundaries so as to render it at once an example and fit instrument for introducing the same absolute rule into these Colonies:

For taking away our Charters, abolishing our most valuable laws, and altering fundamentally the Forms of our Governments:

For suspending our own Legislatures, and declaring themselves invested with power to legislate for us in all cases whatsoever.

He has abdicated Government here, by declaring us out of his Protection and waging War against us.

He has plundered our seas, ravaged our Coasts, burnt our towns, and destroyed the lives of our people.

He is at this time transporting large Armies of foreign Mercenaries to complete the works of death, desolation and tyranny, already begun with circumstances of Cruelty and perfidy scarcely paralleled in the most barbarous ages, and totally unworthy the Head of a civilized nation.

He has constrained our fellow Citizens taken Captive on the high Seas to bear Arms against their Country, to become the executioners of their friends and Brethren, or to fall themselves by their Hands.

He has excited domestic insurrections amongst us, and has endeavored to bring on the inhabitants of our frontiers, the merciless Indian Savages, whose known rule of warfare is an undistinguished destruction of all ages, sexes and conditions.

In every stage of these Oppressions We have Petitioned for Redress in the most humble terms: Our repeated Petitions have been answered only by repeated injury. A Prince, whose character is thus marked by every act which may define a Tyrant, is unfit to be the ruler of a free people.

Nor have We been wanting in attentions to our British brethren. We have warned them from time to time of attempts by their legislature to extend an unwarrantable jurisdiction over us. We have reminded them of the circumstances of our emigration and settlement here. We have appealed to their native justice and magnanimity, and we have conjured them by the ties of our common kindred to disavow these usurpations, which would inevitably interrupt our connections and correspondence. They too have been deaf to the voice of justice and of consanguinity. We must therefore, acquiesce in the necessity which denounces our Separation, and hold them, as we hold the rest of mankind, Enemies in War, in Peace Friends.

WE, THEREFORE, the REPRESENTATIVES of the UNITED STATES OF AMERICA, IN GENERAL CONGRESS, Assembled, appealing to the Supreme Judge of the world for the rectitude of our intentions, do, in the Name, and by the authority of the good People of these Colonies, solemnly PUBLISH and DECLARE, That these United Colonies are, and of Right ought to be FREE AND INDEPENDENT STATES; that they are Absolved from all Allegiance to the British Crown, and that all political connection between them and the State of Great Britain, is and ought to be totally dissolved; and that as FREE AND INDEPENDENT STATES, they have full Power to levy War, conclude Peace, contract Alliances, establish Commerce, and to do all other Acts and Things which INDEPENDENT STATES, may of right do. And for the support of this Declaration, with a firm reliance on the protection of Divine Providence, We mutually pledge to each other our Lives, our Fortunes, and our sacred Honor.

When the time came for signing the Declaration, John Hancock's was the first and largest signature. Hancock, in a magnificently cavalier gesture of defiance, made his signature twice its normal size, explaining that he didn't want to force the king to have to use his eye glasses to read and recognize it. Hancock added, "We must be unanimous. There must be no pulling a different way. We must all hang together." To which Benjamin Franklin replied with masterful double entendre, "Yes, we must all hang together, or most assuredly we shall all hang separately."

When Hancock asked Charles Carroll of Maryland whether he would sign, Carroll answered unhesitantly, "Most willingly." He was the only signer who signed with more than his name, "Charles Carroll of Carrollton," to distinguish himself from his father and another Carroll of the same name.

Stephen Hopkins of Rhode Island had the disease of palsy, which plagued his body with uncontrollable tremors. His signature is shaky scratching. Approaching the desk to sign, he said, "My hand trembles, but my heart does not."

Three weeks after the signing of the Declaration, King George announced that the colonies were in open rebellion, and he declared every rebel in the land to be a traitor. The King also issued special orders to his troops to relentlessly hunt down every signer of the Declaration, placing big money rewards on their heads for their capture.

Is it beginning to dawn on you yet, that your personal decision regarding whether a reformer or a revolutionary is a patriot or a traitor is wholly dependent on whose side you voluntarily choose to be on? The colonists were split into three distinct factions: the rebels, the neutrals, and the loyalists. There were no Democrats and Republicans at that time, thank God.

The rebels were Americans, the neutrals were nothing, and the loyalists were loyal to the King. Once a war starts, shooting or otherwise, neutrality is a dangerous luxury indulged in only by short-sighted fools. Once a war starts, safety can only be found by aligning yourself with either warring side. Neutrals are understandably abused by both sides.

So what eventually happened to the signers of the Declaration? Not only were they hunted down by English soldiers, but many were betrayed by spiteful loyalist neighbors, who marked the signers for special vengeance and frenzied attack. What happened to the signers is a sad story. What a price they paid! But every one of them kept their promise to each other. Some lost their lives, some lost their fortunes, but all of them kept their sacred honor.

Six weeks after the Declaration, 25,000 English soldiers and Hessian mercenaries landed on Long Island where they proceeded to kill, wound, or capture 1600 of Washington's men, most of whom were under 15 or over 50 years of age. With Washington forced to retreat, the Redcoats and Hessians swarmed all over Long Island, pillaging, looting, and wreaking havoc.

Washington desperately needed to know where the English intended to strike next. He asked for volunteers to serve as spies on the English. Only one officer volunteered, Captain Nathan Hale, only 21 years old, and a graduate of Yale. When the English captured Hale and were about to hang him, the commanding English officer asked Hale for his last words before he was hanged. American Captain Nathan Hale said, ''I only regret that I have but one life to lose for my country.''

The English continued their rampage in New York. The Redcoats plundered and burned New York signer Francis Lewis' home, and carried his wife off as a prisoner. The Redcoats confined Mrs. Lewis in a filthy barracks for months. They refused to give her a bed to lie on or sleep on, and they refused to give her a change of clothing. The Redcoats treated her with such great brutality, that they ruined her health, which she never was able to regain. She died two years later.

Loyalist neighbors took over New York signer William Floyd's home, stole his farm equipment, livestock, and everything of value in his house. Luckily, Floyd's wife and children escaped unharmed but were exiled from their home for seven years.

Redcoats took over New York signer Philip Livingston's home and place of business. Luckily, Livingston and his family escaped but they never again returned to their home. Livingston died before the Revolution ended.

Redcoats took over New York signer Lewis Morris' home. They destroyed valuable timber and crops and drove off his livestock. But he did get his home back seven years later.

When the Redcoats drove Washington's forces out of New York, Washington retreated across the river into New Jersey. But the Redcoats crossed over to the Jersey side in hot pursuit. The pursuing Redcoats chased Washington's retreating army across the entire colony. The Redcoats got so close at times that Washington's rear guard could actually see them. And many of Washington's men had so worn out their shoes that they had to march barefooted in the white snow, leaving a clearly marked trail of red blood from their bleeding feet for the Redcoats to follow.

New Jersey loyalists welcomed the Redcoats and their Hessian mercenaries with open arms, and these same loyalists helped the enemy to track down the "traitors" who had signed the Declaration.

John Hart was one of the five New Jersey signers. Hart was 65 years old and lived near Trenton on a large farm with several grist mills for making flour from grain. While his wife lay on her deathbed, with him at her side, Hessian troops invaded his property, devastating his farmland and destroying his mills. Hart was forced to flee into the woods. This 65 year old patriot was hunted like a dog. He avoided capture by hiding in caves. Returning some time later to his home, broken in health by anxiety and hardship, he found that his wife had died, and that his 13 children had scattered in every direction.

New Jersey signer Abraham Clark had two sons who served in the Continental Army. The Redcoats captured both of them. The enemy had no real interest in keeping American prisoners alive, and the Redcoats would confine American captives on prison ships docked in coastal harbors. Rarely and poorly fed, being confined on a Redcoat prison ship was tantamount to a death sentence, and a fast death at that. On the prison ship "Jersey" alone, docked in New York Harbor, over 11,000 American prisoners of war perished. New York Harbor smelled of the stench of death.

Imagine Clark's horror when he learned that the Redcoats were keeping his two sons aboard the "Jersey," and that they were suffering extra special hardships because of their signer dad. The English offered to release Clark's sons if he would publicly renounce his cause in favor of King and Parliament. Clark rejected the enemy's offer, and the fate of his sons is unknown.

New Jersey signer Richard Stockton was a member of the New Jersey Supreme Court. Fearing capture, he and his wife and children moved out of their own home to hide in the home of a brave and trusted friend, but a loyalist informant betrayed him. In the middle of the night, Redcoats showed up at his friend's house, dragged him from his bed, brutally beat him, threw him into prison, and nearly starved him to death. Returning to his real home, the Redcoats burned all of his furniture and clothing, and his library collection of the finest books, stole his horses and family silverware. He died a short time later before the war ended.

Redcoats looted the home of Pennsylvania signer George Clymer and destroyed all of his furniture, but Clymer and his family luckily escaped with their lives.

Pennsylvania signer John Morton was the first signer to die. He expired in April, 1777, just eight months after he signed. Morton thought like a loyalist for quite a while, like almost all of his neighbors in his vicinity near Philadelphia. He was a sensitive, introverted man. When he changed his mind and became vocal for independence, many of his relatives, friends, and neighbors turned on him. Those who knew him well said that this social ostracism killed him. On his deathbed, his last words were, ". . . tell them that they will live to see the hour when they shall acknowledge it to have been the most glorious service that I ever rendered to my country."

Redcoats burned down the home of Rhode Island signer William Ellery, who had 17 children.

Mysteriously, someone set fire to and burned down the home of New Hampshire signer Doctor Josiah Bartlett.

South Carolina signers Arthur Middleton, Edward Rutledge, and Thomas Heyward became officers in the Continental Army and the Redcoats captured all three men during the seige of Charleston, and jailed them aboard a prison ship.

Georgia signer George Walton joined the Continental Army. The Redcoats wounded him badly at the battle of Savannah and took him prisoner.

The Redcoats completely destroyed the home of Georgia signer Doctor Lyman Hall.

Georgia signer Button Gwinnett was the second signer to die. He was the President of Georgia and the Commander-in-Chief of Georgia's military forces in the Continental Army. A suspected loyalist political adversary challenged him to a duel in which he was badly wounded. He died a few days later in May of 1777.

Virginia signer Thomas Nelson, Jr. was the Governor of Virginia and Brigadier General of the Virginia militia in the Continental Army. By mortgaging all of his own property, he personally raised and contributed over $2,000,000 to the war effort. After the war ended, when he could not repay the loans, he was forced to forfeit all of his property. He lost everything.

Nelson participated in the last major battle of the Revolutionary War at Yorktown, Virginia. The Redcoat high command under English General Cornwallis had taken up residence and headquarters in Nelson's own stately mansion. When Nelson noticed that his men were firing their cannons on his neighborhood but in a pattern carefully designed to avoid hitting his mansion, he angrily asked one of the gunners, "Why do you spare my house?" "Out of respect to you, sir," the gunner replied. "Give me the cannon," Nelson ordered, and he began to direct the firing upon his own house, after which Cornwallis surrendered.

With a war being fought on your own territory, and with the possibility and probability that enemy soldiers will be invading your own hometown and neighborhood, could you leave your family to defend themselves while you fought elsewhere as a soldier in your army? This about that question for a while. It's pretty heavy, isn't it?

What kind of sacrificial dedication do some people possess to leave to fight elsewhere while their mothers, fathers, brothers, sisters, aunts, uncles, grandparents, friends and their own wives and flesh and blood children are so vulnerably exposed to the terrible dangers inherent in warfare? Many of the signers had this type of dedication.

What kind of dedication to a cause is necessary to risk hanging for treason when you have a wife with little kiddies at home? The 56 signers had a combined total of 325 children! Can you believe it? Only two were bachelors, and 16 had married twice. Regarding the children, the signers reasoned that it was more important to worry about the KIND of world their children would have to GROW UP IN, rather than worrying exclusively about their physical safety and material well-being.

The signers were fighting to prevent their children from becoming slaves. Think you could make that type of decision about your children based on higher values and eternal principles? One of our founders, John Dickinson, summed up their thinking this way: "It is not our duty to leave WEALTH to our children, but it is our duty to leave LIBERTY to them. We have counted the cost of this contest, and we find nothing so dreadful as voluntary slavery."

After focusing on the suffering of some of the signers of our Declaration, not to be forgotten are the unsung heroes of any war, who are always the thousands and thousands of nameless, faceless, little guys, the dogs of war, whose bravery and gallantry ultimately make the victory possible. If they survive the combat, they receive personal recognition ONLY from family, friends, and neighbors while they live, and are forever lost to history. They live with the only recognition that really counts: WHAT YOU THINK OF YOUR-SELF. And those anonymous thousands who died in battle. . . .

While the fighting continues, equally heroic are the warrior's loved ones who live every conscious second of their lives with a feeling in their being which no words can describe.

What kind of courage is required for people to face the possibility that a .75 caliber lead ball could enter their bodies any place, at any time, hitting them between the eyes, in the lungs or stomach, or in the genitals? What kind of courage is required for people to face the possibility that cannon explosions will tear off their arms, legs, or both? The human body is a fragile thing. What kind of courage is required for people to face the possibility of the enemy plunging a 16 inch steel bayonet into their chest, belly, or back? What kind of courage is required for people to risk death by hanging for the crime of treason, where a thick rope snaps their necks, or slowly strangles the breath from their lungs? What kind of courage is required for people to face the possibility that they could freeze to death, or starve to death? Do you possess these kinds of courage? Our founders did.

What kind of courage would it take for you to kill another human being because you had to? Only an animal would escape semi-permanent psychological trauma from such a horrible life experience. Our founders also had this kind of courage.

What kind of courage would it take for you to withstand the social ostracism associated with your taking a firm position on a controversial issue? Our founders also had this kind of courage.

Our founding mothers and fathers had every kind of courage they needed. Freedom isn't free. COURAGE was the price they paid for freedom. Do you think that this price was too high? If you were living at that time, would it have been too high for you to pay? Think about that.

Remember: courage is not the absence of fear, but the mastery over it. And that RESISTANCE TO DOMESTIC TYRANNY, EVEN UNTO DEATH, is a fundamental aspect of Americanism. Never forget that, as resistance to domestic tyranny was what our Revolution was all about. Resistance to domestic tyranny is what the fight for freedom is always all about. Resistance to domestic governmental tyranny is the essence of pure Americanism.

Two of the most courageous signers of the Declaration of Independence were John Adams of Massachusetts and Thomas Jefferson of Virginia. Jefferson, of course, authored the document, and John Adams' speech inspired the unanimous vote to pass it.

George Washington became our first president. John Adams became our second president. Thomas Jefferson became our third president.

During our entire Revolutionary War, Adams and Jefferson were best of friends, but became bitter enemies after the Revolution. When Adams was leaving the office of president, he even refused to attend the presidential inauguration of Jefferson.

But time is the greatest healer. Years before their deaths, they became close friends again, and regularly exchanged long, philosophical letters.

When Adams died in Massachusetts at the age of 90, his last words were, "Thomas Jefferson still lives." Actually, Jefferson had died in Virginia at the age of 82, five hours earlier, but the news had not yet reached Massachusetts.

Both Adams and Jefferson died on the exact same day in 1826. The day was July 4th, 1826, the 50th anniversary of the Declaration of Independence.

Just a coincidence, of course.

Chapter 5

Mary Ball

*All the flowers of all the tomorrows are in
the seeds of today.* —*Chinese proverb*

There is an age-old cliché which women understand
and appreciate much better than men. It is: the hand
which rocks the cradle rules the world. What does
this mean? It used to mean that your mother made
you who you are. Today it could mean your babysitter,
housekeeper, nursery school or day care center made
you who you are.

Whoever spent the most time with you from the
time you were born, until you stopped dirtying diapers,
made you who you are.

A newborn baby's brain is like a sophisticated computer. Believers in the concept of heredity would say
that each baby's computer brain is hardware with its
own internal, unique, burned-in, built-in, permanent
hard-disk programming. Doubters of hereditary gene
transmission or blank chalkboard theorists would say
that each baby's computer brain is exactly like every
other baby's hardware, with different attitudes, instincts, and intelligence occurring only from the external input of the varying types of software programming
they experience from their environment. Whatever.

But there is no question that mothers raised the
earlier generations of infants, and that these mothers
did the critical early programming of their children.
The person their mother was, her beliefs, values, and

instincts, would mainly determine the person who these children sooner or later turned out to be.

There was a baby girl born in the new England colony of Virginia in 1704 whose one humble life would change the course of history forever. Her name was Mary . . . Mary Ball.

Unfortunately, history has not left us as much information on her life as we desire regarding so important a human being. We do know that Mary Ball's ancestors came to America from England in 1650. We know Mary's father died when she was still just a little girl, and that her mother died when Mary was a 22 year old young woman.

Mary Ball was so much responsible for our victory over the English during our American Revolution that grateful citizens in 1894, 105 years after her death, erected a granite obelisk monument in her honor over her grave site in Fredericksburg, Virginia, standing 11 feet square at its base and towering 50 feet into the sky. Her name and title are inscribed on one side of the shrine, while on the opposite side the inscription simply reads, "Erected by her countrywomen."

The tremendous work she performed to help us to win the American Revolution is too much forgotten or too little recognized by our modern generation.

Supposedly Mary Ball was a tall and pretty young girl, but she had very little formal education. But then again, neither did Daniel Boone, Abraham Lincoln, Davy Crockett, and hundreds of other great Americans. When Mary Ball was 17, she wrote a letter to her brother Joseph who was living in England. This letter still survives. In it Mary says, "We have not had a schoolmaster in our neighborhood until now in four years."

Etymologists have fantasized on the interesting coincidence to them of the great leader or savior stories of Mary Ball and the one of almost two thousand years ago. Both stories somewhere contain the words: virgin (Virginia), Mary, and Joseph.

Although history is dark on the thousands of minor details of Mary Ball's life, it is crystal clear on the one point that matters to her story: Mary Ball was an intensely spiritual soul. It is said that Mary felt the constant presence of God at her side at all times. It is said that Mary believed that God instantly knew every thought in her head, that God instantly heard every word the moment she uttered it, that God saw every move she made as soon as she made it, that God was all-knowing, ever-present, all-powerful, and that God was in such total control of the people and world that He created that EVERY HUMAN ACTION WOULD PRODUCE THE RESULTS THAT GOD INTENDED.

Mary Ball was so spirit-filled, that she could probably be accurately described as a mystic. If you have ever met such a person with this degree of spirituality, you would instantly recognize that you were NOT in the presence of an ordinary human being. Cynics might say that you had met a "space cadet." To say the least, such an experience is spooky.

How you feel about a mystic depends on who you are, or whose side you choose to be on. The enemies of certain historical mystics have accused such people of being insane, or of being "religious fanatics," or of being "possessed by the devil." The historical mystic, Joan of Arc, helped to change the course of history, and was later burned at the stake. Friends of the mystic or the mystic's cause believe that the mystic is "possessed by God," or is on a mission from God.

If you ever meet a mystic, you should somehow feel it. People somehow felt the mysticism and magnetism of Abraham, Moses, Jesus, Mohammed, Gandhi, Mary Baker Eddy, Joseph Smith, Charles Fillmore, and other prophet types. One of Mary Ball's relatives described his feelings about her in this way: "I was ten times more afraid (of Mary) than I ever was of my own parents. She awed me in the midst of her kindness, for she was indeed truly kind. In her presence we were all as mute as mice, and even now, when time has whitened my locks and I am the grandparent of a second generation, I could not behold that remarkable woman WITHOUT FEELINGS IT IS IMPOSSIBLE TO DESCRIBE."

People have reported feeling this way after meeting the Pope or Mother Theresa.

When our Revolution ended, the Marquis de Lafayette, the French hero who fought so gallantly for the American cause, came to visit Mary to pay his respects and to receive her blessing. History records that he experienced a tremendous sense of wonder, and left her struck with awe, and spread her reputation all over France upon his return.

Mary Ball believed that God was the ultimate Truth. Mary Ball believed that it was everyone's duty to serve God on earth. To Mary that meant being truthful, just, charitable, kind, and brave, NO MATTER WHAT THE COST, and that in conducting your life in this manner, God would protect you, or harm you, all according to His own will.

Mary Ball believed that God wanted everyone to struggle to do the best that they possibly could in everything that they attempted, but whether they won, lost, or drawed, IT DIDN'T REALLY MATTER, as God had the outcome all planned the way it came out. What mattered was that you felt that what you were doing was right, and that it was in sync with God's divine principles of goodness. Mary believed that if you were on God's side, that you couldn't lose, no matter what happened. Psychologists might label Mary's philosophy as being "fatalistic."

But the quintessent key to Mary Ball's philosophy was this: FEAR WAS A SIN NO PERSON SHOULD EVER COMMIT. She believed that the human emotion of fear was man's greatest foolishness, and the absolute height of useless stupidity. Mary Ball believed that for man to be afraid of anything was tantamount to his doubting the existence and nature of God. Why be afraid when God is in charge of everything that is? So Mary Ball believed that everyone, everywhere, should practice the mastery over the emotion of fear.

The mastery over fear . . . the mastery over fear . . . the mastery over fear. Does that sound familiar? Think. The mastery over fear is the definition of courage. Remember? Courage is not the absence of fear, but the mastery over it. Remember?

One hundred and fifty two years after Mary Ball died, a famous president of the United States said, "There is nothing to fear, except fear itself." Could this mean that Mary Ball is right?

Because of Mary Ball's spiritual beliefs, she held that for man, COURAGE was the highest virtue. Mary Ball believed that man had to practice the mastery over the emotion of fear to become courageous. She believed that man had to practice both physical courage and metaphysical courage. The definition of physical courage is self-explanatory and easy to understand, but what is this metaphysical courage? Metaphysical courage is conquering your fears enough to be able to stand up for what you believe in. To not only possess convictions, but to verbally express them. And if need be, to defend these convictions even at the risk of your life. Included in Mary's definition of metaphysical courage is the practice of NEVER GIVING UP, never quitting, ever, no matter what, when you felt that you were doing right. Metaphysical courage gives you the strength and fortitude to persevere, no matter what obstacles and hardships you meet in life.

In modern terminology, Mary Ball believed that you could master the emotion of fear by tapping into the power of positive thinking and understanding that the Force is with you.

Mary Ball married at age 26 and died at age 85 of breast cancer. She died in 1789, the first year that we would be living under our newly-ratified Constitution. Just a coincidence, of course.

So what did this woman mystic, Mary Ball, ever do to earn the love and respect of all Americans? What did she do to help us achieve our independence from England? How did she help us to win our Revolution?

The hand which rocks the cradle rules the world. There was a baby girl born in the new England colony of Virginia in 1704, whose one humble life would change the course of history forever. Her name was Mary . . . Mary Ball . . . and she was the mother of George Washington.

Chapter 6

The Father of Our Country

To trust the soul's invincible surmise
Was all his science and his only art.
                    —*George Santayana*

Augustine Washington married Mary Ball on March 6, 1730, and her first child, baby George, was born two years later. His father died when little Georgie was ten years old. When George reached manhood, except for his loving kindness, George remarked that he remembered little of his father, as Augustine left the management of children entirely to his mother. George grew up as an obedient and devoted son who always venerated his mother.

There is only one person in this whole wide world who will ever completely understand who you really are. And total understanding is total love. No matter what you ever become, no matter what you ever do, no matter what you ever think, no matter who or what your best friend, husband, wife, or children ever think you are, there is only one person in this whole wide world who will ever know who you really are. It's your mother. No one understands the program better than the programmer. So to completely understand George Washington, you would have to be Mary Ball.

Intelligence or I.Q. is one thing. Attitude or instinct is another thing. Mary Ball instilled in young George a unique attitude and instinct system regarding four major areas of his life: ACHIEVEMENT, FREEDOM, FEAR, and DESTINY. She planted the exact same seeds in her five other children, but these seeds took, grew, blossomed, and bore excellent fruit only in George, her firstborn. No other Washington child achieved any prominence. It is unexplainable why only young George's dust was fertile ground.

Mary taught young George that it was his duty to do his best, to try his hardest, to be an achiever. She taught him that being cooperative was not always a virtue, and that being competitive was not always a vice. But becoming a CONFORMIST was always wrong, and being an independent INDIVIDUALIST was always right.

Mary taught young George that it was his duty to be free, and that when he eventually became a man, he would never again have to ask anyone for permission to act. He would possess the God-given right to just act.

Mary taught young George that it was his duty to recognize when he became afraid of anything, to analyze the fear he felt, to consider it wisely, to gradually become insensitive to fear by placing it in its proper perspective according to God's wishes, and to eventually MASTER, overcome, control, and eliminate it entirely from his life.

And finally, Mary taught young George that it was his duty to believe in the principle of divine destiny. That meant that young George should always strive to say and do whatever he felt was true, fair, good, right, and just, and after his acting this way, that God would determine the outcome of everything. If he succeeded, God wanted him to succeed. If he failed, God wanted him to fail. If he received pleasure or pain, God willed it. Mary taught young George to pray as if the outcome of everything depended on God, but to act as if the outcome of everything depended on his own actions.

The principle of divine destiny is the principle of letting the force be with you. It is the principle of understanding and accepting that the force controls everything, but acting as if you control everything. Accepting the principle of divine destiny means that you should always say and do the right thing as you see it, and then let the chips fall where they may.

Practice makes perfect, and as a little child, young George began to practice, and practice again, and practice over and over again. He practiced trying to be an achiever. He practiced trying to be free and not asking permission to do things. He practiced trying not to be afraid of anything. He practiced trying to calmly accept the consequences of all his words and actions as being God's divine will. He practiced everything his mother taught him. Use it or lose it.

It should now be easier for you to understand why historians have reported that George Washington was a completely fearless man, totally courageous, unselfish, sacrificial, treated both pleasure and pain the same, and why he would never give up, no matter what. George was an exact copy of his mother, Mary Ball. The force was with him too, and growing gradually to understand and practice these divine principles as well as his mother did, George acted accordingly. You needn't wonder anymore how he became known as the Father of our Country.

Young George grew up normally though, but everyone who encountered him felt he was somehow different, somehow special. Consciousness evolves slowly until it crystalizes. By his teenage years, George's sense of pride made him feel that he was somehow different, somehow superior to other human beings in so many respects, but his sense of humility and immaturity caused him to attribute his superiority to his just being lucky. And even after George became a full-grown man, when he fully understood that his superiority wasn't really just luck but that it was God using him as an INSTRUMENT for God's own divine purposes, George would still tell people around him that he was just lucky. How can you explain your superiority to your fellow human beings who are plagued with insecurity, jealousy, envy, inferiority complexes, and the full gamut of uncontrolled human frailties that you are superior because you are a mystic, without their thinking that you are insane?

So young George grew up normally, living on a large farm, learning how to plant and produce vegetables, grains, fruits, and tobacco. He loved to fish, hunt, and go rowing and sailing on the Rappahannock River. He especially loved music, and loved dancing with pretty girls. He also loved to play cards and billiards for money. He developed a lifelong love for horses and the great outdoors. He also loved to barbeque, take a drink or two or three, and smoke or chew. And he had a great sense of humor, a dry wit, and he loved to smile and laugh at good jokes.

George grew up normally. He occasionally came down sick with common colds, fevers, and the small pox. In fact, the small pox left a few tiny scars on his face which he carried for the rest of his life. And he started shaving his face at age 16.

George grew up so normally that he even experienced the excruciating pains of love sickness. He flirted with several girls as a teenager, but at age 20, he fell madly in love with 16 year old Betsy Fauntleroy, and proposed marriage to her on two different occasions. So he must have kissed her on the lips. Both times Betsy refused the hand of this 6 foot, 4 inch, brown-haired, blue-eyed, 175 pounder. Could it be that she detected divine providence intervening and was intimidated by some unexplainable traits in George's character which we have been talking about? George sadly described Betsy's rejections of his love as a "cruel sentence" which he would have to endure. Is there an emotional pain for young people greater than unrequited love, or for anyone of any age, for that matter?

Yes, young George grew up normally, but like his mother, Mary Ball, he was not to be an ordinary human being. Just listen to the flavor of a sample from a little book of rules for personal behavior which young George wrote for himself when he was about 9 years old:

> *"Turn not your Back to others especially in Speaking, Jog not the Table or Desk on which Another reads or writes, lean not upon any one.*
>
> *Use no Reproachful Language against any one, neither Curse nor Revile.*
>
> *Play not the Peacock, looking every where about you, to See if you be well Deck't, if your Shoes fit well, if your Stokings Sit neatly, and Cloths handsomely.*
>
> *While you are talking, Point not with your Finger at him of Whom you Discourse nor Approach too near him to whom you talk especially to his face.*

> *Be not Curious to Know the Affairs of Others,
> neither approach those that Speak in Private."*

Yes, this George Washington was normal, but he would be different.

The royal colony of Virginia was a vast and unexplored wilderness when George Washington was born, and savage Indians were a constant menace to the early settlers. As a little boy, George remembers English naval and army officers visiting his home. He remembered listening to conversations regarding naval battles and also the English Army's attempts to protect the colonists from the numerous scalping incidents and horrible Indian atrocities, and he attributed his strong liking for the military life to these tales. They seemed to give young George a purpose he could dedicate his life to, a valid cause to live for.

As the twig is bent, so grows the tree. Because young George was trained by his mother, and because of his athletic talents and intensely competitive spirit, he very early developed a reputation which became widespread in his neighborhood and throughout all of the neighboring counties in Virginia. His reputation was this: that young George Washington had a courageous disregard for danger and hardship, and an immense desire for adventure, and probably feared BOREDOM more than death.

At age 14, he wanted to quit school to join the Royal English Navy, but his mother would not permit it. What a prophetic refusal her decision would be. At age 14, he still felt he needed his mother's permission. But one year later, he would not feel this way.

In school, since young George excelled so much in math, geometry, and trigonometry, he decided to become a civil engineer, or surveyor, which profession was in great demand and consequently was very lucrative in the unsurveyed and rapidly expanding new country. Individual private property holders and budding real estate companies desperately needed maps drawn of the boundaries of their land holdings, but competent surveyors were hard to find with enough guts to risk arrows in the back, tomahawks in the head, and fatal haircuts. The pay was understandably high because of the risk-reward ratio of entering hostile Indian-infested territory and having to sleep overnight outdoors for weeks at a time. Would you work for the minimum wage if chances were high that you could get killed while you were performing your work, or possibly killed on your way back home? Would any hazardous duty pay be high enough for you?

Practicing his freedom, George did quit school at age 15, and began his surveying career. His reputation for intelligence, bravery, and technical surveying accuracy grew so rapidly that Lord Fairfax sent George into the wilderness with a few assistants to complete a survey, when George had but turned 16 years old by one month.

After George successfully completed the survey for Fairfax, his never forgotten attraction to military life led him to join the Virginia colonial militia, which is similar to the citizen soldiers in your state's National Guard. Militiamen, like modern National Guardsmen, hold full-time civilian jobs, but participate occasionally in group military-exercise training and band together for common defense during a perceived emergency. The militia was sort of like your local volunteer fire company or first aid squad (and only as good as each individual).

Over the next four years, George endured extreme hardships, but became one of the most respected surveyors in the royal colony of Virginia, and by the age of 20, he had also risen to the rank of Major in the Virginia Militia.

As a point of interest, George had been making good money as a surveyor for five years, in addition to his having inherited valuable property. By the age of 20, he was a wealthy man. He could have decided to live the "good life" of a country gentleman, living off of a prosperous farm. But his own radar or the force's radar was compelling him towards the military, or the "hard life." George was more cause-oriented, wanting to add meaning to his life, rather than simply being money-motivated.

In the following year, Major Washington, at the age of 21, would get his first chance to fulfill his romantic illusions for chivalry. His Majesty the King's Royal Governor Dinwiddie of Virginia would provide George with his first windmill or vision quest. It would be George's first military mission.

War is hell. Young women always knew that, but young men never did until after they personally experienced it. Although it would probably be inaccurate to say that young men used to consider the thought of going to war to be fun, it certainly would be accurate to say that young men then considered the thought of war to be romantic, chivalrous, adventurous, and glamorous. Young men then found it especially glamorous to fight bullies, and then even young women approved of that kind of fight.

England and France had fought bloody wars against each other on the European continent for centuries, and considered themselves traditional enemies. English trading companies and French trading companies both were establishing settlements in North America for similar economic reasons. It was probably inevitable that a clash of interests would break out between the two powers in colonial America.

In 1744, the Royal Governor of Virginia bought miles and miles of Ohio River land for English settler occupancy from the Iroquois Indians, one of the six Indian nations inhabiting the continent, and paid them 100 pounds of pure gold. Today, 100 pounds of pure gold would be equivalent to approximately $650,000. But as English colonists moved in to settle this land, they were constantly harrassed, raided, and massacred by the French with their non-Iroquois Indian allies. The French refused to recognize the validity of the English purchase because the French big businessmen trading companies in control of the French government knew that the English wanted to clear the land for homes and farms, thus hurting the French fur hunting and trapping business, as cutting down the forest always drives the animals away.

Nine years after the English purchased the Ohio River land from the Iroquois, in October 1753, Royal Governor Dinwiddie of Virginia asked for a volunteer to deliver his written message to the French military commander of the Ohio River Valley, located in a fort the French had built near the present site of Erie, Pennsylvania. Dinwiddie's message expressed "surprise and concern" that the French had invaded and occupied His Majesty the King of England's purchased territory, and the message contained a warning that the French should withdraw their troops and vacate the area, pronto. You can see what's coming.

Major George Washington of the Virginia Militia volunteered to deliver this message for Governor Dinwiddie. At the age of 21, this would be George's first military mission, being in command of a seven man contingent.

George left in early November from Virginia, and arrived at the French fort in the middle of December. He had to ride a horse for 41 DAYS (oh, my aching . . .) through 500 miles of mostly unbroken wilderness. How would you like to try that one? Think about it. Think about knowing that you would have to turn around in cold, snowy December to make the same trip back home. Today you could make this same trip by car in one day, and by plane in a few hours. Incredible.

The French commander accepted George politely, but rejected Dinwiddie's warning, explaining that his orders were to take control of the entire Ohio River Valley. The Frenchman gave George a letter to bring back to Dinwiddie which would basically say "up yours."

Remember, George was Mary Ball's son. He had physical courage and metaphysical courage. He was resigned to both pleasure or pain. He understood that God was in control. He had mastered the emotion of fear to such a point that he practically had eliminated it entirely from his life. He would always try to do his best, and the rest was up to God. What God wanted to happen, would happen. And George knew that the force was with him. Amen.

With George's mission completed, he began his long trek homeward. This trip back from Erie to the capital of colonial Virginia in Williamsburg in the dead of winter would prove again what George had been experiencing all of his young life: THAT THE FORCE WAS WITH HIM.

When the first group of horses gave out after several days and fresh mounts could not be found, George and one companion pushed ahead on foot through the wilderness because of George's sense of urgency to report the bad news to Dinwiddie regarding French intentions. While on foot in the wilderness, they met an Indian who said that he would show them a shortcut. Instead, the Indian actually tried to get them lost. When they expressed their suspicion to the Indian, an argument ensued. The Indian started shooting at very close range, first at George and then at his companion. No bullets hit them and they subdued and captured their assailant. Never thought Indians were such bad shots. Must have been just a coincidence, of course.

Contrary to the violently expressed wishes of his companion, George spared the Indian's life and sent him on his way. Caught fish thrown back seem to miraculously return to the good sports when they need them. George believed what goes around, comes around. You'll soon see that he was right. Another Indian would soon try to kill George Washington.

Still on foot, George and his companion came to the partly frozen Allegheny River by nightfall. They slept upon the bank of the river in cold, deep snow, weary and hungry. At daybreak, with only one hatchet, they cut down several small trees to build a crude raft to cross the river. Building the raft took them from sunrise to sunset. In the darkness, they finally launched the raft on to the turbulent water, which was very much over their heads. In the darkness, in the swift current, in mid-stream, huge blocks of rapidly moving icebergs rammed into and capsized the raft, throwing George and his companion overboard into the treacherous and icy water.

Fully clothed, drowning seemed imminent. In the pitch darkness with negative visibility, and in turbulent waters, in the middle of the river, an island appeared (who is this guy, anyway?), and George and his companion drifted safely onto it, where they spent the rest of the night, wet to the skin, with no spark of fire, with their clothing frozen stiffly upon their backs, and with the unpleasant thought, that if they survived the night, of the impossibility of their getting to the other side of the river at daybreak without a raft.

During the night, the temperature dropped to even more extreme cold. People do die of hypothermia, but they didn't. In the morning, the biting cold which didn't kill them had frozen the whole river, and they walked across the ice to the other side. Must have been just a coincidence, of course. Who is this guy, anyway?

The trip home to Williamsburg, Virginia took about 6 weeks. George never lost the French letter, never lost the maps and surveys of the terrain, and never lost the notes he took regarding the strength and disposition of the French forces. It was January of 1754, and George Washington's first military mission was over.

Arriving in Williamsburg, George delivered his report and all of the papers to Governor Dinwiddie proving that the French would resist with force any English attempts to populate the Ohio Valley they had purchased from the Iroquois. Governor Dinwiddie immediately promoted George from Major to the rank of Lieutenant-Colonel in the Virginia Militia.

When George arrived in Williamsburg, the Virginia legislature was in session. He went unannounced into the gallery for visitors and spectators to observe the proceedings. The presiding officer spotted tall George and spontaneously proposed to the legislature that "the thanks of this house be given to Major Washington, who now sits in the gallery, for the gallant manner in which he has executed the important trust lately reposed in him by his excellency the governor."

George was completely surprised. Every legislator and spectator in the hall rose to their feet and broke out in tumultuous applause.

George could not have been more embarrassed by this unexpected praise. When the clapping and cheering finally died down, and everyone had resumed their seats, George rose to his feet, and unaccustomed to public speaking, unsuccessfully tried to utter a few coherent words of humble thanks, but his choking-up tied his tongue.

The presiding officer who had caused this sensation decided to rescue George from the situation he had helped to place George in. "Sit down, Mr. Washington," he said politely, "your modesty equals your valor, and that surpasses the power of any language that I possess."

Stories of George's mission were published in London, coming to the immediate attention of the King, Parliament, the business and professional community, and to all of the English people. Stories of the mission were also published and widely distributed throughout all of the colonies. George Washington's first military mission put him on the map in a big way, making him a more well known star. But he had not yet been in his first battle, and had not yet been in real combat.

George recommended that Governor Dinwiddie send men to construct a fort at the strategic site where the Monongahela River and the Allegheny River met the Ohio River. This three rivers triangle site would later come to be known as the city of Pittsburgh, Pennsylvania. Within five days of George's return, Dinwiddie sent 40 colonial carpenters with a small escort of Redcoats to build the suggested fort.

While cutting down trees and sawing logs for the fort, several hundred French and Indians arrived and demanded that the Redcoats and colonists surrender immediately, which they did, reasoning that they were so hopelessly outnumbered that resistance would be suicidal. It was April of 1754, and the war to determine the French or English possession of the North American continent had begun. It became known as the French and Indian War, which was to last for 9 years.

The French used the captured logs to construct Fort Duquesne on the three rivers site, and they were ready for war.

The telegraph and telephone had not yet been invented, so it took a long time for the news to travel that the French had captured the three rivers fort site. Before Royal Governor Dinwiddie discovered this bad news, he gave George his second military mission: to recruit a troop of colonials and march them to Pittsburgh to man the new fort he assumed his carpenters would have completed.

George Washington's second military mission would be the prophetic event which would shock his eyes open for the very first time regarding what to

George was an inconceivable idea: that the King and Parliament had a demeaning, degrading attitude towards colonists, considering them second class English citizens.

George always considered himself to be a loyal Englishman, with the only difference being that he was living in the English state of Virginia in the country of America. He was loyal to the King, loyal to the English Parliament, and loyal to the English people. To better understand how George felt, think of it this way: if your father's business company in the United States relocated him to work in the island state of Hawaii, and you were born and raised while your mother and father were still living there, wouldn't you still consider yourself to be an American, loyal to the President, Congress, and to the American people? Sure you would.

But seeds would now be planted in George's mind which would later bear fruit.

As George began to recruit his fellow Virginia colonials to march to man the Pittsburgh fort, he was shocked when Dinwiddie and the Redcoat English regular soldiers treated him personally with discrimination, and like a second class Englishman. Dinwiddie refused to pay George and his colonial militiamen on the same pay scale as the Redcoat regulars, though the colonials would have to face the exact same dangers and hardships. Also Dinwiddie informed George that every Redcoat officer would automatically outrank any colonial officer of any rank. So a Redcoat lieutenant would be considered the superior officer or boss in charge of a colonial General. George believed that these policies were grossly unfair, and unreasonably discriminatory, and that they should definitely be changed. George believed in equality—or equal pay for equal work, and equal respect for equal rank.

Prejudice hurts. George was temporarily very mad. There is a legitimate place for justifiable pride. He wrote that "my services will equal those of the best." He was particularly irritated that, as he put it, "any whipper snapper" of a regular outranked him. Incidently, George was only 22 years old when he wrote this. Who does this guy think he is anyway? A mystic? What stainless steel round ones.

George almost told Dinwiddie to shove it, but he recovered. But he would never forget the insult, and he stored it in his memory bank.

The colonial militiamen resented the discrimination in pay and rank between themselves and the Redcoats, so George had a difficult time recruiting men for the mission. He was able to persuade only 160 men to go along, and they disembarked in April of 1754.

When George and his men were still 200 miles from the fort, they learned that the French had captured it, and renamed it Fort Duquesne. George's original orders read that when he reached and occupied the fort that he should "be on the defensive . . . to repel force by force." But the situation had obviously changed, and having no new orders to cover this new development, George decided to create his own new orders. Typical George Washington initiative, heh? Instead of turning back, the fearless spirit decided to move forward. George believed in reality, not technicality. Technically, war between the English and French had not been officially declared, but in reality, what do you call it when the enemy captures your fort? Pattycake?

George marched his men forward towards French

occupied Fort Duquesne. Within two weeks, he and his men were within a few miles of the fort, and their advanced scouts reported back to George that a small platoon of French soldiers were camped ahead of him, directly in the path of George's march.

Now what?

What else? These French were enemy trespassers on English territory. In George's mind, the war had started. Here comes George's first combat experience. After making battle plans, George attacked the French platoon. Surprising the French troops, George and his men waded into them, killing 10, wounding 1, and capturing 21 prisoners. George lost only one of his own men killed.

Lieutenant-Colonel George Washington afterwards wrote a letter to his brother describing his first experience with combat as "a most signal victory." How would you feel before fighting your first battle? Most people experience dry mouths, shakes, and queazy stomachs. Can you imagine? You realize that if a musket ball hits you, it will blow a mighty big hole in you, right? Remembering all of this, get ready for George's next line. He went on to say: "I heard the bullets whistle, and, believe me, there is something CHARMING in the sound."

Charming? Is he joking? Sure he is. To George, the emotion of fear was a joke. When you know the force is with you, guess you're not afraid of being hit. Who is this guy anyway?

By this time, George, through practice, had achieved so much mastery over the human emotion of fear that he felt nothing but contempt for it. In fact, he had practically eliminated his emotion of fear, and hated to see it in anyone else, since it was such an anti-God emotion. The emotion of fear makes COW-ARDS out of men and women. George Washington hated the emotion of fear with a passion.

George's original mission from Dinwiddie was to occupy a fort. Not willing to risk an attack on well-fortified Fort Duquesne with just 160 men, George took the initiative again and marched 60 miles to the south, and built and occupied what he called Fort Necessity. You see, George was not suicidal, just unbelievably courageous, and it is apparent that George believed that discretion is SOMETIMES the better part of valor. It was June of 1754.

Soon, about 180 Virginia militiamen and a few dozen friendly Indians arrived at Fort Necessity as reinforcements, bearing the news that George had been promoted to the rank of full Colonel. But by June 14, George and his men were out of food, and nearing starvation. Now what? There was no McDonald's or Burger King in the area. But remember, somebody up there likes George.

So what happens? About 100 Redcoat regulars, commanded by a captain, arrive unexpectedly at Fort Necessity with needed supplies. Just a coincidence, of course, which brings George's troop strength up to 450 men.

The titularly underranked Redcoat captain, according to policy, informed militia Colonel Washington that he was taking command of Fort Necessity and all of its men. George explained no way José. There was a deadlock. The Redcoats wouldn't take orders from George, and the militiamen wouldn't take orders from the Redcoat captain. Meanwhile, 100 men were sick, and all of the rest were still relatively hungry.

On July 3, about 2,000 French and Indians attacked

Fort Necessity, killing 30 and wounding 70. And George's men had eaten no bread for several days. By nightfall, a torrential rainfall appeared from nowhere, leaving George with no dry gunpowder. With more than half of his men sick, killed, or wounded, and the rest starving, and with wet gunpowder making it impossible to fire another shot, and with no cooperation from the Redcoat captain, George Washington surrendered in humiliation on July 4th. This surrender date is probably just a coincidence, of course. And notice again, George is not suicidal, just courageous. And his second experience with combat was over.

The French permitted George to evacuate the fort with his men and guns, and George marched back to Williamsburg, arriving two weeks later, madder than Bobby Knight for losing, and embarrassed to tears. After making his report to Governor Dinwiddie, he went home to Mount Vernon, Virginia to lick his wounded pride and to get some needed rest.

Two months later, George returned to Williamsburg where Dinwiddie informed him that London had ordered the reduction of rank of all colonial militia officers, so that George Washington must be lowered from his recently received promotion to the rank of colonel, back to the rank of captain. Could this action have been a punishment for George's argument with the Redcoat captain at Fort Necessity? Maybe.

Rather than accept a demotion, George angrily resigned his commission, and returned home to Mt. Vernon as a civilian. He later wrote that the English were behaving "like Fools."

George Washington at age 22 was experiencing the idiotic discipline of bureaucrats for the very first time, and he refused to docilely submit to it. George was learning that desk jockeys in their ivory tower offices love to protect their own jobs and feather their own nests by harrassing the productive field staff people doing all of the real work.

Five months later, English General Braddock, sent from England with 1,000 trained Redcoat regulars, arrived in Virginia. His assignment was to capture Fort Duquesne. General Braddock sent a message to George, asking him to help him to succeed in this mission.

George still yearned for the military life, so he viewed Braddock's request as a unique opportunity, perhaps to secure for himself a royal commission, instead of the second class colonial commission. So he agreed to accompany Braddock, but only as a civilian aide to the General, and George even agreed to serve without pay, thus avoiding any possible confrontations.

The march to Fort Duquesne began in June of 1755. Braddock also took along about 300 Virginia colonial militiamen, bringing his troop strength up to 1,300 men.

George tried hard to explain to General Braddock what he had learned at Fort Necessity, that the French and Indians fought guerilla style warfare, hiding and shooting concealed behind trees, and using the tactics of ambush. They would not fight politely standing up in columned rows, a la European style. Because of these facts, George suggested that Braddock should think of changing his battle style.

All of George's warnings to Braddock fell on deaf ears. Braddock had graduated from the finest English military academies, and he prided himself on his technical military education. He only had contempt for rag-tag colonials. What did they know? His self-conceit and bureaucratic arrogance amazed and insulted young George Washington.

Braddock marched his Redcoats, supply wagons, and artillery pieces out in the open, in one long column, as if they were going on a picnic. And the color red of their uniforms made a very visible target against a tree green background. Fearless George couldn't believe Braddock's recklessness, and continued to counsel caution in the form of several separate columns, spread safely apart. Braddock mockingly laughed at George's concern.

Braddock foolishly expected the French to politely wait for him snuggled safely in their fort. On July 9, when Braddock and his forces were only 8 miles away from Fort Duquesne, a few hundred French and Indians ambushed them. Simultaneously, shots rang out in the front, in the rear, from the left, and from the right. And Braddock's men could not even see the enemy. Within minutes, 800 of the 1300 lay dead or wounded. The French and Indian musket balls were hitting their targets at close range.

Being unfamiliar with this type of warfare, and still not being able to see the enemy, the Redcoats broke up in a wild panic. What a bloody massacre! Braddock himself was mortally wounded and died three days later, but not before he apologized to George Washington for not heeding his advice and not before bequeathing his finest horse to so wise an aide.

In the heat of his third battle, what did the fearless spirit do? George tried valiantly to rally the remaining Redcoat regulars, but none would listen to a colonial, especially a colonial who was technically a civilian, but all of the colonial militiamen would. George ordered the colonials to position themselves to fight from behind trees. From there, the colonials drove back the charging Indians several times. George called up the artillery and actually fired several cannon blasts himself. George rode horseback up and down the entire column to rally all of the survivors to fight. George's gallant efforts saved the remaining live Redcoat soldiers from a total massacre.

When the French and Indians realized that they could not completely finish the kill, they retired back to Fort Duquesne.

With George in command, the colonials protected the rear of the retreating Redcoats all the way back to Williamsburg.

Describing the disaster, George later wrote: "We were attacked by about 300 French and Indians. Our numbers consisted of about 1300 well armed men, chiefly regulars, who were immediately struck with such a deadly panic that nothing but confusion and disobedience of orders prevailed amongst them . . . the English soldiers broke and ran as sheep before the hounds . . . The General (Braddock) was wounded behind in the shoulder and into the breast, of which he died three days after."

George was not impressed with the discipline and fighting ability of the Redcoats at Fort Necessity, and he was even less impressed with these same traits of the Redcoats under Braddock's command. He filed these thoughts of military disrespect for the Redcoats in his memory bank.

Still describing the Braddock fiasco, George matter-of-factly wrote regarding himself: "I luckily escaped without a wound, though I had four bullets through my coat and two horses shot under me." You see.

It was luck. He says so himself. What else could it be? Who is this guy anyway? Four bullets through his coat, two horses blown apart under him, and he doesn't even get a scratch. Somebody up there must like him.

Years later, George found out who was shooting at him. You read that right. What do you think are the odds of an expert sharpshooter specifically assigned to kill you in a battle because of your recognized reputation, years later, travelling for weeks through the wilderness to find you again to tell you that he was the sniper shooting at you during the Braddock massacre? One in a zillion? Well, it happened. And guess what? He was an Indian.

George and his crew were surveying farmland in Western Virginia along the Kanawha River when an old Indian walked into his camp. The old Indian told everyone that before he died he had to speak to the man, as he said, "with the charmed life." Every man knew to whom the Indian was referring. Why did this old Indian feel that before he died that it was his mission to see George Washington? What compulsion drove him? What was burning inside this Indian that George Washington just had to hear?

This Indian told George that he was the sniper specifically ordered to shoot him during that battle. This Indian explained that the French gave him the assignment because of his reputation for never missing a target. This Indian went on to explain how he took careful aim on his first shot, how he squeezed it off, and how he couldn't understand why George wasn't knocked off his horse. This Indian couldn't believe that he had missed. To his amazement, George kept on fighting.

This Indian explained how he reloaded, took careful aim again, and how he squeezed off a second shot. George kept fighting. This Indian scratched his head.

This Indian explained how he reloaded again, took careful aim again, and how he squeezed off a third shot. George kept on fighting. This Indian was getting spooked.

This Indian explained how he reloaded again, took super careful aim, and how he squeezed off a fourth shot. And George kept fighting.

This Indian explained that he deliberately stopped firing at George after four bullets failed. Indians are superstitious folks, ain't they?

This Indian had no idea that all of his bullets did in fact hit George, but passed through his coat. Just a coincidence, of course.

This Indian explained to George that he had come to tell him that Washington would never die in war. This Indian knew that the force was with George, and of course, this Indian's prophesy would be correct. This Indian delivered his prophetic message to George before the French and Indian War ended.

Throughout the colonies and overseas in England, George had become a living military legend after he rescued the Redcoat survivors of Braddock's massacre. His reputation for fearlessness and valor in the face of the enemy was unchallenged. He was a hero, but a few weeks after Braddock's defeat, he retired to his Mt. Vernon home. He was only 23 years old, and in a letter to his brother, this living military legend reviewed his military career like this: ''I was employed to go a journey in the winter (when I believe few or none would have undertaken it) and what did I get by it? My expenses borne! I then was appointed with trifling pay to conduct a handful of men to the Ohio. What did I get by this? Why, after putting myself to a considerable expense by equipping and providing necessaries for the campaign, I went out, was soundly beaten . . . came in, and had my commission taken from me, or in other words, my command reduced, under pretense of an order from home . . . I have been on the losing order ever since I entered the service." And regarding the Braddock defeat, he referred to the "dastardly behavior of the Regular troops" and the "cowardly Regulars . . . Shamefully beaten, by a handful of men."

George rested at Mt. Vernon for only two weeks, when Dinwiddie persuaded him to accept back his colonial militia commission again at the rank of colonel. George's new military mission was to defend Virginia's western frontiers against French and Indian attacks. This he did for three full years, fighting through many more bloody battles without ever being wounded, but finally he resigned and retired again in 1758 at the still young age of 26. The French and Indian War would last for five more years, but George Washington would choose not to be an active participant in that war ever again.

When George retired at age 26, he was thoroughly convinced of two things: the English Army could be beaten, and if a colonial war against England ever materialized, that he was the person who would know how to beat them.

In the next 17 years, George would marry the widow Martha with two young children, run for office and serve in the Virginia legislature and win re-election every time, and manage his farming business—but would participate in no more soldiering for the English Empire.

Why would a dedicated soldier like George decide to stop fighting for the English Empire when the French and Indian War was not over and would last for five more years? It doesn't make sense. Good question. Wasn't he a war lover? Why would he quit? Seems totally out of character for a man who thinks the sound of bullets whistling past his head is music to his ears, doesn't it?

The answer to why George decided to stop fighting for the English Empire will become more obvious to you if you understand the fundamentals of the great American game of baseball: three strikes and you're out. George graciously gave the English 33 strikes, and in his mind, they always struck out. They always made the exact same errors over and over again. They always dropped the ball. They would never accept any coaching or advice. They were uneducable. You can't make chicken salad out of chicken feathers. There were a lot of streets named after them: one way. Theirs. They were legends in their own minds. Their door was always closed. Their game is called: breaking your will to resist—you can't beat us, you have to join us. Take it or leave it.

GEORGE DECIDED TO LEAVE IT.

Have you ever dealt with people like that? Autocratic. Authoritarian. Dictatorial. Snobby. Egotistical. Manipulative. On a power trip. Thinking their hotdogs are ice cream. Getting off on controlling people. Keeping them on a short leash. Well I'll be damned . . . bullies! You understand? Perfect rectal orifices.

If you've ever experienced people like that, saw

them operating in several different situations, how long did it take you to realize that they were professional screw job artists? Only masochists hang around these types for very long, patiently waiting to be their next victim.

George was not a masochist. Are you?

George believed in the good principle of motivation, as opposed to the bad tactic of manipulation. When you are being motivated, the motivator is influencing you to do something beneficial for yourself. When you are being manipulated, the manipulator is deceptively influencing you to do something which will benefit the manipulator. George quit fighting for the English when he felt that they were manipulating him for their own hidden purposes.

George loved a challenge, and was willing to pay any price necessary to achieve a goal he believed in. But there comes a time when you lose faith in something or somebody. There comes a time when you don't need each other anymore. And then it's sayonara time.

You can practice manyana for just so long. When that process starts, sayonara is around the corner. Bridges are there to cross . . . when you're ready to . . . when you're mature enough to . . . and you should never look back in mid-stream. It's O.K.

George lost faith, and didn't think it was wise to risk his life fighting for an English Empire which would continue to consider him and all colonials as second class citizens. He remembered the pamphlet published in 1694, "A New Discourse of Trade," which expressed the big business philosophy which caused Parliament to pass the laws forbidding the colonials to manufacture and sell their own products, and which forced the colonists to depend on items imported from the big English businessmen. Those obnoxious laws had multiplied and become more restrictive by 1758, and had created a dedicated colonial group of discontented reformers. George Washington was one of them.

In 1758, reformer George Washington would try to do HIS PART to VOTE the colonies out of their mess by his becoming a Virginia legislator. He was elected to the Virginia House of Burgesses in that year and would be re-elected every time. He would serve in that capacity for the next consecutive 15 years, where he would discover that it was IMPOSSIBLE to achieve justice for the colonies from England through a voting process, OBVIOUSLY controlled by the greedy, bully, English big businessmen.

In 1769, after operating as a dedicated reformer seeking justice for the colonies through voting for 11 long years, George Washington was 37 years old. He was still the best known man in Virginia, and still the best known man in all of the thirteen colonies. And he had not fought a military battle for 11 years.

In that year of 1769, the Virginia legislature voted to protest the unfair taxation the colonists were subjected to by the big business-controlled English Parliament. You know George voted for that. The new Virginia Royal Governor, Lord Botecourt, as a punishment, locked the doors of the legislative chambers, and refused to let the Virginia representatives meet in legislative session.

Because of this obnoxious tyranny, George Washington called a meeting in a Williamsburg tavern with several other like-minded legislators, where he was the first colonist to suggest the use of force to, as he said, "maintain liberty." Remember his mother had taught George that being free was his duty. In April, 1769, George wrote: "That no man should scruple, or HESITATE A MOMENT to use arms in defense of so valuable a blessing (liberty), ON WHICH ALL THE GOOD AND EVIL OF LIFE DEPENDS, is clearly my opinion; yet arms, I would beg leave to add, should be the last . . . resort."

His remark made it obvious that George Washington had lost faith in the reformer's approach to voting yourself out of a mess. He realized that the bullyism of the English would never change, and that the only thing that a bully understands is a hard punch in the nose. George had become a REVOLUTIONARY.

In the next few years, George would hear the news of the Boston Massacre, the Boston Tea Party, and the Boston Harbor closing. George would write: ". . . shall we supinely sit and see one province after another fall a prey to despotism?" George is no doubt suggesting arms. It was 1774.

The Virginia legislature again protested the English tyranny in Boston. The new Royal Governor, Lord Dunmore, again dismissed the legislature. With Boston under martial law and occupied by thousands of Redcoats, reformer-legislator-George-turned-revolutionary volunteered to recruit an army and march to the relief of the Boston colonists. The fearless spirit was beginning to scare the less fearless.

With Boston under English seige in 1774, George was elected to be a delegate to the First Continental Congress which met in Philadelphia in September. Six months later, the Virginia legislature left Williamsburg to avoid dismissal by Dunmore and met for a meeting in Richmond, Virginia. It was March of 1775, and George would sit in the audience and listen to his friend, Patrick Henry, deliver his stirring "We Must Fight" speech, which Henry closed with the inspiring words, "Give me liberty, or give me death." Then two weeks later, in April 1775, the shots heard 'round the world were fired at Lexington and Concord, Massachusetts.

One month later, on May 10, 1775, the Second Continental Congress met in Philadelphia, the central location of the colonies, to formulate a plan of action. Delegate George Washington again attended. After talking, and talking, and talking, and talking about the problem for two weeks, revolutionary George Washington did something unusual and special. He wouldn't talk anymore. He went silent. All he would do was to listen, and listen, and listen, and listen some more. The other delegates became unnerved by his behavior.

The English were occupying Boston, and starving the Bostonians. Brave men had fired shots at Lexington and Concord. Remember, George didn't believe in technicalities, but he believed in reality. In his mind, the war against England had started. Talk was cheap. It was time for action. But most human beings crave authority to act, crave permission to act.

A picture is worth a thousand words. The nervous, vacillating delegates were acting as if they needed a sign from heaven that it was O.K. to fight. And one came. Delegate George Washington showed up in uniform one day. It was his blue and red colonel's uniform from the French and Indian War that he had not worn for 17 years. He was silent, and gave no explanations. He wore the uniform every day for the next two weeks, and wouldn't speak. No one dared to ask him if he thought he was attending a Halloween Party. Would you have?

On June 14th, the Second Continental Congress would unanimously elect George Washington as Commander-in-Chief of all colonial armed forces. He was then 42 years old. In his acceptance speech, delivered on June 16th, he said:

> *"Mr. President, Though I am truly sensible of the high honor done me in this appointment, yet I feel great distress, from a consciousness that my abilities and military experience may not be equal to the extensive and important trust. However, as the Congress desire it, I will enter upon the momentous duty, and exert every power I possess in their service, and for the support of the glorious cause. As to pay, sir, I beg leave to assure the Congress that, as no pecuniary consideration could have tempted me to accept the arduous employment at the expense of my domestic ease and happiness, I do not wish to make any profit from it. I will keep an exact amount of my expenses. Those, I doubt not, they will discharge, and that is all I desire."*

He also added: "I beg it may be remembered by every gentleman in the room, that I this day declare with the utmost sincerity, I do not think myself equal to the command I am honored with." The man was truly modest. He knew who he was. And he marched off to war.

The cardinal rule of warfare is this: know your enemy. No one knew the English enemy better than George Washington. No one in the colonies had more experience with the English military mind, the English legislative mind, and the English personality mind than George Washington. When it's a country of 3 million people fighting against a country of 10 million people, it is a David against Goliath affair. George Washington would be the right David.

George would spend the next 8 years fighting for his country. He would not return to his beloved Mt. Vernon home for the next 6 years, nor would he get the chance to vote for and sign the Declaration of Independence since he would be in the field fighting the war.

For some reason, the force would always be with this man. He would always lead a "charmed" life. It was proven again and again throughout the entire war. Who was this guy anyway?

In September of 1777, the Redcoats massively assembled around Wilmington, Delaware were getting ready to march a few miles north to attack the rebel capital of Philadelphia, the seat of government of the Continental Congress, the members of which were already evacuating the town in anticipation of an almost certain English victory. George would try to stop the English a few miles southwest of Philadelphia near the Brandywine River.

George was the type of great leader who would never ask his men to do something which he would never consider doing himself. And all of his men knew this about him. Five days before the battle, George and an assistant rode out of their camp to scout the terrain of Brandywine so he could intelligently plan the battle strategy and tactics himself. During this scouting and reconnoitering trip, George would accidentally meet an enemy English soldier named Patrick Ferguson.

Patrick Ferguson just happened to be the man who had designed and invented the most accurate rifle in the world at that time, but he could not succeed in getting the English Army to adopt its use for their armed forces, possibly because certain big English businessmen might lose too much money if they couldn't keep selling the military their extensive inventory of obsolete muskets.

Ferguson had joined the English Army at age 15, and in 1777, he was already a 20 year veteran at age 35. His theory was this: give your infantrymen an accurate rifle, and they will win your wars for you. The English infantry was using the Brown Bess musket which weighed 14 pounds, and a soldier might be able to fire 3 shots a minute, maybe, and with no accuracy. The Brown Bess was so inaccurate that the English weapons training manual for new recruits even left out and eliminated the command of "aim," using the suggestion to "point" the musket in the general direction of the target before squeezing the trigger.

Compared to the Brown Bess musket, Ferguson's breech-loading-rifle invention was half its weight (only 7 pounds), could fire double its shots (6 a minute), and was extremely accurate up to an amazing 300 yards (that's 3 football fields).

Patrick Ferguson had earned the affectionate nickname of "Bulldog" during his demonstrations of his rifle to the English Army High Command because he would lie backwards, prone on his back, and shoot perfect "bullseyes" at 100 yards. Standing, off-hand, he would shoot perfect bullseyes at 300 yards. Armed with his fabulous rifle, Bulldog Ferguson was far and away the best marksman in the entire English Army.

Rather than make a commitment to go into immediate production to arm every Redcoat with Bulldog's rifle, the English Army High Command sent Ferguson to America in 1776 to train and lead a small handful of sniper marksmen to operate against the rebels.

On September 7, 1777, Ferguson and a few of his snipers, armed with Bulldog's rifles, went out to scout the same Brandywine area that George Washington was scouting, and for the same reasons. When Ferguson got a quick glimpse of two horses approaching from a distance, he instructed his men to hide in the bushes. Ferguson later wrote, "We had not lain long when a rebel officer passed within a hundred yards of my right flank," riding a huge bay charger horse, with the officer wearing a "remarkably large cocked hat."

Ferguson also wrote, "I ordered three good shots to steal near them and fire." But seconds after he issued that order to his men, he retracted it, explaining that "the idea (of an ambush) disgusted me (probably as not honorably sporting). I recalled the order."

Ferguson later reported to his superiors that he thought that he had our Commander-in-Chief in his rifle sights that day because he knew that Washington's forces were camped and staging nearby preparing for the imminent battle, and also because he felt that he recognized Washington, since he had seen picture prints of George dozens of times, since these cheap prints of our famous leader sold for pennies and were tacked up everywhere in the colonies for inspirational purposes. Besides, Ferguson understood that the average height of a colonist was 5 feet 4 inches tall, and that the rebel officer with the large cocked hat, riding the classy bay charger, looked like a giant (remember George was 6 feet 4 inches tall and weighed 200 pounds now).

So Ferguson decided to take George Washington as a prisoner. He wrote, "I advanced from the woods towards him. He stopped, but after looking at me, proceeded. I again drew his attention and made signs to him to stop, but he (again) slowly proceeded on his way."

Nobody could intimidate our fearless spirit. And besides, George knew that he was a hundred yards away from his challenger, and without ESP which would have told him that the best marksman in the English Army armed with his own Bulldog rifle was addressing him (who ever said George had no ESP?), George probably reasoned that this enemy could never hit him with a Brown Bess shot from that distance anyway. Ferguson wrote, "I could have lodged a half-dozen balls in or about him before he was out of my reach."

After watching George Washington slowly and calmly ride out of sight, Ferguson wrote, "It was not pleasant to fire at the back of an unoffending individual who was acquitting himself very coolly of his duty, SO I LET HIM ALONE." Guess George was just lucky again.

God bless Bulldog Ferguson. Five days later, George would lose the Battle of Brandywine, and retreat to spend the terrible winter at Valley Forge, while the English captured and occupied Philadelphia.

For the entire war, the force would still be with George. His army would fight the entire war lacking food, clothing, and ammunition. George would endure disease, army desertions, mutinies, and plots to turn him over to the English enemy for hanging. The old Indian was right—George Washington would not die in battle. He would never even be wounded, nor would he even break a bone. And George was no armchair general. He was in the thick of every important battle, shooting his pistols, brandishing his sword, whipping his horse and sometimes his men, wading into the enemy, riding up and down the whole front issuing orders and rallying his troops, leading his men through artillery barrages exploding all around him, etc., etc., etc.

George Washington legitimately became the symbol of our Revolution in the minds and hearts of our people. Through thick and thin, victory or defeat, misery and despair, George was always there.

War is hell. George rode into hell, hunted for the bogeyman, and when he found him, George said to his face, "Boo," for 8 years. In 1777, the newspaper, the Pennsylvania Journal, wrote concerning George: "Had he lived in the days of idolatry, he had been worshipped as a god." In the same year, the heroic Frenchman who fought for us, the Marquis de Lafayette, wrote to George saying, ". . . if you were lost for America, there is NOBODY who could keep the Army and Revolution for six months."

When our Revolutionary War ended in 1783, George retired at the age of 51 to his home in Mt. Vernon. After a tearful farewell to his officers, George appeared before the Continental Congress on December 23, 1783 to resign his commission as Commander-in-Chief of all of the armed forces. This is what he said: "Having now finished the work assigned me, I retire from the great theatre of action, and bidding an affectionate farewell to this august body, under whose orders I have so long acted, I here offer my commission, and take my leave of all the employments of public life.''

His former brown hair had turned completely gray, and his sky blue eyes needed glasses to read.

Four years later, in 1787, George was UNANI-MOUSLY ELECTED PRESIDENT OF THE CON-STITUTIONAL CONVENTION MEETING IN PHILADELPHIA TO WRITE OUR CONSTITU-TION. Unanimously electing George Washington as president of the group assigned to write our Constitu-tion should prove beyond the shadow of a doubt that our founders were truly freedom lovers in every re-spect, because one year earlier, in 1786, the future president of our constitutional convention, charged with the responsibility to write our Constitution, wrote a letter to Declaration signer, Robert Morris, which was well publicized, concerning his hatred for the institution of slavery. George Washington wrote: ''There is no man living who wishes more sin-cerely than I do to see a plan adopted for the aboli-tion of slavery.'' So you no longer have to guess who the man was who led the charge to write that abolition of slavery into our Constitution. Unfortu-nately, George failed to accomplish this, one of his desired objectives.

It is here interesting to note, however, that many decades later, a future president of the United States would proclaim that his greatest hero, and the one man whose life would have more influence on this future president's life than any other man in recorded history was George Washington. That future presi-dent's name was Abraham Lincoln.

In February of 1789, after our Constitution was ratified by the states, and in force, George Washington, at the age of 57, was unanimously elected as the first President of the United States of America.

After serving two terms, 8 more long years, as our President, George retired to his home in Mt. Vernon in March of 1797, at the age of 65. His former gray hair was now completely white.

What were his last public remarks to his countrymen? What did he say in his Farewell Address? What advice did he think current and future generations of loyal Americans would need to remember?

In George's 6,000 word Farewell Address, he preached that all loyal Americans should firmly support our Constitution, and he warns us NEVER to allow a change in it unless by the AMENDMENT process. If presidents, senators, congressmen, or bureaucrats go around our Constitution by passing laws or making regulations not specifically authorized by our Constitution, George refers to this unAmerican, illegitimate lawmaking as evil "usurpation" of power, which appears that it "in one instance may be the instrument of good, it is the CUSTOMARY WEAPON by which free governments are destroyed."

George warns against our allowing our government to build up a HUGE NATIONAL DEBT that future generations of Americans will have to be taxed heavily for to repay.

He warned us that political parties, if not downright evil, are at least EXTREMELY DESTRUCTIVE AND DANGEROUS to the freedoms of individuals within our Republic; and you should understand that when he used the word, "republican," that he was not referring to the non-existent-at-the-time political party of that name, but to the unique form of our government known as a Republic.

George warned us that INTERNATIONAL TREATIES, AGREEMENTS, AND ALLIANCES with agencies or foreign governments are ALL dangerous to America, and should be kept to a minimum. But definitely have entangling alliances with none. He suggests that it is much safer for our free businessmen to make relationships with their free businessmen counterparts in foreign countries than it is for our government to make relationships with foreign governments. He is suggesting here an American governmental foreign policy of isolation as the smartest course of action for America, always.

And when foreign countries are fighting a shooting war against each other, George said that it is in America's best interests TO STAY OUT OF IT COMPLETELY, and to thereby maintain our STRICT NEUTRALITY in all such cases.

George Washington loved his country, America, and its people, first, last, only, and always. He was a nationalist, and a Real American, and proud of it.

Human nature never changes. Never. Not since Adam and Eve. Never. In his Farewell Address, George was giving us "straight talk" from his vast experiences with human nature for 65 years, from his vast experiences with every sort of person in every sort of situation. George was talking about human nature. His advice is timeless, and wise FOREVER. His advice in his Farewell Address is part of the essential fundamentals of the philosophy of Americanism.

Two years and 9 months later, at Mt. Vernon, Virginia, on December 14, 1799, at the age of 67, George fell gravely ill from strep throat. Without the antibiotics we have today, a strep infection can stop the beating of your heart. George knew he was dying.

Do you fear the unknown? THIS IS WHY YOU FEAR DEATH. But George feared nothing for all of his adult life, least of all death. How could he change now? And he didn't. Maybe he understood something about death which we don't understand.

On his sickbed in the afternoon, when he could hardly speak, he whispered to his doctors, "You had better not take any more trouble about me, but let me go off quietly. I cannot last long."

About 10 P.M. on his deathbed, with his wife, secretary, and doctors surrounding him, the fearless spirit calmly said, "I am just going. Have me decently buried, and do not let my body be put in the vault in less than two days after I am dead." And interestingly enough, he added, "Do you understand me?" His secretary said, "Yes, sir." George then said, " 'Tis well," and he expired. Mary Ball's son, George Washington, was dead. On December 18th, the fearless spirit's human remains were placed in the tomb at Mt. Vernon, where they still repose.

But George Washington's spirit is with us everyday, and every American carries his picture in their pocket, purse, or wallet.

Chapter 7

To Choose, or Not to Choose

The hottest places in hell are reserved for those, who in times of moral crisis, do nothing.
                                                   —*Dante*

William Shakespeare had Hamlet say: "To be, or not to be. That is the question." He could have had him say it differently, but meaning about the same thing, "to choose, or not to choose, to decide, or not to decide." This modern variation is a similar question, and it causes a similar madness.

To choose or not to choose is a tricky question which confuses most people, because it looks like you are faced with two things, when in reality, you are confronted with three.

"To choose" contains two parts, and "not to choose" contains only one part, so . . . we're talking about three parts.

To positively choose something is the first act, which automatically means when you do so, that you have negatively chosen to reject the other alternatives, which rejection constitutes a second act. And not to choose is a choice in itself to remain neutral, which is a third act.

In other words, "to choose" contains a pro and a con side. "Not to choose" contains only one side, but is a choice nevertheless. That makes three.

Are you still following this analysis? Hang in there. It's important. You'll see.

There are several major choices you MUST make for your life, and once you get by the majors, all of the other choices are minor and routine.

Major choices you will have to make are: should I go to college, or just work? If college, which one? If work, where? What career should I pursue? Should I go into business for myself? Should I marry or stay single? If it's to marry, who? Should I have children, and how many? Should I buy a home, and where?

Once you've made these major decisions or choices, which are tough, all of the other decisions are easy, minor, routine, and no-brainers, like what should I eat for lunch, or should I cut the grass today.

Nobody likes to make tough decisions. That's natural. Having to make tough decisions is emotionally painful. Facing tough decisions makes you fear, doubt, and worry, the three biggest demotivators. Having to make a tough decision sells more wine and beer than commercials. But everyone usually survives the tough decisions that they have to make. It all depends on your upbringing, and who you are. No doubt you've heard of the expression: when the going gets tough, the tough get going. Well, there's a more realistic one: when the going gets tough, the tough get drunk or high, and after they later sober up, they get going.

When you are confronted with having to make a tough decision, you normally tend to procrastinate, hoping things will slowly clear up in your mind, so you can decide to do the right thing with more confidence. But sometimes you have to make a tough decision with little or no confidence that you are right. You sometimes just have to go on your instincts, your gut feelings. That's life. Sorry 'bout that.

In fact, sometimes you can even make better decisions on tough choices using your INSTINCT rather than your LOGIC.

Allright, allright already, what the hell is this all about, damn it? It's about the tough choices each colonist had to make regarding whose side they would be on during our controversy with England.

It's really all about the loyalists or tories during our reform and revolutionary period. Both words describe the same people. The descriptive words, loyalist and tory, are synonymous and are used interchangeably, like soda and pop, or surf 'n turf and steak 'n tail. But "loyalist" is a more easily understood word, with a more obvious meaning which causes no confusion. So it's more useable and will be used herein.

A loyalist was a man or woman living in one of the thirteen colonies in America in the late 1760's and all of the 1770's and early 1780's who made the personal choice to remain "loyal" to the King and Parliament, and who refused to support the patriotic reformers and rebels who were fighting for our freedom and eventual American independence from England.

That is an objective definition of the term, loyalist.

We may as well get right into it, the nitty-gritty if you will. Try this next definition on for size. Hold on to your seat. The patriotic rebels defined a loyalist as "a thing whose head is in England and its body in America and its neck ought to be stretched." Get the picture? Pretty heavy stuff, no? If you refer to people like they are objects (things), and when referring to them you use the impersonal pronoun (it), this is the height of disrespect for these people.

Deep down in your belly, have you ever whispered

to yourself regarding a controversial situation: "I don't want to get involved?" Welcome to the club. Smart people often say, "Leave me out of this one. I don't want to get in the middle of this thing. It's really none of my business anyway, and I like to mind my own business."

Usually, this non-involvement attitude is a wise course of action. You have to pick and choose your OWN battles, and not drift into and get caught up in other people's fights, which can often result in both sides getting mad at you.

It is smart for you to be practical and pragmatic, and for you to be primarily concerned with your own enlightened self-interest. That's O.K.

But sometimes, just sometimes, and it rarely ever happens, but sometimes in a particular controversy you MUST choose sides, because like it or not, you ARE involved. Sometimes in a controversy you must choose sides. Do you agree?

Sometimes it is wise to decide that this or that particular controversy IS your fight. Sometimes you will decide to get involved just on principle. Sometimes you will decide to get involved out of your own enlightened self-interest. PRINCIPLE or SELF-INTEREST sometimes forces you to get involved in a controversial situation.

Therefore, sometimes it is stupid of you NOT to get involved in a particular controversy, once you understand it well enough. Do you agree?

Once you understand that you are involved in a controversial situation whether you like it or not; and once you understand that you should choose a particular side; and once you understand which side you favor in the controversy; you will make only one of two choices: you will choose to join the side you favor, or you will choose to remain neutral.

The emotion of fear is the enemy which makes you lean towards neutrality. Your fear tends to overcome your intelligence. Your fear can turn you into a coward, and a fool.

The virtue of courage is the friend which helps you to join a particular side. Your courage reinforces your intelligence. Your courage makes you become a hero or a heroine.

Remember the definition of courage: it is not the absence of fear, but the mastery over it. You can be a hero or a heroine and still be scared poopless. But if your fear overcomes you, you become a coward.

Your emotions of fear, doubt, and worry incapacitate you. They all prevent you from doing something. They all tend to make you do nothing. They all tend to keep you in the middle. They all tend to discourage you from acting, and keep you only reacting. They keep you in neutral, in a coma, in a passive trance, or make you mentally run away from choosing to live up to your true responsibility to protect yourself and your loved ones.

The natural human emotion of doubt is really only a degree of the natural human emotion of fear. The natural human emotion of worry is also really only a degree of the natural human emotion of fear. So fear itself is the octopus enemy with the different tentacles of doubt and worry.

Why all this discussion about making choices, and the destructive emotion of fear? What does it all have to do with anything? The answer is: it has everything to do with everything.

By 1765 in the colonies, every colonist, every man and woman, every young person, everyone with an I.Q. above room temperature, was discussing the subject of freedom. And guess what? Everyone agreed with everyone else. Everyone wanted to be free. Naturally. The colonists disagreed only on the best methods to restore and maintain their freedom from interference by Parliament and the King's agents.

Every colonist was aware of and concerned about the obnoxious new laws, rules, and regulations which Parliament was imposing on the colonists, which the King supported, and which restricted the colonists' freedom of action.

And dedicated reformers were multiplying.

Conversations, arguments, and debates all centered around each one's own personal opinions regarding the best way to restore their lost freedoms. The colonists understood that they all had a right to their own opinions, and they all proudly exercised that right, and that right to their own opinion was mutually respected by all.

But personal opinions inside your brain will eventually translate themselves into a specific pattern of action. As you think, so will you act.

When Parliament passed the tax laws in 1765 to be imposed on the colonists, retail businessmen in the colonies were faced with a tough decision. Most of the smaller businessmen who were not members of the big businessmen trading company club decided to take a stand against the taxes out of principle. All of the bigger businessmen who were members of the big businessmen trading company club decided to cooperate with the taxing policy out of self-interest.

The smaller businessmen who felt that taxation without representation was tyranny, and who had the courage of their convictions to live up to their principles, refused to import and sell the taxable items. These small businessmen refused to become tax collectors, and they refused to become, in essence, agents of the English government.

The bigger businessmen who were members in good standing of the big businessmen trading company club, operating out of self-interest, decided to conduct "business as usual," and continued to import and sell the taxable items, thus becoming tax collectors and, in essence, agents of the English government.

Parliament's passing of the tax laws, and the big businessmen's self-interest decision to cooperate with their execution and enforcement, heated up the debate on the subject of freedom in the colonies, and created a heated major division among the colonists.

The word "loyalist" took on a more well-defined meaning. Anyone supporting the taxation policy was referred to as a loyalist. Businessmen who charged and collected the taxes, and their friends and customers who did not oppose the taxes, were considered to be loyalists.

The colonists who loudly protested the Parliament's imposition of the taxes, and loudly protested the businessmen's cooperation in charging and collecting the taxes, and who loudly protested the bureaucrats' enforcing of these tax laws, began referring to themselves as the Sons of Liberty.

The votes in Parliament to pass the obnoxious tax laws were in the bag, so-to-speak, bought and paid for, all sewed up. The big English businessmen took care of doing that to make sure that the colonists would be paying for their own enslavement. But as a cover-up, the Parliamentarians had to follow the phony procedure of ''open'' debate and discussion on the floors of Parliament regarding the tax laws, which were called the Stamp Act, primarily sponsored by the big businessmen-bought politician, Charles Townshend. Big businessmen-bought politicians alway conduct ''open hearings'' or ''public debate and discussion'' on controversial legislation to fool the people into believing that the politicians arrived at their final decisions ''democratically,'' when in reality the votes were all rigged in the cigar smoke-filled back room.

Catch Townshend's demeaning, condescending attitude towards the colonists by what he said on Parliament's floor on February 7, 1765, minutes before the final vote on his tax bill. He said:

> *''These children of our own planting, nourished by our indulgence until they are grown to a good degree of strength and opulence, and protected by our arms, will they grudge to contribute their mite to relieve us from the heavy load of national expense which we lie under?''*

The bastard. The snob. The snobby bastard.

Isaac Barre, a freedom-loving Parliamentarian who refused to sell out to the big businessmen, had been warning the Parliament to, as he put it, ''keep your hands out of the pockets of the Americans and they will be obedient subjects.'' Barre quickly jumped to his feet to refute Townshend's argument, beautifully demolishing its faulty logic, and exposing it to be the scurrilous lie and hypocrisy that it was. Barre said:

> *"Children planted by your care? No! Your op-position planted them in America; they fled from your tyranny into a then uncultivated land, where they were exposed to almost all the hardships to which human nature is liable, and, among others, to the savage cruelty of the enemy of the country-a people the most subtle, and, I take it upon me to say, the most truly terrible of any people that ever inhabited any part of God's earth; and yet, actuated by principles of true English liberty, they met all these hardships with pleasure, compared with those they suffered in their own country from the hands of those that should have been their friends.*
>
> *They nourished up by your indulgence? They grew by your neglect of them. As soon as you began to care about them, that care was exercised in sending persons to rule over them, in one de-partment and another, who were perhaps the dep-uties of some deputy member of this House, sent to spy out their liberty, to misrepresent their ac-tions, and to prey upon them, men whose behavior, on many occasions, has caused the blood of those Sons of Liberty to recoil within them, men pro-moted to the highest seats of justice: some, to my knowledge, were glad by going to foreign countries to escape being brought to a bar of justice in their own.*
>
> *They protected by your arms? They have nobly taken up arms in your defense, have exerted their*

*valor, amidst their constant and laborious indus-
try, for the defense of a country whose frontiers,
while drenched in blood, its interior parts have
yielded all its little savings to your enlargement;
and, believe me, remember I this day told you
so, that the same spirit which actuated that people
at first will continue with them still; but prudence
forbids me to explain myself any further. God
knows, I do not at this time speak from motives
of party heat. What I deliver are the genuine
sentiments of my heart; however superior to me
in general knowledge and experience the respectable body of this House may be, yet I claim to
know more of America than most of you, having
seen and been conversant in that country. The
people there are as truly loyal, I believe, as any
subjects the king has; but a people jealous of
their liberties, and who will vindicate them, if
they should be violated. But the subject is too
delicate. I will say no more."*

Could you recognize that Barre was implying something ominous? Could you catch his drift? Barre had
been a career military man who had fought along
side the colonists as a Redcoat officer in the French
and Indian War. This soldier-turned-statesman knew
well the colonists' freedom-loving attitude. He also
knew that every colonist owned guns, was heavily
armed, and was not afraid to use them. His common
sense told him, "Never push a man with a loaded
gun in his hand."

But politicians are jerks. They feel that they are
in the protected position to afford the luxury of pushing

armed men with the law, because the politicians are not the enforcement agents who have to face the possible bullets.

So bought-Parliamentarians voted in favor of the tax act. This obnoxious action had the cause-and-effect relationship of giving birth in the colonies to the historical phenomenon of vigilantism.

Vigilantes are people who consider themselves to be free spirits, non-conformists. They possess the courage, and have the nerve to punish their perceived enemies by themselves, without feeling the need to have the protection of legal authority to do so. They just need to feel that what they are about to do is right. Vigilantes practice their hobby by themselves as an individual, or as a group with other free-spirited vigilantes who agree on a common target.

Vigilantes operate outside of the law. They consider themselves to be good outlaws. They are willing to break the law, and risk capture and punishment, for the sake of what they consider to be justice.

Vigilantes operate secretly, usually under the cover of darkness. They are night people who do their deed, and usually disappear into the night without getting caught.

There are good vigilantes, and there are bad vigilantes, basically because there are good laws, and there are bad laws. Good laws protect good people and punish bad people. Bad laws protect bad people and punish good people. How you feel about a vigilante depends mainly on how you feel about the laws you live under. How you feel about a vigilante also depends on how you feel about the vigilante's purpose, goals, or mission. If you support their goals, their breaking of laws to accomplish their mission doesn't bother you, and you consider the vigilantes to be good. If you don't support their goals, their breaking of laws to accomplish their mission bothers you, and you consider the vigilantes to be bad.

So you see, we're back to the issue of choices again.

If you read Margaret Mitchell's classic, GONE WITH THE WIND, you could appreciate how living either in the North or South after our Civil War would automatically color your opinion of the Ku Klux Klan. It all became quite relative. Scary no doubt, but understandably relative.

Vigilantism in the colonies was conducted by patriotic rebels against the loyalists, especially against loyalist businessmen who were willing to sell imported English products with taxes attached, because these were the very items which Parliament had forbidden the colonists to manufacture locally for themselves. Vigilantes also operated against loyalist politicians, bureaucrats, and law enforcement agents.

If you were a colonial political reformer seeking relief from the Parliament's unjust laws, you loved the vigilantes. If you were a loyalist, you hated the vigilantes.

The vigilantes in the colonies were known as the Sons of Liberty. The loyalists referred to them as the Sons of Licentiousness. Again you see, everything is relative, and your feelings about controversial matters depend entirely on whose side you choose to be on. One person's dream is another person's nightmare.

Government is usually the mid-wife of the vigilante. Unfair, unjust, tyrannical government laws, rules, and regulations will ALWAYS produce vigilantes.

Vigilantes are different from a mob. Mobs are always bad, because riotous mobs destroy people and property indiscriminately. Vigilantes, on the contrary, focus on specific targets and are single-minded as to their purpose. Vigilantes have ethics, while mobs do not.

You could legitimately consider vigilantes to be decent people because they give their targets a fair chance to repent, or to escape. Vigilantes warn their targets to cease persecuting the innocent population, or warn their targets to stop supporting the government which is persecuting the innocent population. The vigilantes go into action only if their courteous warnings go unheeded. So vigilantes are even different from assassins, who kill you by surprise.

Do you remember John Hancock, the wealthy and very respectable chairperson of the Continental Congress which produced our Declaration of Independence? Remember that Hancock was the first signer, and that he deliberately made his signature the largest so that the King could read it without having to use his eye glasses. This is why you are sometimes asked for your "John Hancock" instead of your signature. This is how the synonymous expression originated. Hancock would later serve as the first elected governor of the state of Massachusetts.

Well, John Hancock was a vigilante, proving that vigilantes are not all dirtbags. He was one of the main organizers and an actual participant in the (famous for a rebel, infamous for a loyalist) vigilante action of the revolutionary period, the Boston Tea Party.

Vigilantes are romantic figures who fire the imaginations of the innocent victims of government persecution because of the sweet and legitimate revenge they inflict on tyrants. Vigilante actions against oppressive government agents and their friends inspire the victim population to resist oppression. Vigilante action slows up the government's oppression of the people by reminding the government agents and their friends who are "just doing their jobs" that vigilantes can visit them at any time, in any place, at their office, at their home, at a bar, or on the street to inflict retribution. Vigilantes remind government agents and their friends that there is a potentially high price for administering and enforcing bad laws on the population, and for "just doing their jobs." The vigilante is the tyrant's bogeyman, and also the tyrant's agents' bogeyman.

Probably, vigilantes were most popularized by the legends of Robin Hood in England and Zorro in Mexico. What exciting guys! They were real heroes, proving again that under the right circumstances, vigilantes can be good folks who have mastered their emotion of fear to the point of fearlessness to defend their countrymen and women against government-inflicted unfairness. Vigilantes can be true champions of the little people.

Vigilante action against the loyalists by the Sons of Liberty first began rather peaceably with the traditional warning tactic of hanging their loyalist targets in effigy. Stuffing paper into the shirt and pants of a dummy with the loyalist target's name pinned to its shirt, and then with a rope around the dummy's neck, hanging it from a tree or pole, is the traditional warning that freedom-lovers everywhere always issue to their enemies. The targeted enemies of freedom get the message that somebody out there doesn't like them very much, and that maybe the next time, the neck stretching from the end of the rope may not be that of a symbolic dummy.

People hung in effigy usually have trouble sleeping. Remember that the vigilante is the tyrant's bogeyman.

If the hanging in effigy warning tactic did not deter a particular loyalist from his obnoxious course of action, the ante was upped. Under the cover of darkness, the vigilantes would throw rocks at the windows of his home or business, thus smashing them, and then disappearing into the night. Glass was expensive and hard to obtain as it was one of the taxed items forbidden to be manufactured in the colonies, and it had to be imported from England.

Sometimes at night the vigilantes would smear the loyalist's windows with feces—you know, the solid variety of human waste. This fertilizer was abundantly available and free for the taking as indoor plumbing had not yet been invented. To relieve themselves, the colonists had to leave their buildings and go outside to their out-houses, their outdoor bathrooms.

In the morning, cleaning this dried-on malodorous substance off of their windows was not an easy or pleasant chore.

If the warnings of hanging in effigy, or breaking and smearing windows didn't work its magic, the vigilantes got real serious about hurting the loyalist. Vigilantes would raid the loyalist's home, which was usually isolated in the country and outside of the business district. They would rampage through the house, completely wrecking it, and sometimes burning it to the ground. God forbid that the loyalist and his family were at home. Although women and children were always off-limits from harm, some adult male loyalists did lose their lives under these circumstances.

But the vigilantes saved the most terrible punishment for the most vicious, undiscourageable loyalists. It was an extremely painful, and sometimes fatal procedure known as tar-and-feathering, using hot pine tar and goose feathers. Anyone who ever witnessed a man treated with this torture could never forget it.

The vigilantes would kidnap the loyalist and bring him to a remote location where other vigilantes were heating a huge kettle of black tar over an open fire. When the tar came to a bubbling boil, it was ready for application on the loyalist.

The loyalist would be stripped naked, and a vigilante using a big cup, long-handled ladle would scoop up the boiling, smoking, red-hot tar, and pour it first over the loyalist's shoulders, then his chest, then his back.

If you have ever accidently burned yourself with boiling water, you know how painful it is. But the pain doesn't last that long if you get yourself to ice or cold water. Think of how long you would feel the excruciating pain of burning with boiling sticky tar clinging to your skin. No comparison. The loyalist's screaming could be heard for miles.

Next, the burning tar would be poured on top of the loyalist's head, and would drip down his face, usually permanently blinding him in one or both of his eyes. And last, but not least, the burning tar would be poured on his genitals, usually rendering him impotent for life.

If the loyalist was to be displayed to the town's people in the fashion of a spectator sport, goose feathers were then applied to make him look ridiculously dressed up for the festive occasion. If a mocking parade was not planned, the vigilantes would forget the feathers and just dump the loyalist into a ditch for possible later recovery by any of his friends who would dare to attempt his rescue.

If the tarred-and-feathered loyalist didn't die, and quite a few did, can you imagine how difficult it was for him to later remove the tar from his body parts? The clean-up process usually took weeks, and the skin would often come off with the tar.

Before using this tar-and-feathering technique on the most obnoxious loyalists, the vigilantes would give the loyalist target the courtesy of a chance to move out of town before they executed the sentence. A vigilante would place a little cold feathered tar ball in his hand in a public place, and then the vigilante would disappear into the crowd. Or the vigilantes would send the tar ball to the loyalist in an envelope or package, by messenger or by mail. If the loyalist didn't respond to this type of warning by moving out of town, well . . . tar baby here we come.

The vigilantes operated for 10 years (1765–1775) against the loyalist businessmen and loyalist enforcement agents who were implementing the big businessmen-controlled Parliament's oppression on the colonists. That oppression was, of course, Parliament's refusal to allow the colonists to manufacture and trade certain essential products among themselves and with foreigners, and Parliament's insistence that the colonists must ship to England all raw material needed for the production of these forbidden essentials. That oppression was also Parliament's insistence that the colonists must then import these subsequently finished essential products back from England, and pay the taxes on them. In a nutshell, the vigilantes were protesting this government-imposed form of slavery designed to keep the big businessmen rich, while forcing the victims to pay for all of the enforcement expenses associated with their own enslavement.

For 10 years the arguments among the colonists centered on freedom: freedom to produce and sell what you wanted to and to sell it where you wanted to, freedom from unfair taxation without representation, and freedom from unfair government interference.

During this 10 year period, the loyalists were a distinct minority, obviously acting against the colonists, and cooperating with the King and Parliament out of vested self-interest. The rest of the colonists who loved freedom but lacked the guts to be active with the other distinct minority of vigilantes, argued among themselves regarding the most potentially effective methods to obtain relief from their grievances against the King and the Parliament. The different opinions regarding the best method of insuring justice and restoring their freedom ran the whole peaceful gamut of their advocating that every colonist should write a personal letter to the King and every leader in Parliament to express their opinions; or that every colonist should sign a commonly circulated petition for redress of grievances and that the petition be sent to the King and Parliament; or that every colonist should boycott and not purchase the taxed items; etc., etc., etc. Many colonists did in fact use these peaceful methods, but to no avail.

Then the shooting incidents at Lexington and Concord in April of 1775 added a whole new frightening element to the controversy over freedom. Freedom itself was no longer the only issue to discuss. Whether governments had the right to oppress its citizens was not the only issue to consider any longer. The hot issue to discuss, and the issue on which each freedom-loving colonist would have to make a tough decision was war or peace. Should the colonists fight a shooting war to bring the King and Parliament to their senses to restore freedom to the colonists? Or should the colonists continue for a much longer time using the peaceful methods of letters, petitions, and boycotts, hoping to make the King and Parliament see the light.

The shooting and killing at Lexington and Concord (where 65 Redcoats and 49 patriotic rebels died) drew the lines, the very unmistakable, definable lines of the argument: are you willing to kill your government enemy if he persists in taking away your freedom? Yes, no, or maybe?

As an aside, how would you yourself personally answer that question today, right now at this moment? Tough choice. Tough decision. Ever think of that question before now? Think about it.

Would you kill your government enemy if he persists in taking away your freedom? That's an easier question to answer if your government enemy is a foreigner who doesn't speak English, doesn't look like you, doesn't dress like you, doesn't eat your foods, and doesn't worship the same God. Would you kill your government enemy if he persists in taking away your freedom? That's a harder question to answer ''yes'' to, if your government enemy speaks English, looks like you, dresses like you, eats the same food, worships the same God, and is not a foreigner, but is an Englishman just like you.

The harder question was the difficult decision facing each colonist. That question facing the colonists THEN is analagous to your being asked TODAY if you think you could kill Americans in your own government and their enforcement police, army, and bureaucrat agents if these Americans persisted on a course designed to take away your freedom, and in essence, to make you a virtual slave of the government, all the while hiding behind the excuse that they were "just doing their jobs." Hard question, no? That's about an EXACT parallel to the situation each colonist was facing back then.

Enough answered "yes" back then. That's why we are Americans now, not Englishmen. Our founders set the example, and established the AMERICAN principle that it is LEGITIMATE to kill your own government's agents forcing their will on you because they are "just doing their jobs."

Are you willing to kill your government enemy if he persists in taking away your freedom? That was the question on every freedom-loving colonist's mind after April 19, 1775. That was the tough decision every freedom-loving colonist had to contemplate. That was the tough choice all freedom-loving colonists had to make for themselves. NO ONE COULD HIDE. NO ONE COULD ESCAPE THE NECESSITY OF MAKING A DECISION ON THIS QUESTION. EVERYONE WAS INVOLVED, WHETHER THEY LIKED IT OR NOT, WHETHER THEY WANTED TO BE INVOLVED OR NOT. EVERYONE WAS INVOLVED. ACTUAL REVOLUTION HAD BEGUN.

After Lexington and Concord, everyone living in the colonies was involved. It was analogous to your being a passenger aboard an ocean liner at sea that was on fire. Only a bozo wouldn't feel involved.

A shooting war had started. George Washington would soon be commanding a revolutionary army which would be trying to break the English seige of Boston. The war had begun.

To choose, or not to choose, to decide, or not to decide? That is the question. Holy mackerel. Now what? What madness!

I'm a peaceful reformer. Should I become a revolutionary? These nuts have gone too far, damn it. Do they really think they can beat the mighty English Army? What are they, crazy? Maybe I'll turn neutral. Can I stay a reformer now? Son of a female dog! Maybe the loyalists are right. Things aren't that bad. Not bad enough to kill for freedom, damn it, are they? Pass the whiskey.

To choose, or not to choose, to decide, or not to decide? That is the question. Holy mackerel. Now what? What madness!

I'm a neutral. I haven't been involved. Can I stay that way now? Maybe I should join the reformers? But is that course still an option? The reformers are the ones who got us into this mess anyway. Those revolutionaries are fanatics. Maybe the loyalists are right. I'll think about all this later. Pass the beer.

To choose, or not to choose, to decide, or not to decide? That is the question. Holy mackerel. Now what? What madness.

I'm a loyalist. This war is great news. We'll show these traitors. Our Redcoats will destroy these damn fools within two weeks and the revolution will be over forever. But what if it lasts longer? What if the rebels win? They can't win. If they win, they'll kill me. If they know they're losing, they might try to kill me anyway. Damn it, this whole thing might be bad for business. I think I'll have a spot of tea.

To choose, or not to choose, to decide, or not to decide? That is the question. Holy mackerel. Now what? What madness.

I'm a revolutionary. We have no representation in Parliament, so we can't vote our way out of this mess. We have to shoot. I'm joining the Continental Army. But wait. I have responsibilities at home. But they'll understand. I think. It's now or never, isn't it? Nobody lives forever. What will I later tell my children if I don't fight now? Tyrants don't see the light until they feel the heat, damn it. Pass the whiskey, pass the beer, and later, get me a cup of strong coffee. And may God be with us.

The battles at Lexington and Concord divided the colonial population into three distinct factions: patriotic rebels, neutrals, and loyalists. From colonial enlistments in the new Continental Army and colonial militias, and from outspoken supporters of the King and Parliament published in newspapers, historians estimate that 5% of the colonists were patriotic rebels, 90% were neutrals, and 5% were loyalists. That meant, of course, that out of a colonial population of three million, 150,000 people supported the concept of killing government agents to obtain freedom, 2,700,000 people weren't sure, and 150,000 people supported the government agents.

It is significant that you realize that of the 5% (150,000 colonists) with patriotic rebel sentiments, less than 10,000 actually picked up their muskets and marched off to war right after Lexington and Concord. Most of these patriotic rebels waited, like all of the neutrals, and all of the loyalists to see if this "war" would be "a flash in the pan" which would terminate soon.

With only a handful of revolutionaries actually fighting the war, the months dragged on enough to convince the entire colonial population that these revolutionaries were really serious about fighting for freedom to the death, and that this rebellion would not be a temporary affair. The 5% patriotic rebels thought, "Go for it!" The 90% neutrals thought, "Umm . . . interesting." The 5% loyalists thought, "Why can't our Redcoats beat these idiots!?"

But most of the 5% rebels, and all of the 90% neutrals and 5% loyalists, watched, waited, and argued. Then a brand new topic surfaced in the arguments: independence. Independence from England.

To choose, or not to choose, to decide, or not to decide? That is the question. Holy mackerel. What next? What madness. Give me a break.

Regarding the subject of independence from England, the 5% rebels thought, "Why not." The 90% neutrals thought, "Ummm . . . interesting." The 5% loyalists thought, "Treason!" The arguments raged on.

Then finally, on July 4, 1776, after 14 months of shooting warfare, the Continental Congress declared our complete independence from England. This revolutionary action caused ALL DEBATE TO CEASE. No more talking was necessary. Everyone felt that the Declaration of Independence meant that TOTAL WAR was on, and that all arguments would now have to be settled on the field of battle.

Our Declaration of Independence was the action which caused a realignment of attitudes among the three factions of colonists. What previously to the Declaration was 5–90–5 became 33 ⅓–33 ⅓–33 ⅓ AFTER the Declaration. The previous 5% rebel and 5% loyalist sides remained stable, but nearly 30% of the neutrals joined the rebel side, and another nearly 30% of the neutrals joined the loyalist side. This still left 33 ⅓% who decided to remain neutral. It was John Adams, signer of our Declaration and the future second president of the United States, who estimated that popular sentiment in the colonies became divided into equal thirds after the Declaration. That meant that 1,000,000 colonists supported the principles of freedom and independence even if it meant having to kill your own government's agents; 1,000,000 were cowards who supported nothing; and 1,000,000 supported the existing establishment under the King and Parliament.

Isn't it incredible that one third of the population (1,000,000 people) would, in effect, lock themselves in their rooms aboard a burning ocean liner in deep water, acting like ostriches, holding on to the illusion that all the trouble would disappear without their having to do anything?

The neutral third of civilian colonists would go with the flow to survive. They shut their mouths tightly, expressing no opinions to anyone. They did the bidding of whichever side controlled their town. They were gutless chameleons. If the Redcoats and loyalists controlled their town, the neutrals would outwardly act like good loyalists. If the Continental Army and patriotic rebels (now called Americans) controlled their town, the neutrals would outwardly act like good Americans. Neither side would trust or respect the neutrals, and both sides would use them as they saw fit. Nothing the neutrals owned was safe. Everything they owned was subjected to being "borrowed." The neutrals were typical victims of wartime occupation, battered by both sides. Neutrals lived in fear like slaves for 8 years.

War is hell, especially war on your own soil, because of the tragedy of civilian involvement. War on American soil is inconceivable to the modern generation because they missed the three wars actually fought here: our War for Independence, the War of 1812, and our Civil War. Americans in a dozen of our states never think about it, that every day they walk or drive over sacred ground where deceased Americans actually spilled their blood in war defending our freedom.

Americans, however, did experience two major revolutions in the last 30 years, complete with shooting, killing, burning and terrible violence on our own soil on a widespread scale. These very real revolutions did not, however, materialize into full scale civil war. Nevertheless, Americans were fighting Americans. American revolutionaries were killing government agents, and government agents were killing American revolutionaries. These two revolutions were the Black Civil Rights Movement, and the anti-Vietnam War Movement (also known as the Peace Movement). The Black Civil Rights Movement was seeking full equality under the law for all black Americans. The anti-war-peace movement was seeking an end to the war in Vietnam.

The Black Civil Rights Movement of the 1960's, with the burnings and killings in the Watts area of Los Angeles, California, Newark, New Jersey, Detroit, Michigan, and in hundreds of other major American cities around the country did have the potential for full scale civil war again on our own soil. Black American revolutionaries like Jesse Gray, Stokely Carmichael, H. Rap Brown, Malcolm X, and others, abandoned Martin Luther King's peaceful reform approach to constructive change, and traveled around the country preaching violent revolution.

When a shooting war erupted from all of this peripatetic incitation, government authorities mobilized the police, national guard, and federal army troops to suppress the revolution.

Discussions, debates, and hot arguments concerning this controversial issue raged among all Americans, but especially among Black Americans. Family members, neighbors, and friends were divided. Every American was involved, and forced into taking a definite position on the issue. A tiny percentage of Americans sympathized with the violent black revolutionaries. A larger percentage sympathized with the peaceful black reformers. But the largest percentage, just like after Lexington and Concord, chose a neutral position.

The violent black revolution known as the Civil Rights Movement did not result in full scale civil war, and died a natural death after Congress passed new civil rights laws insuring full equality under the law for all black Americans. The violent revolutionaries had achieved their objectives, thus eliminating the need for further violence.

By the 1970's, another violent revolution was raging in America. It was the anti-Vietnam War Movement, also called the Peace Movement.

Like the black revolutionaries, the activist revolutionaries in the anti-war-peace movement came mainly from the ranks of the young people. But while the black revolutionaries took their violent battles exclusively to the streets, the anti-war-peace revolutionaries took their violent battles to college campuses as well as to the streets. Ohio national guardsmen wounded and killed several people during the violent revolution at Kent State University.

Discussions, debates, and hot arguments concerning this controversial Vietnam War and the anti-war-peace revolutionaries raged again among all Americans. Family members, neighbors and friends were divided again. Every American was involved again, and forced into taking a definite position on the issue. A tiny percentage again sympathized with the violent anti-war-peace revolutionaries' efforts to end the war. A larger percentage again sympathized with our government's position to continue the war. But the largest percentage, again, just like after Lexington and Concord, chose a neutral position.

The violent anti-war-peace revolution movement did not result in full scale civil war, and died a natural death after President Nixon ended the Vietnam War. The violent revolutionaries had achieved their objective, thus eliminating the need for further violence.

And we have not experienced a violent revolution in America since then. But the black revolution of the '60's, and the anti-war-peace revolution of the 70's taught us again the valuable lesson that violent revolution works. It does scare people. It forces people to take sides. But it works to achieve objectives. Violent revolutionaries force bureaucratic government to grant concessions. And it could happen again in America. And full scale revolutionary war in America should never be considered inconceivable, since our country was originally founded on the principle of violent revolution.

But back to 1776.

After our Declaration of Independence, every civilian AMERICAN (1,000,000 of them) considered every civilian LOYALIST (1,000,000 of them) to be a traitor. By the same token, every civilian loyalist considered every civilian American to be a traitor likewise. You see again, whom you consider to be a traitor depends entirely on whose side you choose to be on. And the eventual winners in the conflict, of course, arrange the treason trials. But neither side waited for the war to end before executing sentences. Both sides, the Americans and the loyalists, hanged plenty of captured prisoners as traitors before the war actually ended.

Civilian populations suffered greatly in some areas for their beliefs. The Redcoats believed in a "scorched earth" policy. They burned down certain towns completely to the ground, like Charlestown, Massachusetts; Portland, Maine; Norfolk, Virginia; New London and Fairfield, Connecticut; and Esopus, New York.

New York City was the loyalist stronghold throughout the entire 8 year war. Loyalists from every other colony migrated to New York for safety reasons. Early in the war, George Washington seriously considered a plan to burn the city to the ground, but rejected the idea on principle.

There was no mandatory military draft back then, so every American soldier was a volunteer. It is estimated that of the 1,000,000 American civilians, only about 50,000 of them (5%) actually participated in the struggle as armed soldiers, willing to kill their own government's agents for freedom.

It is also accurately estimated that our Declaration of Independence caused 50,000 loyalist civilian volunteers (out of 1,000,000) to join the English Army. This means that 50,000 civilian loyalists (5%) actually became Redcoats or members of special loyalist militia units who were willing to kill Americans for the English government.

Once you overcome your fear and thereby decide to get personally involved in a controversial and dangerous situation, you will do so out of principle or self-interest, one of the two, or possibly a little bit of both, but mainly one, more than the other.

American soldiers in uniform and loyalist soldiers in Redcoat uniform, on either side of this conflict, willing to face and to shoot each other, were probably motivated more out of principle (since they were volunteers) than out of selfish self-interest. They both really believed that what they were doing was right, and they both were willing to die for those beliefs. Honor and ease are seldom bedfellows. Therefore, volunteer soldiers on either side of a war deserve our respect. These people are pullers at the oars, not passengers in the boat. They're just in different boats, going in different directions.

It almost goes without saying that neutrals deserve no respect, and that the same type of respect due to volunteer civilian soldiers is NOT due to the rest of the able-bodied Americans and loyalists who wouldn't take up arms. But to both their credits, for courage, many Americans and loyalists remaining behind in their respective enemies' occupied territory did operate in the underground as saboteurs.

People motivated primarily out of principle act in a very predictable fashion, and such people can be trusted to act as they believe, and you have to respect them.

Activists in a conflict of any kind operating mainly out of self-interest deserve less respect. People motivated primarily by self-interest act less predictably, and can never be completely trusted.

Human beings are complex creatures. Human nature being what it is, there are very few people who act from principle 100% of the time. Conversely, there are very few people who act from self-interest 100% of the time. The truth of the matter concerning motivation for human action lies somewhere in the middle, and you should accept the fact that when situations change, minds often change. Situation ethics is a fact of life. And fatigue and stress also change minds. Anyway, it's important for you to remember that RESULTS COUNT MORE THAN MOTIVATION.

During our Revolution, the classic example of the complex character of human nature and of minds changing is the case of Major General Benedict Arnold, one of the most brilliant battlefield strategists and tacticians of all time. Starting out originally as a patriotic rebel for the American cause, presumably out of principle, he later became a traitor out of vested self-interest. For the first 5 years of our 8 year war, Arnold repeatedly risked his life on the battlefield and fought valiantly for the American side.

During one heated battle against the Redcoats, Arnold was severly wounded in the leg, which would cause him to limp for the rest of his life. Limping around frozen Valley Forge, Pennsylvania with George Washington during the frigid winter of 1778, Arnold signed an oath of allegiance to the United States, and continued to fight for America until 1780, when Washington discovered that Arnold was about to betray his country. Arnold intended to turn over his military command at West Point, New York to the English as his entry price into the English Army as a Brigadier General, but his treacherous plan failed when Washington accidently uncovered his traitorous plot.

But Arnold did manage to escape, and fought the remaining 3 years of the war for the English side.

George Washington had complete faith and trust in Benedict Arnold, since Arnold had proven himself in so many foxholes, so many times. But human beings have no defense against betrayal by a Judas. When Arnold's betrayal of America was unmistakably confirmed, Washington, in complete shock said, "And now whom can we trust?"

To choose, or not to choose. Why did Arnold choose to change sides? Probably because he came to the conclusion that the Americans were doomed to lose the war, and he wanted to be on the winning side. His motivation switched from acting out of principle, to acting out of self-interest. He became a believer in the theory that the first few rats to desert a sinking ship are the ones most likely to survive, rather than being true to principle, in which case, he would have reasoned all the way that this is my ship, and come hell or high water, I'm staying to bail it out till my last breath.

Today in modern America, if you choose to remain in a neutral position, you suspend your opinion of Benedict Arnold in mid-air. If you choose to be an American, you believe that Benedict Arnold was a traitor. It's that simple.

Fighting in the South for the English Army for most of the rest of the war, Arnold led the Redcoats to a smashing victory over American forces in a particular battle in Virginia. His Redcoats took many American soldiers as prisoners that day. One of our POW's recognized General Arnold and bravely yelled out loud, "Traitor!" Arnold limped over to that brave POW and playfully asked him what the Americans would do to Benedict Arnold if Arnold were captured. The brave POW smartly replied, "We'd cut off the leg that was wounded in the service of your country, and we'd bury it with full military honors, and then we'd hang the rest of you." Guess that says it all in a nutshell.

Results count more than motivation, but if determining a person's motivation is important to you, there is an almost fool-proof method which has always stood the test of time. This method is the BEST way to predict on whose side of a controversy an individual will likely tend to be on. This method entails asking yourself this test question: who signs their check? Down through history has come this brilliantly logical cliché: whose bread I eat, his song I sing.

This theory proved valid during our entire Revolution. With few exceptions, all officeholders, bureaucrats, agents, police, and soldiers in charge of administering, bookkeeping, and enforcing Parliament's laws remained loyalists, and supported the status quo, since it was in their own vested self-interest to do so. Anyone who depended on the existing government system for their salaries and livelihood remained loyalists. Few quit their jobs out of principle. Even most of the Church of England (Episcopalian) ministers who depended on the English government for their salaries remained loyalists. And the businessmen who were dependent on the English government for their profits remained loyalists.

Anyone the English government was feeding, directly or indirectly, tended to remain a loyalist. And remember, results count more than motivation.

Talking about feeding, there is an old cliché concerning warfare which comforted every loyalist, but scared the hell out of every American. The truth that this cliché expresses so well is probably one of the main reasons that the loyalists assumed that the war would definitely end in a few weeks. That cliché is: an army travels on its stomach. It is a medical fact that you can starve to death in one week without food. Without enough food for proper bodily fuel for simple survival, where can you even find enough energy to fight?

Have you ever gone without food for even one day? Completely without food? Not even so much as a cracker, or a piece of bread? In modern America, three square meals is a daily ritual. When you happened to miss just one meal, can you remember how ravenously hungry you became, and how much you pigged-out at the next meal?

The loyalists were confident that their English Army Redcoat allies would win the war quickly, not only because of their superior numbers, superior training, superior experience, and superior equipment and military supplies, but also because the Redcoats would always have a superior, solid, stable food supply, and a superior logistical distribution system in place to make sure that every Redcoat had a full belly of rations at all times.

And guess what? The loyalists were right about the food, and they were also right about everything else mentioned above, while the Americans fought almost the entire 8 year war in a state of near starvation and deprivation regarding food, men, guns, ammunition, and clothing. But the Americans still won. Incredible.

To a loyalist for the longest time, it was inconceivable how the Americans could even physically survive, much less fight a war. Where would the Americans obtain enough supplies for their soldiers?

Necessity is the mother of invention. George Washington invented a navy. In fact, he invented three navies: a Continental, militia, and a private one to raid the enemy English ships bringing massive supplies to the Redcoats. Whatever supplies Washington could not procure locally from friendly American farmers and equipment producers, and also, whatever supplies he couldn't obtain through the spoils of victorious battles, Washington would steal the other necessities from the English enemy at sea.

Also on November 10, 1775, the Continental Congress ordered the establishment of a special fierce fighting group of soldiers which would be aboard the Continental ships as a military detachment, and which would forever become a permanent part of our naval forces. This was the birthday of the United States Marine Corps. Semper Fi.

You can understand the existence of a federal Continental navy, and the existence of a navy for each state. But do you understand what Washington's private navy was? They were politely called privateers. This was a euphemistic way of saying "pirates."

Yes, George Washington unleashed American pirates on the English enemy, promising these adventurous patriots that they could keep half of any booty they captured and brought into any American-controlled ports. Color that fabulous incentive for swashbucklers. From the beginning of the war to the end of the war, and especially when American soldiers were in dire need, these patriotic pirates supplied our Continental soldiers with food, clothing, guns and ammunition. In the critical first three years of the war alone, American pirates had sunk or captured 559 English vessels, thus keeping our war effort alive. 13,000 American pirates, operating on 175 sailing ships, with 2,000 cannons, raided English shipping during the entire war. We could have easily lost the war for freedom without them.

The loyalists also underestimated the desire, ability, and ingenuity of the freedom-loving civilian population with American sentiments to produce supplies for the war effort. Civilian Americans dug up the earth to find saltpeter to manufacture gunpowder; they knitted socks, shirts, pants, hats, gloves, and blankets for Washington's army; they melted down leaden statues, fishing sinkers, window leads, and pewter dishes and cups as materials for bullets. In fact, the leaden statue of King George in New York City was melted down into exactly 42,088 bullets.

The loyalists also never expected foreigners to help the American cause with men and supplies. The English could afford to pay gold to German mercenaries called Hessians to assist in the fighting, but the American rebels were too poor to do that. And the loyalists could not believe that foreign businessmen would take the extreme risk of selling supplies on credit to a wild bunch of ragtag rebels who only had two chances of winning: slim and none, against all odds.

The loyalists never anticipated that foreign military officers would come to America for the sole reason that they simply loved freedom. That thought was inconceivable to a big-government-lover. Freedom-loving foreigners like Frenchman Lafayette, like Germans DeKalb and Steuben, and like Poles Pulaski and Kosciusko, were motivated out of pure principle, and the desire to help their fellow human beings in their glorious quest to live free or die. DeKalb and Pulaski actually lost their lives here in battle.

In April of 1777, the French military officer, the Marquis de Lafayette was barely 19 years old when he left his wife and year-old daughter to come to America to join the fight for freedom. The French government tried to stop him. His family tried to stop him. But he still came here to fight for freedom anyway, although he couldn't speak even one word of English.

In a revealing letter to his young wife, asking her for forgiveness for his deserting her so abruptly, he said: "As a defender of that liberty which I adore, coming as a friend to offer my services to this most interesting republic, I bring with me nothing but my own free heart and my own good will, no ambition to fulfill and no selfish interests to serve. The happiness of America is intimately connected with the happiness of all mankind. She is destined to become the safe and venerable asylum of virtue, of honesty, of tolerance, of equality, and of peaceful liberty."

What prophetic insight, proving that Americans have no monopoly on the universal desire for freedom which has always and will always exist among all mankind.

Young Lafayette became one of George Washington's most brilliant commanding officers, valiantly leading his troops in several major battles for the remaining 6 years till the war's end.

While the war was still raging, Lafayette reluctantly attended a dance given in his honor in American-occupied Baltimore, Maryland, but he was very noticeably acting about as uncomfortable as a fully clothed person at a nudist camp. Freedom-lovers sometimes can't forget the freedom battle that they are engaged in, even for a moment, until it's over. Lafayette was such a mentally and emotionally consumed person. When the ladies who planned the party for him asked him if he was having a good time, Lafayette found it impossible to give a polite answer. He said: "You dance very prettily; your ball is fine; but my soldiers need SHIRTS."

The women who sponsored the party became so embarrassed that the party soon broke up, and everyone went home. However, a few weeks later, bundles of shirts arrived at Layafette's camp site.

But back to the loyalists. After we won the war, eight of the original states published the names of identifiable loyalists whom these states were officially banishing, thus forbidding these condemned loyalists to ever live in these states again. These eight states then confiscated the property of these loyalist exiles, sold it at auction, and would forever refuse to make any form of restitution. The other five states virtually did the same thing, and took similar actions against the loyalists, but with slightly less formality.

When George Washington's army forced the English Army to leave Boston in 1776, 1,100 loyalists boarded ships with them to retreat to Canada out of the very real fear of retaliation. It was March 17, 1776, and for the next one hundred years in the United States, that day, March 17th, would be merrily celebrated as Evacuation Day, commemorating the anniversary of the liberation of Boston by the English departure. Modern Americans of every race, color, and creed, celebrate every March 17th as the Irish holiday of St. Patrick's Day. From now on, on March 17th, many Americans will be drinking a few extra green beers to AGAIN celebrate that date as Evacuation Day also.

When Washington's army finally forced the English to evacuate Philadelphia, where the English with active loyalist assistance had been long brutalizing American civilians with starvation, imprisonment, and hundreds of hanging executions, angry Americans burned hundreds of loyalist homes, and killed many of their owners.

When the war ended in 1783, and George Washington marched his army triumphantly into New York City, 12,000 loyalists boarded ships and left for relocation to Canada.

By war's end, over 100,000 loyalists had been forced to evacuate America out of fear of retaliation. Most fled back to England or went to Canada, but thousands relocated to Bermuda, Jamaica, Bahamas, and to the territory which in the future would become the sunny state of Florida.

If only 100,000 loyalists out of the estimated 1,000,000 of them actually left our shores by war's end, what became of the estimated 900,000 remaining loyalists who supported the government coercion exercised against Americans by our English enemies, and who refused to support the freedom fighters? Nobody knows for sure. They could have relocated within our growing country, where as strangers they could have concealed their old identities and traditions. And, of course, their blood descendants must still be among us.

Chapter 8

Principles

> *Patriotism means to stand by the country.*
>
> *It does not mean to stand by the President or any other public official save exactly to the degree in which he himself stands by the country.*
>
> *It is patriotic to support him insofar as he efficiently serves the country. It is unpatriotic not to oppose him to the exact extent that by inefficiency or otherwise he fails in his duty to stand by the country.*
>
> *In either event, it is unpatriotic not to tell the truth—whether about the President or anyone else.*
>
> —President Theodore Roosevelt (1901–09)

The men and women who established our country and helped to produce America's founding documents (the Declaration of Independence, our Constitution and the Bill of Rights) were brilliant students of recorded history. They studied the leaders, people, and events which occurred in ancient Greece, Rome, and other civilizations. They also studied the reasons for the rise, falls, and aftermaths of these former societies. If you studied over 6,000 years of eye-witness accounts of unfolding history, do you suspect you might learn a few of history's little known secrets?

From their extensive historical research, they distilled dozens of history's lessons down to their fundamental essence, and the abuses which they were actually experiencing from the English government only re-proved as positively true the revealing theory which they discovered from history: that MAN'S GREATEST ENEMY HAS ALWAYS BEEN HIS VERY OWN GOVERNMENT.

This revelation is shocking news if you're hearing it for the first time, but it's an undeniable fact. Man's greatest enemy was never poverty, ignorance, disease or war. Your thinking needs to be reversed. In fact, it was usually man's own government which actually created these other horrible conditions.

So let's define what government actually is, always was, and always will be: legalized force or power. Nothing more, nor less. It's that simple. A so-called government that passes laws or decrees for its citizens, but which has no police or army with deadly weapons to enforce them, is NO GOVERNMENT at all. Citizens could laugh and not obey a so-called government without raw power to convincingly threaten, or actually force citizens to comply with its legislation.

To help you to better understand the definition of government as legalized force, try thinking of it in this way: creating a government is similar to your placing a loaded gun in someone else's hand, and giving him permission to hold that gun to your head to make you obey the laws he passes. Does this analogy help? It's pretty exact.

Government is legalized force or power. Put in other words: government is force made legal.

George Washington understood this obvious principle, and warned us: "Government is not reason. It is not eloquence. It is force. Like fire, it is a dangerous servant, and a fearful master."

So America's founders fully understood what history and their own actual experience proved: that all government is dangerous, at best a necessary evil, always to be watched closely, and NEVER TO BE TRUSTED.

Fully understanding that all government was potentially oppressive, our founders still had the awesome responsibility to form one. Put yourself in their shoes, feeling the same way they felt about government, and knowing that you had to set one up. What kind of government would you have established? An easy job? Where would you have begun?

Our founders were inspired by one principle, a principle so unique that it simplified their job of forming a government. This principle was such a fantastic revelation, was so revolutionary, that NO GOVERNMENT HAD EVER BEEN BASED ON IT BEFORE. This glorious principle became and remains the very essence of Americanism. Our founders discovered the greatest secret, the only true answer to the fundamental question: where do rights come from? Man's right to life, liberty and property?

Where do rights come from? All of history provided one loud and clear answer: the government. History taught that rights come from the government. Sometimes the government was called the Pharoah. Rights come from the Pharoah. Sometimes the government was called the Emperor. Rights come from the Emperor. Sometimes the government was called the King. Rights come from the King. Sometimes the government was called the Senate, or Parliament, etc., etc., etc.

History taught that rights come from the government, and since the government granted rights to its citizens, government could also take them away, any time they wanted to. . . . and government always did take rights away from its citizens.

This principle of rights coming from government made government everyone's boss. "Power corrupts, and absolute power corrupts absolutely." This historical principle of rights coming from government should help you to better understand why government has always been man's greatest enemy. Get the picture? The government has always pointed a gun at its citizens and, in essence, has said: "Obey, or else."

Our founders discovered and had the audacity to proclaim the magnificently simple truth: rights DO NOT COME from government, RIGHTS COME FROM GOD. This previously unheard of principle became the basis of Americanism: rights come from God, not from government.

And if it makes you feel more comfortable to substitute your own synonym word for God, like Creator, Force X, the Deity, Supreme Being, etc., go right ahead, it doesn't really matter since these other words will also be referring to the exact same spiritual entity which our founders were talking about. There's no rational need here to get hung up on semantics, right?

Thomas Jefferson proudly announced in our Declaration: "We hold these truths to be self-evident, that all men are created equal, that they are endowed by their Creator with certain unalienable rights, that among these are life, liberty, and the pursuit of happiness."

If rights come from God, then what is the legitimate function of government? Jefferson adds: "That to secure (protect) these (God-given) rights, governments are instituted among men . . ." So the proper role of government is TO PROTECT MAN'S GOD-

GIVEN RIGHTS. Period. This concept is fundamental to the philosophy of Americanism.

Once a government is formed by the people, where does this government get ITS rights to do anything? Jefferson adds that government gets its "just powers from the consent of the governed." In other words, PEOPLE GRANT LEGITIMATE RIGHTS TO GOVERNMENT. What a magnificent reversal! Government does not grant rights to people. People grant rights to government.

Summing up, God grants rights to man, then man grants rights to government. This means man is the legitimate boss of government, operating on the logical principle that the creator is the boss of its creation. Man should always be pointing the gun at government, not the other way around. This concept of man being the boss of government is also fundamental to the philosophy of Americanism.

Although it may seem absurd to ask a ridiculous question, only to answer it with an obvious answer, we need to make the point here anyway. Of what is a government composed? Only men and women, people like you and me. Nothing more than that. Only humans. Nothing magical or mystical. Just flesh and blood like yours and mine.

Collective words like group, class, team, and others representing more than one person, exist exclusively in the mental realm of your own mind. Only individuals really exist in the material world. A teacher teaches a "class" only in her own mind. She really teaches only individual students in the material world. A coach coaches a "team" only in his own mind. He really coaches only individual players in the material world. Your mind automatically collectivizes, categorizes, and classifies more than one individual into a word which simplifies the communication process among ourselves. It would be impossible to talk to or write to anyone if your mind didn't do this. But using the collective word "government" tends to evoke false impressions in you of awe and fear which are deceptive and misleading. So there exists a critical need to demystify the word "government."

For truth and clarity's sake, you should always mentally translate the collectivized word "government" into its material reality as "the humans whom WE ALLOW to run the government for us." If you think of the word government in this way, the word government tends to lose much of its witch-doctor, bogey man imagery, doesn't it? It's sort of like what Dorothy did to the Wizard of Oz when she pulled away the curtain. Remember?

Keeping that thought in mind, that government is composed of people just like you and me, let's address a self-evident principle of pure logic which our founders fully understood: YOU CAN'T GIVE WHAT YOU DO NOT HAVE. This principle is universal, and holds true for the material world as well as the abstract world.

To illustrate, if you don't possess a $100 dollar bill, you can't give a $100 dollar bill to anyone. You can't give what you do not have.

If you get tricky and say, "But I may be able to get a $100 dollar bill from somewhere, so I can give it to someone," you still haven't disproved the principle that you can't give what you do not have, because you'd have to get the $100 dollar bill first. Then you'd have it, you'd possess it, and then, of course, you could give it away because you'd have it.

If you don't possess the right answer to a question, you can't give that right answer to anyone. You can't give what you do not have.

If you get tricky and say, "But I may be able to get the right answer from somewhere, so I can give it to someone," you still haven't disproved the principle that you can't give what you do not have, because you'd have to get the right answer first. Then you'd have it, you'd possess it, and then, of course, you could give it away because you'd have it.

Get the picture? You can't give what you do not have! THERE ARE NO EXCEPTIONS. None. This principle ALWAYS holds perfectly true. Always. Do you agree?

Let's apply this logical principle to the humans whom we allow to run the government for us, because our founders DID when they wrote our Constitution to form our government.

Our founders asked themselves: what rights should these humans whom we allow to run the government for us have? What should WE ALLOW the newly created American government to do?

The principle: you can't give what you do not have, applies to rights. We cannot give a right to the humans whom we allow to run the government for us which we ourselves, as individuals, do not possess. Obviously. Do you agree? Bow to the principle. You cannot give what you do not have.

In plain English, if you can't do it, the humans whom you allow to run the government for you can't do it either. Can you understand and accept that? If you as an individual have no legitimate God-given right to do something, then the humans whom you allow to run your government for you have no legitimate man-given right to do that something either. Where else could the humans whom you allow to run the government for you possibly get that right if that right didn't come from you? Magic?

Remember, the government is only human beings who receive their right to do something FROM YOU, and you can't give them the right to do something unless you AS AN INDIVIDUAL possess that same right. Simple, isn't it? This concept is also fundamental to the philosophy of Americanism.

To illustrate: you as an individual possess a God-given right to defend yourself from bodily harm. Therefore, because you possess it, you can grant your self-defense right to the humans whom you allow to run the government for you. If you had to stand in front of your home every day with a baseball bat, or gun, or knife to defend yourself, your family and your property, how could you earn a living to support yourself? So you wisely grant this self-defense right that you possess to the humans whom you allow to run the government for you. You freely choose, in effect, to hire a policeman to perform a function that you have a right to perform yourself, so that you can go to work with some measure of peace of mind.

Another example along similar lines: you as an individual possess a God-given right to protect yourself from murderers and other criminals, even if it means killing the potential murderers or quarantining criminals so they lose their ability to hurt you. So you wisely grant this self-defense right to the humans whom you allow to run the government for you. You freely choose, in effect, to hire judges and wardens to establish courts, jails, and other punitive or rehabilitative facilities.

As an aside, granting a right to the humans whom you allow to run the government for you DOES NOT MEAN that you therefore lose that same right. It does not mean that you lose your own right to exercise it. On the contrary, you ALWAYS possess this God-given right FOREVER. It is unalienable, meaning that you can never lose it, and that nobody can ever take it away from you.

If you hire policemen, judges, wardens, etc., who is the BOSS? You or them? Guess. You are also the boss of all politicians and government workers, elected (hired and payed for) or appointed (hired and payed for). You are the boss of the humans whom you allow to run the government for you. The humans whom you allow to run the government for you are NOT the bosses, and never should be. This concept is also fundamental to the philosophy of Americanism.

Summing up, the humans whom you allow to run the government for you can only legitimately do what you as an individual can legitimately do. If you as an individual have no legitimate right to do something, then the humans whom you allow to run the government for you have no legitimate right to do it either. Understand? EVERY law or regulation passed by the humans whom you allow to run the government for you, authorizing them to do something that you as an individual have no legitimate right to do, is un-American. EVERY law or regulation, passed by the humans whom you allow to run the government for you, prohibiting you from doing something that as an individual you have no legitimate right to prohibit others from doing, is also un-American.

This American principle of government has been lost and forgotten by this generation. It must be re-learned and applied to EVERY law and regulation passed by the current so-called American government at every level: federal, state, county, and city.

The key to better understanding the universal principle that you can't give what you do not have, when you're discussing applying this principle to the humans whom you allow to run the government for you, rests with the word "force." The humans whom you allow to run the government for you can have NO legitimate man-given right to FORCE you to do anything, if you as an individual have NO legitimate God-given right to FORCE your neighbor to do that same anything. Conversely, the humans whom you allow to run the government for you can have NO legitimate man-given right to forbid you from doing anything using the threat of FORCE, if you as an individual have NO legitimate God-given right to forbid your neighbor from doing that same anything using the threat of FORCE.

Where could the humans whom you allow to run the government for you possibly get such rights when you don't have them to give? You can't give what you do not have. Remember?

Let's use two specific examples for each case to illustrate the point of when the humans whom we have allowed to run the government for us have IL-LEGITIMATELY acted in an un-American manner, positively to order and negatively to forbid. We'll look at one positive and one negative example on the federal level, and one positive and one negative example on the state level.

Everyone knows that the humans whom we allow to run the government for us at the federal level have sent billions of dollars in foreign aid to foreign countries. Apply the principle. Do you as an individual have a legitimate God-given right to do this? Yes, you do. Do you as an individual have a legitimate God-given right to FORCE your neighbor to help you to pay for this? No, you don't. Then the humans whom you allow to run the government for you can have NO legitimate man-given right to FORCE you to pay (taxes) for this action. Where could they possibly get it from if you yourself don't have it to give? It is an un-American action. When you as an individual exercise your legitimate God-given right to send aid to foreigners, it is charity. When the federal government does it, it is ILLEGITIMATE FORCE.

If you as an individual FORCED your neighbor to help you to pay for this foreign aid, it would have to be considered stealing, or theft, wouldn't it? When the humans whom we allow to run the government for us do it, it also has to be considered theft, but the humans whom we allow to run the government for us pass a law to make the obvious theft legal. So it becomes legal theft! But it's theft nonetheless. If it would be theft for you, face it, it HAS TO BE theft for them also. Think about it.

Everyone knows that the humans whom we allow to run the government for us at the federal level created an era known as Prohibition. Apply the principle. Do you as an individual have a legitimate God-given right to FORCE your neighbor not to drink alcoholic beverages? No, you don't. Then the humans whom we allow to run the government for us can have NO legitimate man-given right to do that either. Where could they possibly get it from if you yourself don't have it to give? This was an un-American action.

Everyone knows that the humans whom we allow

to run the government for us at the state level build and operate civic centers, sports arenas, stadiums, racetracks, convention centers, and cultural arts centers. Apply the principle. Do you as an individual have a legitimate God-given right to do this? Yes, you do. Do you as an individual have a legitimate God-given right to FORCE your neighbor to help you to pay for this? No, you don't. Then state governments can have NO legitimate man-given right to FORCE you to pay (taxes) for these actions. Where could they possibly get it from if you yourself don't have it to give? It is an un-American action. When you as an individual exercise your legitimate God-given right to do this, it is business. When state governments do it, it is ILLEGITIMATE FORCE.

Everyone knows that the humans whom we allow to run the state government for us operate lotteries or numbers games. This is obviously gambling, but they forbid you to do this yourself. Apply the principle. Do you as an individual have a legitimate God-given right to FORCE your neighbor NOT to gamble or make money bets with someone? No, you don't. Then state governments can have NO legitimate man-given right to forbid you to gamble either. Where could they possibly get it from if you yourself don't have it to give? It is an un-American action which constitutes an ILLEGITIMATE MONOPOLY.

Think. Think hard. Apply this American principle to other governmental actions such as: the social security system, welfare system, banking system, the military draft, gun control, zoning, transportation systems, farming, alcoholic beverage sales, public school system, etc., etc., etc. Think American and see what you get. How many of these programs are illegitimate force, or legal theft, or un-American monopolies?

Now let's suppose that you as an individual have no PARTICULAR God-given right to grant to the humans whom you allow to run the government for you. So you can't give what you do not have, right? And if you as an individual don't have a particular God-given right to grant to those humans whom you allow to run the government for you, then no other individual has it either, right? Not so fast, you say.

What if you got together with five of your friends. Would that very act of associating with OTHERS IN AGREEMENT obtain that non-existent right for all of you? What if you got together with a hundred people, or a thousand, or a million, or a hundred million people? Would that very act of associating with others in agreement OBTAIN that non-existent right for all of you? No. How could it?

If you as an individual have no particular God-given right, then no other individual human being will have it either. Numbers don't matter, even large numbers. Logical principle matters. A hundred million people without a particular God-given right are simply a hundred million people who have no particular God-given right to grant to the humans whom we allow to run the government for us. If none of them have it, none of them can give it. So the principle that you can't give what you do not have applies PERFECTLY to the plural, as well as to the singular, ALWAYS. Simple, isn't it? Bow to the principle.

We have actually been discussing the differences between a type of government called a republic, and a type of government called a democracy. In a republic, the God-given rights of just one individual citizen cannot be taken (voted) away by the majority. The humans whom we allow to run the government for us in a republic protect the God-given rights of even one citizen from a majority vote. What if that one citizen were you? Would you want protection? God-given rights are unalienable, remember, and IT IS CONTRADICTORY TO EVEN CONSIDER THEM SUBJECT TO ANY HUMAN VOTE, EVER.

In a democracy, the majority rules because the people living in a democracy DO NOT UNDERSTAND that rights come from God. People living in a democracy believe rights come from the MAJORITY of the people themselves. In a democracy, whatever the majority decides, it goes. If the majority decides you are not allowed to have a boyfriend or a girlfriend until you are 30 years old, then the democracy government enforces that majority decision. If the majority decides you cannot marry until you reach the age of 35, then the democracy government enforces that majority decision.

If the majority decides to execute by firing squad, anyone caught in the act of sexual relations with anyone not their marriage partner, then the democracy government enforces that majority decision. If the majority decides to outlaw divorce under penalty of death by electric chair, then the democracy government enforces that majority decision. If the majority decides to forbid telecasting of TV soap operas, or sporting events like football, basketball, hockey, hunting, tennis, horse-racing, fishing, baseball, golf, boxing, and bowling, then the democracy government throws them all off of the TV. If the majority decides to outlaw bingo, then the democracy government outlaws bingo. If the majority decides to forbid travel vacations outside of the United States, then the democracy government enforces that majority decision. If the majority decides to outlaw smoking cigarettes, then the democracy government outlaws smoking cigarettes. If the majority decides that the Masons, Moose, Elks, Rotary and Kiwanis are subversive organizations, then the democracy government passes a law making membership in these groups illegal. Etc., etc., etc.

No one's freedom is protected in a democracy. Every citizen's freedom is subjected to a majority vote, because the people believe that all rights come from and can be taken away by a majority vote. NO ISSUE is off-limits to a vote in a democracy. None, literally. Democracies are so un-American. This fact prompted James Madison, the fourth President of the United States, to say this; "Democracies have ever been spectacles of turbulence and contention; have ever been found incompatible with personal security or the rights of property, and have in general been as short in their lives as they have been violent in their deaths."

Are you beginning to see BY NOW the serious consequences of your belief regarding rights and where they come from? Your individual freedom depends on your answer.

The American belief is that rights come from God. The American belief is that government is established to protect God-given rights. The American belief is that the humans whom we allow to run the government for us get their legitimate rights from us. The American belief is that you can't give what you do not have. The American belief is that if you as an individual

CAN'T legitimately do something, then the humans whom you allow to run the government for you CAN'T legitimately do that something either.

Do you know what a syllogism is? The dictionary defines a syllogism as a three part form of reasoning, in which two premises are made and a logical conclusion is drawn from them. Examples are:

Major Premise:	*All live humans breathe.*
Minor Premise:	*Fran is alive human.*
Conclusion:	*Therefore, Fran breathes.*

Major Premise:	*All dogs can bark.*
Minor Premise:	*Fido is a dog.*
Conclusion:	*Therefore, Fido can bark.*

Major Premise:	*On planet Earth, what goes up, will come down.*
Minor Premise:	*The baseball went up.*
Conclusion:	*Therefore, the baseball came down.*

In a syllogism, if your major premise is true, and your minor premise is also true, then your conclusion WILL ALWAYS BE TRUE.

If you possess a true major premise, you can ALWAYS create a syllogism to arrive at a true conclusion.

Our founders gave future American generations the TRUTHFUL MAJOR PREMISE needed to create what shall henceforth be called the Real-American Syllogism. Dropping the de-mystified but more cumbersome definition of government, this truthful major premise is:

> *If you as an individual have no legitimate God-*given right to do something, then the government

has no legitimate man-given right to do that same something either.

Assuming you understand this formal truthful major premise, let's create a short version which means exactly the same thing, but is even less cumbersome to use:

>*IF YOU CAN'T DO IT, THEN THE GOVERN-MENT CAN'T DO IT EITHER.*

Now let's use this shorter truthful major premise to create Real American Syllogisms out of the four factual political examples used earlier.

Major Premise: *If you can't do it, then the government can't do it either.*

Minor Premise: *You cannot force your neighbor to pay for foreign aid.*

Conclusion: *Therefore, the government cannot force you and your neighbor to pay for foreign aid.*

Major Premise: *If you can't do it, then the government can't do it either.*

Minor Premise: *You cannot force your neighbor to abstain from drinking alcoholic beverages.*

Conclusion: *Therefore, the government cannot force you and your neighbor to abstain from drinking alcoholic beverages.*

Major Premise: *If you can't do it, then the government can't do it either.*

Minor Premise: *You cannot force your neighbor to help you to pay for building and operating recreational centers.*

Conclusion: *Therefore, the government cannot force you and your neighbor to help them to build and operate recreational centers.*

Major Premise: *If you can't do it, then the government can't do it either.*

Minor Premise: *You cannot force your neighbor to abstain from gambling with anyone.*

Conclusion: *Therefore, the government cannot force you and your neighbor to abstain from gambling with anyone.*

Master this Real American Syllogism technique and you will always, FROM THAT DAY FORWARD, be able to determine whether any particular governmental action is American or un-American.

Now, as an aside, using the word "whom" in the de-mystified but more cumbersome definition of "government" is technically correct English, but shall henceforth be dropped, out of poetic license, for more simplicity. English teachers, please note.

Returning to our earlier discussion, what type of government did our founders FINALLY establish? The answer is: they formed what is called a limited government, a government STRICTLY LIMITED to perform only those things which you as an individual have a God-given right to perform for yourself.

The technical name for this type of limited government is a REPUBLIC. This is why, when we pledge allegiance to our flag, we pledge allegiance to the "republic" for which it stands. Remember, "I pledge allegiance to the flag of the United States of America, and to the REPUBLIC for which it stands, one nation under God, indivisible, with liberty and justice for all."

Without going into technical details now, you need to realize that our founders NEVER intended to form, and DID NOT FORM, a type of government called a DEMOCRACY. A republic and a democracy are two distinctly different forms of government. As different as a filet mignon is from a fast-food hamburger. We do not pledge allegiance to the "democracy" for which it stands. Nor have you ever heard of a song entitled "The Battle Hymn of the 'Democracy'." Have you?

In fact, you can't find the word "democracy" in our Constitution, or in any of the Constitutions of our 50 states because it just isn't in there anywhere, but mention of the "republican" form of government which our founders established is. But interestingly enough, you will find the word "democracy" and its definition in the official U.S. Army Training Manual published by our own government in 1928. Read what this official American government publication says 139 years after the ratification of our Constitution about the form of government known as a democracy: "Democracy: a government of the masses. Authority derived through mass meeting or any form of direct expression results in mobocracy. Attitude towards property is communistic, negating property rights. Attitude towards the law is that the majority shall regulate, whether it be based upon deliberation or governed by passion, prejudice and impulse, without restraint or regard to consequences. Results in demagogism, license, agitation, discontent, and anarchy.'' How 'bout that.

America is a republic. In fact, in 1787, when Benjamin Franklin was asked by a Mrs. Powell of Philadelphia, what type of government our Constitution formed, Mr. Franklin quickly replied: "A republic, madam, if you can keep it." Think we've kept it?

Here's how you form a republic, and this is exactly how our founders did it. You take a sheet of paper and write down everything that the humans you are going to allow to run the government for you can do, everything they can't do, and state that the people can do everything else. Now every citizen will be able to understand the rules. That's HOW you form a republic. It's like writing up a legal contract, in case amnesia develops later. In fact, it IS a legal contract between the bosses (citizens) and their employees (government workers). If enough citizens agree with the rules you draw up, you have created a new country. If enough citizens disagree with the rules, you still have chaos, and have NOT formed a new country.

In our case, enough citizens agreed with the rules our founders produced, so the United States of America was born. The rulebook was called the Constitution. It defines exactly WHAT our country is all about, exactly WHAT it is, and exactly WHAT our hired humans we allow to run the government for us, CAN and CANNOT do. In fact, the Constitution ITSELF can, in a REAL sense, BE CONSIDERED OUR COUNTRY. Don't think of the ordinary definition of the word "country" in the geographic sense of mountains, plains, valleys, or oceans. Rather think of the word "country" in the sense of WHAT EXACTLY you are loyal to. Since the Constitution represents the idea, the essential being of our country, it IS our country. It is our country because the Constitution is WHAT our country is. Without the Constitution, we wouldn't be a country. Without the Constitution, the United States of America wouldn't exist.

So why did enough citizens agree with the rulebook of the Constitution? Because the Constitution gave the people the CONFIDENCE that their freedom was GUARANTEED; because the Constitution was primarily written to protect and defend the people's God-given rights from oppression by the humans we allow to run the government for us. Our Constitution guaranteed that the humans who run the government for us could only point their gun at CRIMINALS trying to physically harm us, or at SUBVERSIVES trying to take away our freedom.

How did the Constitution do that? Because the Constitution defined and spelled out in EXACT detail what the new government (the humans we allow to run the government for us) could do, and exactly what the new government (the humans we allow to run the government for us) could not do. The Constitution prevented the new government (the humans we allow to run the government for us) from taking away the people's freedom, ever.

The Constitution listed exactly (literally, exactly) what the Congress could do, exactly what the President could do, exactly what the courts could do, and exactly what they all could NOT do. It also lists exactly those 18 things for which you can be taxed.

Remember that our founders did not trust government, not even the one they were establishing, because they understood human nature, history, and government. Jefferson said: "In questions of power, let us hear no more talk of trust in men; but rather bind them down from mischief with the chains of the Constitution."

The Constitution was written for ALL TIMES because it forever embodies eternal principles which can NEVER change. Specific conditions in future American societies could be covered by the amendment process, but the principles of man's rights being paramount to the government (the humans we allow to run the government for us) could never change.

As an aside, how would you answer this question? The function of the Supreme Court is to interpret the Constitution? True or false?

The answer you give to this important question is indicative of the identity crisis most so-called Americans are experiencing. Ninety-nine percent of the people would answer the question above with a "true" answer, and would be wrong. So if you answered "true," you needn't feel too bad. But the correct answer is "false."

The function of the Supreme Court is NOT to interpret the Constitution. The direct opposite is true. The Constitution is perfectly clear and understandable to anyone of average intelligence, and does not need interpreting. The function of the Supreme Court is to interpret the LAWS Congress passes, to make sure that these laws are Constitutional. In other words, the main function of the Supreme Court is to STAND UP for the Constitution, to DEFEND it, and to STRIKE DOWN any law which the Supreme Court justices perceive as un-Constitutional.

If our Constitution ever needed interpreting, the most AUTHORITATIVE source for this interpretation of the exact meaning and true spirit of each clause in our Constitution comes from what is known as "The Federalist Papers," which is a collection of essays published as newspaper articles to convince each state to ratify the document. The authors of "The Federalist Papers" were Alexander Hamilton and James Madison of the Constitutional Convention which actually wrote the document, and John Jay who became the first Chief Justice of the Supreme Court of the United States. Think these original Americans might have known what they were writing about?

The first ten amendments to the Constitution are called the Bill of Rights. These were passed and became law within 2 years of our Constitution's ratification, and were icing on the Constitution's cake.

Through the Bill of Rights our founders said, in essence, to the new Federal Government (the humans they were going to allow to run the government for us): if we didn't grant you a right SPECIFICALLY, you don't have it. Also, if we forgot to specifically list a right that the people have, the people still have it anyway. In other words, our founders were saying loud and clear to the new Federal Government (the humans they were going to allow to run the government for us): if we didn't specifically grant you a right, you don't have it, but the people still do!

Remember the American philosophy of government. Every right granted to the new Federal Government (the humans we allow to run the government for us) was already possessed by the people as individuals, or else they obviously couldn't grant them to the humans they were going to allow to run the new government. The rights granted to the new government (the humans they were allowing to run the new government for us) fell into a category which could be properly identified as "protective," meaning the new government's function was clearly to protect and defend the people's God-granted rights. The best way to insure the people's freedom and happiness is to create a government whose function is to protect and defend the people's God-given rights.

For the record, your God-granted rights end where mine begin, and vice-versa. The new government's job (the humans who were being allowed to run the government for us) was to protect everybody's God-granted rights by being, in essence, impartial referees. When your understanding of your rights begin to trample on my understanding of my rights, government (the humans we allow to run the government for us) can legitimately get involved between us. Government's job was, and is, to protect you from me, and vice versa. If we lived in peace, government (the humans we allow to run the government for us) shouldn't interfere with us, except to help protect us from criminals.

This is how a republic works. The government's powers are limited to specific functions. The government in a republic is not free, but the people are. In a republic, the government (the humans we allow to run the government for us) is literally the slave of the people. The free people are the supreme masters of the slave government (the humans we allow to run the government for us). The people being masters are free to do practically anything. The government (the humans we allow to run the government for us) being a slave is only free to do what we the people allow it to do. Have you ever considered that everyone working for government is your slave? Interesting, no? This is the American philosophy of government.

Government employees (elected-hired or appointed-hired) work for you and are therefore entitled to be paid a salary for performing their full time duties of protecting the people's God-given rights, just as you are entitled to compensation from your employer for the work that you do.

In order to pay salaries to their employees, businesses charge customers for the services they render. Our founders viewed government in this same light. In order to pay salaries to their employees, government (the humans we allow to run the government for us) charges their customers for the protective services they render. Government charges for services rendered are called taxes. Taxes are the cost to customers for government services, just as business profits are the cost to customers for business services.

You pay for (are taxed for) government services that you could do for yourself. This is the only legitimate American form of taxation. Any other form of taxation is illegitimate, unconstitutional, and un-American.

The Constitution enumerates the specific functions for which you agree to be charged (taxed), and there are only 18 of them. Did you ever realize that? Only 18! There are only 18 governmental functions for the performance of which you agree to be taxed. Check Article One, Section Eight, which is simply one incredibly long sentence. These government functions are functions you yourself have a God-given right to perform.

Again, our founders were not perfect, and a few

brilliant purists make a tremendously interesting case
for the rationale that our founders should have completely abolished TAXATION as the means of financ-
ing a government. These purists claim that the biggest
MISTAKE our founders made, was the fact that they
did not in fact do this, and that they didn't is the
ROOT CAUSE of ALL of our problems today.

Claiming that this theory can be logically derived
from our founders' definitions of freedom and Americanism, these purists argue that every truly legitimate
governmental function could have been and still could
be financed through a voluntary 50–50 type raffle or
lottery, or through a voluntary subscription program.
Raffles and lotteries are self-explanatory, and you can
easily understand the subscription idea by asking yourself why the firemen should show up at your house
to put the fire out if you have not voluntarily subscribed
to their service? Volunteer fire companies take note.

But summing up: if you as an individual have no
right to charge your neighbor for something, then the
government (the humans you allow to run the government for you) can have no right to charge you for
that same something either. Remember the principle?
You can't give rights to the humans you allow to
run the government for you which you yourself do
not have.

Whenever the humans you allow to run the government for you charge you for a governmental service
which you could NOT charge your neighbor to perform
for you, that government charge is illegitimate, unconstitutional, and un-American. AND SO IS THE GOV-
ERNMENT SERVICE IN QUESTION. The government (the humans you allow to run the government

for you) can only legitimately do what you as an individual can legitimately do. And this concept is a fundamental aspect of the philosophy of Americanism when applied to the issue of taxation.

It is amazingly symptomatic of most so-called Americans' identity crisis that they see NO CAUSE and EFFECT relationship between an increase in government services and an increase in taxation. Much less do they ever consider whether the government (the humans they allow to run the government for them) even has a legitimate right to perform the services in the first place. Wanting to have their cake and eat it too, they demand more government services, while simultaneously demanding lower taxes. How can they believe that they can have one without the other? And why do they never ask themselves whether the government (the humans they allow to run the government for them) has a legitimate right to even perform the services in question?

The American principle of government being able to legitimately do ONLY what you as an individual can legitimately do is universal, and applies equally to every level of government: federal, state, county, and city.

Think. Apply this American principle to everything which every level of government does, and you should begin to realize how un-American every level of government has become, and that our Constitution has been trashed, even though every Federally elected official, upon taking office, swears a solemn oath to uphold and defend it.

After our Revolution, original Americans were free. What does that mean exactly? Being free means that you don't need to ask anyone for PERMISSION to do anything. You just do it. Did you get that? You just do it. How do you like that?

Being free means that you are the boss, you are the authority, you have the authority to do what you want without seeking permission. You need authority from no one. You just go for it without permission. You're the authority yourself. You're free. Understand?

If you must seek permission to act, you are NOT free. Slaves need permission. Employees need permission. Children need permission. The boss needs no permission. He's the boss. You are the boss! Original Americans sought permission to act from no one, much less from government (the humans they allowed to run the government for them). Government employees needed and sought permission from original Americans to do anything. The free American people told the humans they allowed to run the government for them what those governmental humans could and could not do. This is exactly what our founders intended.

The great American principle of freedom is this: you never need permission, you grant permission.

If you now feel that you need to ask our governmental humans for permission to act, you are NOT free, and, after asking our governmental humans for permission which is then denied, you really are a slave. Can you dispute this? Feeling a need to ask for permission to act means you are a prisoner in your own mind, a dependent not an independent, and not free. Asking for permission, which is then denied, means you are a prisoner IN REALITY.

Being free means that you just do what you want to without asking for permission to do it. If government (the humans you allow to run the government for you) then issues a "stop" order, your choice is to submit or to fight. Our founders decided that freedom was worth fighting for. Have you ever wondered whether you also would have fought for your freedom?

If you had had the opportunity to be one of the 56 signers of our Declaration of Independence on July 4th, 1776, do you think you would have signed it? Every signer realized that he was signing his death warrant if they lost our Revolution. But they signed it anyway because they all loved freedom that much.

Were they completely fearless? That's doubtful since they were human beings, but they had courage. Courage is not the absence of fear, but the mastery over it.

Among these 56 signers were physicians, businessmen, farmers, and one clergyman. But the largest representation consisted of attorneys—23 of them— which was 41% of those heroes.

Among the 55 delegates who produced our Constitution in September of 1787 were physicians, businessmen, farmers, clergymen, and college professors. But the largest representation AGAIN consisted of attorneys—34 of them—which was 67% of those heroes (and future American attorneys would be taught in law school for the next 150 years that their rightful duty was to uphold Constitutional law, not case or precedent law). And 46 of these delegates, or 84% of them were elected members of their respective state legislatures. Understanding their credentials, can you doubt their competence? And twenty-six year old Jonathan Dayton of New Jersey was the youngest, while eighty-one year old Benjamin Franklin was the oldest.

These 55 Constitution-producing delegates undoubtedly derived much of their courage and conviction from their religious faith. Among them were Baptists, Quakers, Episcopalians, Catholics, Presbyterians, Methodists, Congregationalists, and French Huguenots. Not surprisingly, none were atheists, since what true atheist could possibly admit the American principle that rights come from God?

Before leaving this reference to religion, let's add that one of the heroes of the Battle of Bunker Hill in Boston was Israel Putnam, a Jew, who will always be remembered for his famous remark, prompted no doubt by the patriot's shortage of ammunition, "Don't one of you shoot 'til you see the white of their eyes!"

You are a so-called American. You inherited freedom. That's what our founders fought and died for, so you would never have to ask permission from the humans you allow to run the government for you to do anything. You are free. The government is not. Government (the humans you allow to run the government for you) always needs your permission to do anything. You never need permission to do anything from the humans you allow to run your government.

The American concept of freedom is that you do not need permission from anyone to do anything. You are free. Doesn't that excite you? If not, phone the undertaker.

Damn it! What a glorious feeling it is to be truly free, needing no one's permission for anything! Almost indescribable, isn't it? Can you feel it? Needing no one's permission! Fantasize about it. You're allowed. Get off on it! Go ahead! This is what our Revolution was all about, the quest for freedom, by freedom lovers.

Remember the basis of Americanism: rights come

from God, not the humans we allow to run the government for us. Remember our Declaration: "...endowed by their Creator with certain unalienable rights,...life, LIBERTY, and the pursuit of happiness." Liberty! Freedom! You are born with it. Remember?

Remember that the great American Principle of Freedom is that you never need to ask permission from the humans you allow to run the government for you to do anything. They work for you, not the other way around. Why ask for permission from your employee? Does that make any sense?

Think. Apply this great American Principle of Freedom to your life. See how free you really are.

How many times have you asked for permission from a governmental body to allow you to do something you wished to do, instead of just doing it? Compare this to how many times original Americans asked for permission to act from this hired government.

Would original Americans ever think they needed permission from the humans they allowed to run the government for them to ride a horse? Ha-ha! Have you ever asked the humans you allow to run the government for you for permission to drive a car?

Would original Americans ever think they needed government permission to marry the person they loved? Ha-ha! Have you ever asked permission to marry from a human you allowed to run the government for you?

Would original Americans ever think they needed government permission to build an addition to their house? Ha-ha! Have you ever asked permission from a human you allow to run the government for you to make renovations on your house?

Would original Americans ever think they needed government permission to buy a musket? Ha-ha! Have you ever asked a human you allow to run the government for you for permission to buy a gun?

Would original Americans ever think they needed government permission to go into a business for themselves, manufacturing, servicing, or buying and selling anything? Ha-ha! Have you ever asked a human you allow to run the government for you for permission to become self-employed?

The list is endless. How free do you feel? How many other things that you did required permission from the humans you allow to run the government for you? How many times were you discouraged from even trying some things because seeking and receiving permission from the humans you allow to run the government for you would be too burdensome? How many times were you denied permission to operate from the humans you allow to run the government for you because you couldn't comply with governmental laws, rules, or regulations? And probably the most common abuse of your freedom is legal theft, that you are denied permission from the humans you allow to run the government for you to withhold payment of your own hard-earned money from going to support governmental policies and programs with which you strongly disagree. You are automatically forced to support them. You never even think to seek such permission to withhold your payment because you know it will be denied. So the humans you allow to run the government for you keep passing laws to steal from you legally. How free do you feel? How free are you really?

Original Americans had no identity crisis. They knew who they were, and who they were supposed to be. Original Americans were free. They never needed permission to act from the humans they allowed to run the government for them. They just did it. They could never conceive of having to buy a license from the humans they allowed to run the government for them to exercise their freedom. Inconceivable! Outrageous! And damned un-American.

Think. Apply the Real American Syllogism to the above examples. Can you force your neighbor to buy a license from you to drive a car? Can you force your neighbor to buy a license from you to marry someone? Can you force your neighbor to buy a license from you to renovate a house? Can you force your neighbor to buy a license from you to buy a gun? Can you force your neighbor to buy a license from you to become self-employed? Oh, you can't?

Then how can the humans you allow to run the government for you do this? It is illegitimate, unconstitutional, and un-American. Remember: if you can't do it, then the humans you allow to run the government for you can't do it either.

Remember, you are only free if you don't need permission to act from the humans you allow to run the government for you. You just do it. The acid test in determining whether you are really free involves the issue of control. Who controls whose actions? Do you feel you control the actions of the humans you allow to run the government for you, or do you feel that the humans you allow to run the government for you control YOUR actions? Think about that. What is your answer to this question?

Being free means that you are in complete control of your choice of actions. Not being free means that the humans you allow to the government for you exert control on your choice of actions. Think about it. Which do you feel is the case?

If you're not feeling free right now, it might remind you of how you felt when your parents ordered you to "go to your room and stay there," or when your school teacher gave you detention. Remember that feeling of your lack of freedom, that someone else was controlling your actions, and your needing permission to act from a parental or educational authority? Don't you feel now that governmental authority has become your parental authority substitute? But it's damned un-American.

The men and women who established our country and produced America's founding documents: the Declaration of Independence, our Constitution, and Bill of Rights, understood the true meanings of the words: freedom, patriotism, and Americanism.

Burn these definitions into you soul. Repeat them silently and out loud, over and over again. Memorize them now, and NEVER forget them. If they sound right to you, you may be a Real-American.

Freedom is the condition resulting from never needing permission to act from the humans we allow to run the government for us.

Patriotism is loyalty to our Constitution.

Americanism is loyalty to limited government because rights come from God.

Original Americans were free, patriotic, and loyal to the principles of our limited government, a republic. Because of this, original Americans TRULY lived in the land of the free and the home of the brave. What have we become now?

_____ Part II _____
THE RESULTS

Chapter 9

The American Way of Life

> *Yes, we did produce a near perfect Repub-*
> *lic. But will they keep it, or will they, in*
> *the enjoyment of plenty, lose the memory*
> *of freedom. Material abundance without*
> *character is the surest way to destruction.*
> —*Thomas Jefferson*

We Americans today number only 6% of the entire world's population, and we live on only 6% of the entire world's land mass. But we own 50% of the world's goods, which abundance of goods provides us with the highest standard of living, compared to the living conditions of all of the rest of the world's population.

Did you know this simple fact?

How did we Americans accomplish this incredibly high standard of living? Does the land mass of the United States contain more and better natural resources than those contained in the land masses of Central and South America, Europe, Asia, Africa, the Middle East, Australia, and New Zealand? No. Are Americans stronger and smarter than Central and South Americans, Europeans, Asians, Africans, Middle Easterners, Australians, and New Zealanders? No. Can Americans naturally work harder than all of these other peoples? No.

Then what caused this high standard of living here, higher than anywhere else on earth? The answer is freedom. The degree of freedom for the people was and still is higher here than anywhere else in the world. And remember the American definition of freedom: never needing permission from government to do anything. Freedom for the people caused our abundance. Think about this.

The bottom line is this: our never needing permission to do anything from the humans we allowed to run our government for us was the thing which enabled us to produce the greatest abundance of basic material items like food, clothing, shelter, and the greatest abundance of material luxuries like everything powered by battery, gas, and electric.

Also, our never needing permission from the humans we allowed to run our government for us enabled us to buy this abundant production from, or to sell this abundant production to all of our own people, and to all of the other peoples in the world.

And lastly, our never needing permission from the humans we allowed to run our government for us meant that we as individuals owned and therefore controlled whatever we produced for ourselves, and that we as individuals owned and therefore controlled whatever we purchased from others, and that we as individuals could KEEP whatever we owned and therefore controlled.

So summing up, the freedom we inherited from our American founders enabled us to freely produce material goods, to freely buy them, to freely sell them, and to freely own, control, and KEEP whatever we possessed.

This freedom system which we inherited from our American founders, and which is memorialized for all times in our Constitution, meant that the humans we allowed to run our government for us could NEVER interfere with and attempt to control our lives and our property, EVER. This is the essence of Americanism. These governmental humans had one basic function: to protect from violation by criminals our God-given rights of life, liberty, property, and our individual pursuit of happiness. That's all. And remember, this governmental protective function is the same thing which we ourselves as individuals can perform, and this is also exactly why we can allow our governmental humans to perform this protective function too, remember?

Aside from performing their normal function of protecting us from criminals at all times, in our economic lives, early Americans did NOT expect their governmental humans to do SOMETHING to enable them to produce a high standard of living. THE DIRECT OPPOSITE WAS TRUE. Early Americans expected their governmental humans to do NOTHING, which these early Americans understood would enable them, in their economic lives, to produce a high standard of living BY THEMSELVES.

In other words, the American governmental system of economics was designed by our founders to be PASSIVE, not active. Our founders deliberately designed our economic system this way ON PURPOSE to insure our freedom, because they perfectly understood the principle that freedom from governmental interference in the economic life of the people is the greatest motivating force for human beings to produce a high standard of living for themselves.

Basically, the only thing early Americans allowed and expected their governmental humans to do regarding their economic lives was to mutually formalize a uniform value system for currency, weights, and measures to facilitate trade among themselves, and this action was not viewed as interference.

But how can we be sure that our founders understood the principle that freedom from governmental interference in the economic life of the people is the absolute GUARANTEE of what we shall hereafter label as the HIGH STANDARD OF LIVING FORMULA? Easily. Our founders remembered well the stories of the Jamestown and Plymouth settlements' common experience. And here is what they remembered.

The Jamestown, Virginia settlement was established in 1607 with the Council Compact and with Captain John Smith as its most famous leader. The Plymouth, Massachusetts settlement was established in 1620 with the Mayflower Compact and with Sir William Bradford as its most famous leader.

By common request, the governments of these settlements were the boss of everyone, and these governments established a communal, or collectivistic, or using the appropriately modern terminology, a socialistic economic system.

Economics, of course, is the science of who gets what, when, where, how, how much, for how long, and at what price. MEMORIZE THAT SIMPLE DEFINITION.

This socialistic economic system in Jamestown and Plymouth meant that all land and ''personal'' property were owned, in effect, by the settlements' governments, because everyone had agreed to allow their governmental humans to control everything, supposedly for everyone's benefit.

The acid test of real ownership is always who controls the property? You or the governmental humans? If you allow the governmental humans to control the property, then you really don't own it, the governmental humans do. Understand? The acid test of ownership always entails the application of the principle of control.

All of the settlers at Jamestown and Plymouth worked together at governmentally assigned tasks. They shared and shared alike in the total production of all of the goods for the settlement. And everything which everybody produced (food, clothing, etc.) was brought by each settler to a common warehouse for storage, and for later equal distribution.

At the appointed times, everyone would appear at the settlements' warehouses where the governmental humans would dispense the goods on an equal shares for everybody basis. After all, everyone was equal by law.

So what happened? Did this socialistic economic system work well for everyone's benefit? No. Everyone starved. What? Why?

Because the lazy people realized that no matter how little they produced and brought to the common warehouses, they would still receive the same equal share of all the goods as their more productive neighbors. So the lazy people began to loaf. They didn't do their fair share. You dig?

When the more productive people realized that they were being made by the governments to support the loafers, these productive people began to slow down also, and became less productive. You dig?

As one family after another eased up on their production of vegetables, grains, and meats, less goods went into the common warehouse, naturally, and supplies in the warehouse began to dwindle and dwindle, down to practically nothing.

Soon, starvation threatened to wipe out all of the settlers. Can you see why? It's just HUMAN NATURE, and human nature can NEVER change. So the governmental leaders knew that their socialistic experiment was a failure. Instead of providing ABUNDANCE for all, this socialistic economic system was providing SCARCITY for all.

Something had to be done. A change was necessary. But what were the choices? Only two. The governmental leaders of Jamestown and Plymouth could use their police powers to FORCE productive labor, or these leaders could devise a different system which would hopefully motivate and encourage VOLUNTARY productive labor. Said another way, these leaders could choose to use one of only two forms of human motivation to solve their scarcity problem: the natural human fear of PUNISHMENT, or the natural human desire for REWARD.

Stop here, and ask yourself the following two important questions. Really. Stopping and thinking about your honest answers to the following questions will tell you a whole lot about yourself, about your conditioned mentality.

Here are the two vitally important personal questions.

If you were John Smith or William Bradford, and you had the responsibility to solve this critical scarcity problem, would you use your police powers to try to force productive labor, using the people's natural fear of punishment as their primary motivation, or would you try to devise a different system of voluntary productive labor, using the people's natural desire for reward as their primary motivation? What is your answer? Think about it.

Next question. If you were just one of the settlers, which form of motivation do you think would work better on you to get you to work harder to be more productive to save yourself: the fear of punishment, or the desire for reward? What is your answer? Think about it.

Interesting questions, no? Were you really honest with your answers? Did your honest answers reveal where your head is at? And did your honest answers make you wonder how your head got there? Stimulating, no?

Smith and Bradford considered the thought of using governmental police powers to force people into productive labor to be abhorrent, because they had fled from the old country because it had employed just such an oppressive system. So both Jamestown and Plymouth rejected the use of governmental force, and the natural human fear of punishment associated with such a tactic, to solve the SCARCITY problem.

Jamestown and Plymouth decided instead to abandon their old socialistic economic systems in which the governments decided who got what, when, where, how, how much, for how long, and at what price. They decided to switch to a uniquely free economic system in which each individual would be left completely alone, with no governmental interference at all, so that each individual could decide for himself or herself exactly who got what, when, where, how, how much, for how long, and at what price.

Consequently, the Jamestown and Plymouth governments equally divided up the formerly governmentally owned and controlled pastures and farm lands, and officially announced to all of the settlers that henceforth these properties would now be owned and completely controlled by each individual. These governments also officially announced that each individual could produce whatever goods or services he or she wished to produce, and as much as they wished to produce, and that each individual could exchange these goods or services among themselves according to their own abilities and their own desires. Everyone would have to work, or suffer from a self-inflicted penalty—that of hunger and shame. From this time forth, people would own and control their own private property, and would be totally responsible for themselves. They would be ''on their own,'' ''sink or swim.''

The free economic system was born for the FIRST time in all of recorded history at Jamestown and Plymouth. For the very first time, public property (which is always REALLY government property) was abolished, and for the very first time, the true idea of PRIVATE PROPERTY was established, where individuals could own and therefore completely control their own property, and use it as THEY saw fit, without needing permission from government to do so, and also without having to fear punishment from government for their economic activities of producing, buying, selling, and keeping.

Thus the Jamestown and Plymouth settlements established the forerunners and set the precedents for the free economic system which would eventually become the American Way of Life—memorialized in our Constitution after we achieved independence—of PRIVATE PROPERTY and SELF-RELIANCE—just the opposite of the governmental public ownership system and the people's reliance on government, both of which are characteristic of Socialism.

So what happened then? Guess. You already must know. ABUNDANCE, of course, what else? No more loafers, no more starvation. Prosperity. ABUNDANCE. A high standard of living. The settlers swam, and did not sink.

But why did this new system of private property and self-reliance rather than public property and government-reliance produce the increase of voluntary productive labor, which in turn produced the abundance, which in turn produced the increase in the standard of living? Good question.

Well, the answer is HUMAN NATURE. No wonder the settlers were willing to work harder and harder— ALL of the fruits of their labors were their own. Who can deny this powerfully motivating voluntary labor INCENTIVE which is based on the right to own and control your property yourself, and to control the rewards of one's own labor? NO ONE IN HIS RIGHT MIND.

The greatest voluntary productive labor incentive for an individual to work at his MAXIMUM ever conceived in mortal mind is the God-given right to own and control ALL of your own private property, and for you to be able to KEEP all of the fruits of your own labors. Nothing else works better to motivate you to work at your MAXIMUM productivity. Can you think of a more effective INCENTIVE? No? Then bow to this magnificently simple and true principle. O.K.? Why not?

Why would anyone voluntarily work at their maximum if he or she knew that they couldn't KEEP all of the fruits of their labors? That would definitely be

AGAINST human nature. And fear of governmental punishment can only motivate individuals to work at their MINIMUM. THAT is human nature. And human nature never changes. Human nature will change when a leopard changes its spots.

Here is what Captain John Smith of Jamestown wrote in his diary after they avoided starvation by changing to the new FREE economic system of private property ownership and individual self-reliance:

> *"When our people were fed out of the common storehouse and labored jointly together, glad was he who could slip away from his labor or slumber over his task. He cared not, presuming that howsoever the harvest prospered, the general storehouse must maintain him. Even the MOST HONEST among them would hardly take so much true pains in a week under the public ownership and common storehouse system, as now for themselves they will do in a day. So that, we reaped not so much corn from the labor of thirty as now three or four will provide for themselves."*

Sir William Bradford of Plymouth wrote regarding the same matter:

> *"When the system of private ownership was established, and self-reliance became the rule, the housewife came out of her kitchen and the children gave up some of their play time to work in the fields so the family could produce more, and have more, and live better."*

Why Bradford had to learn his lesson on economics the hard way for himself, instead of learning from Smith's experience is a matter for speculation. But we know one thing for sure: the founders of our Republic and our free enterprise system which they fixed into our Constitution, definitely learned the economic lesson of Jamestown and Plymouth, that the GREATEST voluntary productive labor incentive which will produce ABUNDANCE and a SUPERIOR standard of living will be found in the ideas of private property, self-reliance, and an individual's ability to KEEP ALL of the fruits of his or her own labors.

So our founders were definitely guided in their thinking on economics by this definition of freedom (needing no permission from government), and their studious understanding of the brilliant 4-step High Standard of Living Formula, UNQUESTIONABLY PROVEN at Jamestown and Plymouth.

This 4-step High Standard of Living Formula goes like this: (frontwards) incentive-labor-production-abundance. Again. Incentive produces labor, labor produces production, production produces abundance. Again. The incentive to keep ALL of the fruits of your own labor will motivate you to labor at your maximum; laboring at your maximum will increase your production; your increased production will produce abundance. (Backwards) abundance-production-labor-incentive. Again. Abundance is produced by production, production is produced by labor, labor is produced by incentive. Again. Abundance is produced by your increased production; your increased production is produced by your laboring at your maximum; your laboring at your maximum is produced by the incentive to keep all of the fruits of your own labor.

If one picture is truly worth a thousand words, please look now at the delicately balanced inverted triangle building blocks picture immediately following, which should not only help you memorize the 4-step High Standard of Living Formula, but it will also be the same picture used later on, but with a much different configuration, to perfectly illustrate the essential point on this critical economic subject, without then having to use a thousand more words:

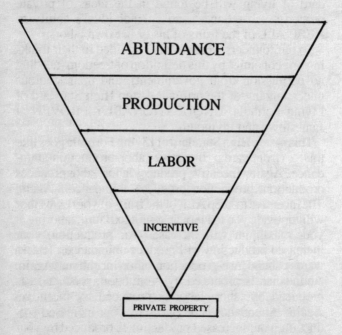

ABUNDANCE

PRODUCTION

LABOR

INCENTIVE

PRIVATE PROPERTY

Our American free economic system based exclusively on the sacred ideas of private property and self-reliance produced almost heaven-on-earth living conditions for the ''common people'' of America when compared to how the common people had ALWAYS lived for the last 6,000 years everywhere else on earth. Even during the height of our great depression, no

American starved, and the average American still enjoyed a higher standard of living than the average citizen living in every other country in the entire world. The sacred American ideas of private property and self-reliance INSURED THE APPLICATION of the 4-step High Standard of Living Formula which was always the KEY to our inherent well-being, and a life of abundance for the common people.

On the contrary, for 6,000 years, the common people everywhere else in the world regularly experienced repeated famines, starvation, and early deaths because their governments ALWAYS controlled everybody and everything, and their governments NEVER really allowed their people to maintain true private property and self-reliance. Consequently, these incredibly similar and typically socialistic governments ALWAYS INSURED that their common peoples would barely be able to scratch out a meager existence, living forever in fear of governmental punishment, and living forever in abject poverty, misery, and scarcity.

We are basically comparing the ONLY TWO essential philosophies and forms of government ever known to man since Adam and Eve. They are Americanism and Socialism. There has NEVER been a third philosophy and form of government, and there NEVER can be. There will NEVER be an exception to this PERFECT rule.

As an important aside, and before returning to the simple but mind-blowing fact that ONLY the essential philosophies and forms of government of Americanism and Socialism have ever existed, and can ever exist, we need to cover the economic subjects of gold, money, and inflation. NORMAL PEOPLE used to find it EASY to understand the subjects of gold, money, and inflation until the INTELLECTUALS worked so hard to confuse everyone on these SIMPLE subjects. The following few pages explaining the simple, fundamental truth regarding gold, money, and inflation will make intellectuals go berserk. Listen up. You'll love it.

Humans desire things which are pretty, useful, and scarce. Humans do not desire things which are plain, useless, and plentiful. Isn't that principle simple to understand? It's just human nature. Gold is pretty, useful, and scarce. Gold is shiny. It is pretty. Gold is the most malleable metal in existence. It is the metal capable of being stretched out the thinnest, and shaped and molded the easiest, almost like bubble gum. In fact, you can stretch a one ounce gold piece into a thin strand for miles. Did you realize this fact? Gold is also virtually indestructible. It doesn't rust or corrode. Gold can lie on the bottom of the ocean for thousands of years, and after knocking the barnacles off of it, it is as pretty and shiny as it ever was. So ancient and modern humans have ALWAYS valued gold as pretty and useful for jewelry, ornaments, statues, decorations, etc. And modern humans value it also to perform critical functions in dentistry and in electronics because of its virtual indestructibility and non-corrosiveness, which no other metal can even come close to equalling. And gold is hard to find, and extremely difficult to mine when found. Gold is scarce. For all of these reasons and more, humans will ALWAYS desire gold. It is pretty, extremely useful, and scarce. Case closed. Simple, no? It's just human nature.

Intellectuals will say, "But you can't eat gold." Normal people answer, "Brilliant observation. Gold is not food. You can't eat diamonds for the same reason, but humans will always find diamonds desirable too.'' Big deal.

With the exceptions of gifts and thefts, economic transactions can only occur in two forms: the barter system, and the money system. The barter system works something like this: ''I'll trade you one hundred potatoes for one hundred carrots.'' Bartering is trading one valuable, desirable commodity for another valuable, desirable commodity. VALUE for VALUE. Something DESIRABLE for something else DESIRABLE. Logical, no? Now, you wanted the carrots, but what happens if the carrot man doesn't want your potatoes? No trade. So you have to offer the carrot man a valuable, desirable SOMETHING ELSE for his carrots, a different medium to encourage an exchange, a trade. These NO TRADE POSSIBLE type of occurrences gave birth to the money system. The money system works something like this: ''I'll trade you one gold piece for one hundred carrots.'' Gold is money, a medium of exchange, the desirable something else which PRODUCES the exchange, the trade. The gold money system, like bartering, is also trading one valuable, desirable commodity for another valuable, desirable commodity. Value for value. Something desirable for something else desirable. Logical, no? It's just human nature. It violates human nature for you to trade something valuable and desirable which you own, for something else which is worthless and undesirable, doesn't it? Think about that for a while.

Gold is HARD money, and for good reasons, gold became the UNIVERSAL, world-wide, acceptable HARD money, which everyone, everywhere, would accept and exchange their carrots for, because they knew that they would be able to exchange that gold for tomatoes, corn, wheat, tools, horses, etc., or anything else, ANYWHERE. And gold pieces were a lot easier to carry around in your pockets than one hundred potatoes. Got it? Convenience.

But for large purchases, like buying land or buildings, etc., heavy gold was difficult or impossible to carry around in your pockets. For large purchases, you needed to transport your heavy gold in horse-drawn wagons. And thieves loved to raid and rob your wagon. Can you dig it?

This extreme difficulty, visibility, and danger of theft when paying large quantities of heavy hard money gold to the sellers of expensive things created the PAPER money system. Here's what happened, and remember that money could be ANYTHING used as an acceptable medium of exchange.

Owners of valuable, desirable gold began to store their gold in guarded warehouses for safe-keeping. The gold owners asked the warehouse operators to give them a written paper receipt, so that these owners would be able to get back their gold whenever they desired, using these written paper receipts as PROOF that the warehouse operators ONLY took temporary possession of the owners' gold for storage purposes ONLY. The warehouse operators naturally charged their storage customers a small fee for this storage service. And, of course, the warehouse operators did not OWN the gold they stored. They were simply guarding and storing it for the owners for a fee. No questions so far, right? Can you see where we're heading?

Obviously, if you require us to define for you the

exact meaning of the word, "receipt," we would appreciate your answering the following question: what planet are you from?

So, let's say that you have stored your valuable, desirable gold in the warehouse, and that you have a receipt to prove it. Now you wish to buy a big house from someone who wishes to sell it. You both agree on the price, and you say something to the house seller like this: "Rather than my going to the warehouse to redeem my receipt to pick up my gold, and then having to transport my gold to you, why don't I just sign over my receipt to you, and then you can go to the warehouse anytime you wish, to pick up the gold, because my signing over my receipt to you means that my stored gold NOW belongs to you?" The house seller says O.K. So you take possession of the seller's house, and the house seller takes possession of your endorsed receipt, drives his wagon over to the warehouse, turns in the endorsed receipt, and the warehouse operators give the house seller the gold which that particular receipt represented. Simple so far, right? Can you see where we're heading now?

The receipt you gave the house seller only represented one of your lots of gold in the warehouse, and you possess several more warehouse receipts, representing several more lots of your stored gold. Now you wish to buy a young white horse from someone else who wishes to sell the beautiful animal. You both agree on the price, and the horse seller agrees to accept another one of your endorsed receipts, representing another one of your lots of gold stored in the warehouse. So you take possession of the beautiful white horse, and the horse seller takes possession of your endorsed receipt, but he's too busy, or too lazy, or too rich, or too tired to ride over to the warehouse to cash in the receipt to pick up the gold which that receipt represents. So the horse seller just keeps that receipt in his pocket.

Now, let's forget about YOU for a while. Let's discuss this horse seller with your endorsed receipt in his pocket. He never goes to the warehouse. He goes out shopping to buy 5 cows so that he can feed steaks, roasts, and hamburgers to the 200 guests he has invited to his daughter's wedding banquet.

He endorses the gold receipt over to the cow seller, and takes possession of the 5 cows. The cow seller accepts the paper receipt ONLY because he believes that that particular piece of paper represents a valid claim on a specific amount of gold in the warehouse. Got it? So, the paper money system starts to flourish. Everyone begins to exchange valuable, desirable commodities for PAPER RECEIPTS which represent valuable, desirable, gold, because it's so convenient not to have to lug heavy, cumbersome gold around.

Can you see now how the warehouses would later change their names to "banks"? Can you also see now how the additional gold you would place there in storage would later become known as "deposits"? Can you also see now how the gold receipts would later become known as paper money or "bank notes"? And a "note" means "debt," which means that if you possess a warehouse note or a bank note, that the warehouse or bank OWES you something which belongs to you, and has a debt TO YOU. Can you dig it? This is how the banking system was born.

To review, money is a valuable, desirable commodity which is an acceptable medium of exchange used to bring about a trade when the barter system fails.

Universal hard money is gold. Paper money is a receipt for gold. A piece of paper is valueless. A piece of gold is valuable. A piece of paper is undesirable. A piece of gold is desirable. A piece of paper only becomes valuable and desirable when it is a receipt representing a valid claim on a specific quantity of valuable and desirable gold. No receipt has INTRINSIC VALUE in and of itself as a piece of paper. All receipts only have value when they can be turned in or redeemed for some COMMODITY of intrinsic value in and of itself, like vegetables, fruits, meats, fish, wheat, tools, lumber, gold, etc. The hardest thing for intellectuals to understand is that paper is paper, and gold is gold. Poor bastards.

Gold became the UNIVERSAL hard money BACKING of ALL paper money receipts because it was a valuable, desirable commodity which wouldn't spoil, or deteriorate like any other backing would. Gold is the most durable commodity on the face of the earth.

Now let's cover the subject of inflation.

Warehouses for gold storage sprung up in every village and town. In larger communities with large populations, several competing warehouses in the same large community were established. So receipts for stored gold, issued by dozens and dozens of different warehouses, began to circulate everywhere, even across town, county, and state boundaries. Can you dig it?

One day, a warehouse operator, and we'll call him by the name of Slick, in one town, made an intriguing observation: no gold owners who stored their gold in Slick's warehouse ever appeared to cash in their receipts to withdraw their hard money gold which the receipts Slick issued to these owners represented.

So Slick had a clever idea, not very honest, but very clever: why not print up additional receipts which will appear to everyone as valid-looking as all of the other receipts he had issued, so that he could use these additional receipts (backed by nothing, not backed by additional gold deposits) as paper money to spend to buy things which he desired? Who would know he did this? Nobody. So he did it.

Thinking of what air inflation does to a balloon, will help you to better understand what monetary inflation does to the paper money supply.

Slick's printing of additional receipts (paper money) backed by nothing of value was INFLATION. Inflation is an INCREASE in the paper money supply which is backed by nothing of value. MEMORIZE THAT DEFINITION. Don't try to complicate it because it really is that simple. Just accept it. The dictionary will tell you the same thing. So this was actually how inflation was born. Slick's printing of 500 new warehouse receipts unbacked by gold is inflation of the quantity of existing receipt supply (existing paper money supply). Got it?

Each phony, unbacked paper money receipt which Slick printed was also what later came to be known as a COUNTERFEIT. Inflation and counterfeiting are EXACTLY the same thing. You can understand this, can't you? This is how counterfeiting was born. And please separate in your mind that the first step of the inflation/counterfeiting is the PRINTING up of the phoney receipts (paper money bills), while the second step involved is the SPENDING of these counterfeits into circulation. Printing counterfeit paper receipts causes no trouble. Spending counterfeit paper receipts into circulation is the action which causes ALL of the trouble.

Slick went on a spending spree, using the counterfeit paper money, and since he loved horses, he started to buy up every horse for sale.

What were the economic results of Slick's spending spree? A noticeable and dramatic effect on the economic laws of supply and demand—the price of horses went higher and higher. What is the economic law of supply and demand? Simple. Supply is the number, amount, or QUANTITY of goods available for sale. Demand is the DESIRE and ABILITY of customers to buy those available goods, and ability is determined by the amount of money which these customers possess.

The supply and demand bottom line is this: if the supply of a good is high, and demand for it is low, the selling price of that good will be cheap; but if supply of a good is low, and demand for it is high, the selling price of that good will be expensive. Think about it. It's just a perfect example of human nature in action.

Another bottom line is this: in a free economy, customers are the ONLY people who determine what the eventual PRICE of goods and services will be, and at what price these things will sell for. If customer demand for a particular product is high, they will buy and buy it causing the supply to get scarcer and scarcer, driving the PRICE of that particular product higher and higher, until the producers increase the supply. If the customer demand for a particular product is low, they will stop buying it, causing the supply to be high, driving the PRICE of that particular product lower and lower, until the customer demand increases. Can you understand that this is simply a human nature process? Like what happens at an auction. Think about that.

So when Slick entered the market with his counterfeit paper money (receipts), and started to buy up every horse that he could, he created a natural shortage of horses which everybody else may have wished to buy, thus driving the price of horses up for everyone else.

Slick had owned 3 horses before his counterfeiting and spending spree began, but after a few weeks, people in town noticed that 50 horses were now grazing in Slick's pasture. The people became suspicious regarding how Slick had become wealthy enough to buy 47 more horses in so short a time period. People became nervous about storing their gold in Slick's warehouse, so they all ran to Slick's warehouse with their receipts (paper money) to withdraw their gold. Not only did Slick's depositors appear at his warehouse, but so did every horse trader holding the receipts (paper money) which Slick had paid them for the horses they had sold him.

People tried to turn in and have 1000 receipts redeemed, which were supposed to represent 1000 separate lots of gold. But Slick was forced to announce that the warehouse contained only 500 separate lots of gold, and that he had counterfeited (inflated) 500 additional receipts, which he had spent. In essence, Slick was admitting that he had stolen and spent half of the gold in the warehouse, and consequently, each receipt was now actually worth half of what it had represented before the inflation and counterfeit spending. In essence, each receipt was devalued by 50%.

Said another way, prior to the inflation, 1 receipt represented 1 lot of gold. After the inflation, 2 receipts represented 1 lot of gold. Think about that.

If nothing were done to correct this situation, sellers realized that just to stay even, they would now have to double their prices of their goods for sale, and ask for 2 receipts for goods, which prior to the inflation used to cost only 1.

So what finally happened to Slick? The furious mob lynched him, hanging him by his neck from the closest tree until he was dead. The horse traders burned their phony game of Monopoly type money receipts to take them out of circulation, and went to Slick's pasture and re-possessed their horses. And after the gold owners withdrew their gold deposits from the warehouse, they burned down the warehouse. Case closed.

Somewhat summing up: EVERY piece of paper money ever printed, in ANY country, at ANY time, yesterday, today, and tomorrow, is a RECEIPT. These receipts are ONLY VALUABLE if you can redeem them for the valuable commodity which these receipts are supposed to represent, and which these receipts are supposed to be backed-up by. These receipts are therefore WORTHLESS if you cannot redeem them for something valuable, because they then represent NOTHING, and are backed-up by NOTHING.

Somewhat summing up: inflation is an INCREASE in the paper money supply, which additional paper money is unbacked by anything valuable, and is actually a receipt for NOTHING, and this counterfeit currency causes trouble once it gets spent into circulation.

Somewhat summing up: inflation ALWAYS causes higher prices. Inflation is the cause, and higher prices are simply the bad effects of inflation. Higher prices are NOT inflation itself. Higher prices are the RE-SULTS of inflation. Inflation is a DISHONEST IN-CREASE in the paper money supply. Inflation is AL-WAYS counterfeiting, pure and simple, and inflation ALWAYS reduces the value of all of the other paper money in circulation, and inflation ALWAYS drives UP the prices of everything.

Continuing the inflation story, warehousemen every-where were ALWAYS tempted to inflate the quantity of the receipts they issued, in order to conveniently steal from their gold storage customers. Some did. Some were caught. Some escaped. And news of this type of counterfeiting always shook the confidence people had in accepting paper money (receipts) as payment for the goods which they sold. After every counterfeiting scandal, sellers would ALWAYS de-mand payment in gold and silver coins ONLY. Natu-rally, this was just a normal human nature reaction. You can understand that, can't you?

So gradually, the people lost a TON of confidence in warehouse (bank) receipts (paper money), but they still didn't want to carry around their heavy gold. So what happened?

Local governments in scandal-ridden areas assumed control, and forbid some warehouses from issuing re-ceipts for the gold deposits in their care, and these local governments assumed the responsibility of an exact accounting and issuing of the only authorized receipts for all warehouse deposits. And, of course, these standard governmental-issued receipts (paper money) were fully backed by the gold stored in the warehouses, and these standard governmental receipts could be redeemed for the gold which these receipts represented. When governments did this, CONFI-

DENCE in accepting these government-issued receipts (paper money) in exchange for valuable commodities was usually always RESTORED.

Some towns, counties, and states issued standard currency (receipts, paper money). But the amount of gold backing on the different governmentally-issued currencies VARIED considerably. This fact created cumbersome confusion in pricing and trading when these different currencies showed up in different areas. Soon, the NATIONAL governments in each country established a standard currency (receipts, form of paper money), backed by gold, and fully redeemable in gold at any time.

Soon, WAREHOUSE paper money receipts disappeared, BANK NOTE paper money receipts disappeared, TOWN-ISSUED paper money receipts disappeared, COUNTY-ISSUED paper money receipts disappeared, COLONY-ISSUED paper money receipts disappeared, STATE-ISSUED paper money receipts disappeared, and ONLY country-wide national FEDERAL GOVERNMENT-ISSUED paper money receipts became ACCEPTABLE LEGAL TENDER for all financial transactions. And this STANDARDIZED national paper money currency was backed by a fixed quantity of gold, or another precious metal of similar desirable qualities like silver, since silver is durable, malleable, the brightest metal known to man, and the best conductor of electricity known to man, and a metal essential to the photographic industry. And this NATIONAL CURRENCY was a receipt backed by gold and silver, and fully redeemable for these valuable, desirable, precious metals.

And please try hard to always remember that the people STILL OWNED the actual gold and silver which these national receipts represented. The government was STILL like the warehouse which did not own the gold and silver, but simply stored these precious metals for their customers, and printed and issued the appropriate receipts.

Governments knew that they had to guarantee the people that their paper money currency could be INSTANTLY CONVERTED into the gold and silver which it represented, or the people would keep their gold and silver at home under their beds, rather than depositing it in the new government warehouses (government banks). Makes sense, doesn't it? Because normal people understand that paper is paper, and gold is gold. But intellectuals can't understand that.

Before government got involved in the storage and receipt issuing procedure, do you think that YOU would deposit your gold for storage in a warehouse whose operators told you, that after you deposited your gold, you could NEVER use your receipt to withdraw it? Give me a break.

As an aside, check Article I, Section 10, Clause 1 of our Constitution, and you will see how NONE of our states could issue their own paper money, or mint their own coins, or LEGALLY FORCE any citizen living in their state to accept any other payment other than gold and silver coins as a form of payment for a debt that somebody owed them. But back to our story.

So what happened after each national government issued national paper currency, which gradually became the ONLY paper currency in circulation? The national federal governments with a MONOPOLY on the printing and issuing of receipts (paper money currency) began to inflate their currencies, with the exact same results of inflation always: reducing the value of each paper money receipt, and driving prices of goods up higher. Governments became LEGAL COUNTERFEITERS, and began to STEAL LEGALLY from their citizens (customers), by devaluing through the inflation process the currency held by their citizens.

Ancient Roman governments stole the private property wealth from their citizens using a gimmick known as "coin-clipping." The ancient Roman emperors would have their bureaucrats shave off tiny bits of gold from the gold coins passing through their hands through taxation, before spending these gold coins back into circulation. This is why the shape of so many ancient Roman gold coins became so funny looking. Ancient Roman emperors also stole the private property wealth from their citizens by keeping ALL of the gold and silver coins in their possession and NOT returning them into circulation, but rather minting and returning into circulation, coins of much less value, like coins made of copper, lead, or iron, but with the same numerals, titles, designs, and words stamped on these baser metal coins that were formerly on the precious metal gold and silver coins in the same denominations. But with the advent of paper money, governments could steal gold easier from their own citizens by simply running the printing presses OVERTIME to produce counterfeit receipts (paper money), and then spending these counterfeit bills into circulation.

Governments have ONLY two methods of stealing from their own citizens: taxation and inflation. Some of the private property wealth stolen by government from their productive citizens winds up in the pockets of government officials, but most of it is usually re-distributed to less-productive citizens, to buy their votes to re-elect the "give-away-artist" politicians. When the productive citizens start to SCREAM LOUDLY about the confiscatory and visible direct taxation, the "give-away-artist" politicians, in order "to take the heat off" themselves, will usually STOP the tax increases, and may even LOWER the direct taxes, but then they will resort to the LESS VISIBLE and INDIRECT FORM of stealing and taxation called inflation.

With the exception of CRIMINAL PRIVATE counterfeiters, inflation (the increase in the paper money supply unbacked by anything valuable) can ONLY be caused by those who CONTROL the money supply. Guess who that is: the federal government, of course.

And it is axiomatic that government inflation of all of the currencies in the world is one of the biggest causes, if not THE biggest cause, of all of the economic ills of the world. Think about that.

Summing up inflation with one final example: inflation of the paper money supply is analogous to and produces a similar effect on the value of the paper money supply, as what adding water to milk does to the milk. Think about that.

Serious students of economics remember the histories of what is called "rapid inflation," which occurred in Germany after WW I, and what it did to devalue the German paper money supply, where a pound of butter, which used to cost 1 mark, wound up costing 5 million marks. Incredible. China after WW II experienced the same type of "rapid inflation." Can you imagine living like a millionaire one day, and a few weeks or months later, not being able to even buy a pound of butter? That actually happened, if the assets you possessed were in the form of paper money. Everyone's savings, bank accounts, and insurance policies were wiped out. Check it out if you're interested. It will blow your mind.

Only those who kept their wealth in the form of gold coins or gold bars were saved. In fact, these gold holders became multi-millionaires during the "rapid" or "runaway inflation," because whenever paper money becomes worth LESS AND LESS because of inflation, gold always becomes worth MORE AND MORE.

Serious students of economics will also remember that gold and silver coins circulated openly and freely in America for over 150 years after the founding of our country, and that our paper money was redeemable by our government for the gold and silver which it represented for an even longer period than that. And that our silver coins weren't replaced by our government in the same denominations by baser copper-nickle coins for at least 175 years after our founding. These serious economic students will also remember how our so-called American government stole most of our gold coins beginning in 1933, and stole most of our silver coins beginning in 1965, and that our so-called American government refused in the 1930's to redeem our paper money currency by returning the gold it was supposed to represent, and that our so-called American government refused in the 1960's to redeem our paper money currency by returning the silver it was supposed to represent. After this theft by our so-called American government, all of America's paper money in circulation which had the words "Gold Certificate" and "Silver Certificate" printed right on it, and which actually had words printed right on it that this paper money was redeemable by our government in actual gold and silver, remained valuable receipts ONLY as "collector's items."

The bottom line is this: every dollar in America today is a WORTHLESS piece of paper, a RECEIPT backed by NOTHING. Check it out. They are all called Federal Reserve Notes. Try to exchange your Federal Reserve Notes, which are simply pieces of paper, for gold or silver, and see what you get. NADA. In fact, if you believe the stuff which comes out of the back end of a bull regarding "fractional reserve banking" or that ou Federal Reserve Note paper money is backed by our Gross National Product, you are a certifiable intellectual. Think about that.

In fact, it will blow your mind when you discover that the so-called Federal Reserve System is not really federal, not really owned and controlled by the government, but is owned and controlled by private individual big businessmen stockholders, who make fabulous profits ONLY from our government's stealing-from-the-people inflation policy. And guess what. The Federal Reserve System has NEVER been audited. Think about that.

How would you feel about your dry cleaner, if, when you showed up to redeem your clothing receipt for your clothing, the dry cleaner told you to drop dead? Or how would you feel about your fur cold-storage warehouse operators, if, when you showed up in the winter to redeem your receipt for your mink or fox coat, the furrier told you to drop dead? These are PERFECT examples illustrating what has been done to America's paper money supply.

But let's return now to the subject of Americanism versus Socialism.

Americanism and Socialism are unchangeable generic terms, representing the ONLY two philosophies and forms of government which have ever existed, and can ever REALLY exist. And the philosophies and forms of Americanism and Socialism are as IR-RECONCILIABLY DIFFERENT from each other as HEAVEN is as irreconciliably different from HELL.

So let's repeat the definition of Americanism in order to correctly establish the true definition of Socialism. Americanism is loyalty to LIMITED government because rights come from God. Socialism is loyalty to POTENTIALLY UNLIMITED government because rights come from the government. The definition of Socialism is that simple.

Confusion in your mind on this subject of the mutually EXCLUSIVE existence of the only two philosophies and forms of government called Americanism and Socialism, with none others possible, can only be created in your mind if you allow intellectuals to create it there by their discussing the matter of DE-GREES of governments.

Intellectuals focus their attention on this matter of DEGREES of governments as their convenient excuse for doing NOTHING about the world in which we live. Intellectuals try hard to convince you that you also, like them, should focus your attention on this same matter of degrees of governments so that you also will be neutralized into doing the same NOTHING about the world in which we all live.

Here's how the scam works. Intellectuals admit that there is a black and a white, but a degree of each called gray. And this, of course, is true. Intellectuals also admit that there is a hot and a cold, but a degree of each called warm. And this, of course, is also true. Intellectuals also admit that there is a good and a bad, but a degree of each called fair. And this, of course, is true. Etc., etc., etc.

So intellectuals will admit that there is an extreme philosophy and form of government called Americanism, and its opposite extreme philosophy and form of government called Socialism. But these intellectuals will then focus their attention and yours on the middle ground of DEGREES which lies between the both extremes.

These intellectuals will admit that the extreme philosophy of Americanism can only truly express itself when it materializes into the actual form of government under which people live called a true republic; and these intellectuals will also admit that the extreme philosophy of Socialism can only truly express itself when it materializes into the actual form of government under which people live called a true dictatorship.

But after admitting this much, these intellectuals will focus their attention and yours on the middle ground of the degrees of both of the materially expressed forms of governments which lie between the extremes of Americanism and Socialism using the terms which they themselves invented, like oligarchy, democracy, monarchy, fascism, nazism, communism, etc., etc., etc.

HONEST intellectuals will admit that the governmental systems labeled oligarchy, democracy, monarchy, fascism, nazism, and communism are ALL simply various forms and degrees of Socialism, and that anyone who believes in any of these forms and degrees of governments is really fundamentally a Socialist.

But DISHONEST intellectuals will NOT admit this truism.

The intellectuals's use of these various governmental terms, describing the degrees of HOW MUCH governmental control of your life that you might be experiencing, diverts your attention away from the facts of whether you, as a non-criminal, should be experiencing ANY governmental control of your life at all, assuming that you are, of course, not a criminal.

The intellectual's riveting of your attention on the DEGREE of government you are currently living under, keeps you from focusing your attention on the essential NATURE of the government you are currently living under.

There are only two essential NATURES of any government you are currently living under. You are either living under a LIMITED government because rights come from God, which makes it American; or you are currently living under a POTENTIALLY UNLIMITED government because rights come from the government, which makes it Socialist. Either you are really the boss of the government you are living under, which makes it American; or the government you are living under is really the boss over you, which makes it Socialist.

Which NATURE of government are you currently really living under, Americanism or Socialism? Forget about DEGREES. What is your answer?

Summing up, intellectuals always claim that NORMAL people always try to find simple solutions to very complex problems. Intellectuals love to play semantic word games. NORMAL people hate semantic word games, but love the bottom line. Intellectuals love to discuss complex theories. NORMAL people enjoy discussing the REALITIES they must deal with on a daily basis. Intellectuals will disagree with NORMAL people who prefer to focus on the true natures of reality, and who understand that since the beginning of time and until the end of time, there has existed and can only ever exist, the two different forms of government materially expressed by the two irreconciliably different philosophies of Americanism and Socialism.

Americanism produces ABUNDANCE for the common people and a HIGH standard of living, while Socialism produces SCARCITY for the common people and a LOW standard of living. Every single factual history book ever written since the beginning of time has proven the unquestionable truth of this statement. Not one factual history book has ever been written since the beginning of time which disproves this statement, because it can't.

Since 1917, the unfortunate Russian people have been living under a TOTALLY socialistic government, where the humans running the government are everyone's boss. Let's compare their standard of living with our own for the 50 years following 1917.

Americans produced 60% more steel; 66% more petroleum; 95% more electric motors; 66% more hydro-electric plants; consumed 90% more natural gas; built 94% more miles of paved roadways; laid 67% more miles of railroad track; built 80% more ships; produced and sold 95% more cars and trucks; produced and sold 40 million more TV sets; produced and installed 90% more telephones; built and sold 70% more houses; and we Americans have never had to import wheat and other grains and foodstuffs to avoid famines and starvation like the poor Russians have had to, even though the Russians have 60 million more farmers than we do; and we never experience the long waiting-lines and empty shelves that the Russians always experience; and our workers do not have to pay three full weeks worth of their total salary, like the sad Russians have to, just to buy a new pair of shoes.

Is there really any comparison between our HIGH standard of living and their LOW standard of living? Obviously not.

Why is there such an obvious difference between our standards of living and theirs? The answer lies in what Karl Marx, the father of modern Socialism, wrote in his Communist Manifesto in 1848. He wrote that the first and most important duty of every dedicated communist is to work for the complete ABOLITION OF PRIVATE PROPERTY. And remember, every communist is a Socialist.

So in 1917 in Russia, the new socialistic government COMPLETELY abolished private property, and OFFICIALLY announced that the socialistic government owns and controls everybody and everything, thereby destroying everyone's natural incentive to work at their maximum to produce abundance and a high standard of living.

Russia in 1917 became like Jamestown in 1607, and like Plymouth in 1620, with the EXACT same results. Famines and starvation have plagued the victim Russian people more than a dozen times since 1917, and STILL plagues them today.

Instead of restoring the principles of private property and self-reliance which have always been the ONLY incentive which is capable of producing abundance and prosperity, the socialistic government of Russia always uses the demotivating principle of the fear of punishment to increase production, but this punitive form of motivation has never worked to solve the constant problem of scarcity, even after the Russian Socialists have murdered in cold blood, more than 100 million of their own people in brutal concentration camps for the exact same reason: these people all wanted to restore their God-given right to PRIVATE PROPERTY. Period. No other reason.

Intellectuals would love for Americans to MERGE our system with these murderous types of socialistic systems to form a so-called ONE WORLD GOVERN-MENT, under the over 40 year old United Nations organization headquartered in New York City. How's that idea sound to you? Do these Socialists appear to you like wonderfully reasonable human beings? Intellectuals will point out that these Socialists do wear beautiful three piece suits, and jackets and ties sometimes. How nice.

It is simply human nature to desire private property, and your right to own and control your own private property is the ONLY incentive which can produce the highest standard of living for all peoples every-where. Jamestown and Plymouth proved the truth of this human nature concept.

Our founders created a UNIQUE form of govern-ment based on the philosophy of Americanism, believ-ing in limited government because rights come from God. Therefore, the proper role of the government our founders established with our Constitution can best be described as PROTECTIVE. In other words, the essential role of our American government is to protect us from being harmed by criminals. PERIOD.

To protect us from criminals, foreign or domestic, who might try to basically do three things to us:

1) inflict bodily harm on us   (life)
2) subject us to slavery or involuntary
   servitude   (liberty)
3) steal our private property (pursuit of happiness)

As an interesting aside, our founders COULD NEVER EVEN CONCEIVE of allowing the humans we allow to run the government for us to pass any laws supposedly designed to protect you from possibly hurting YOURSELF. Our government's passing a law making skydiving illegal because you might possibly hurt yourself doing it, would be totally un-American. And wearing an automobile seatbelt might be smart, but any law forcing you to wear one is totally un-American.

In other words, our founders established our Constitutional government to PROTECT us from criminals who might attempt to VIOLATE our unalienable God-given rights to life, liberty, and the pursuit of happiness (private property). Period.

This means then, that our American government has only ONE proper protective role in our economic activities, that is, to protect our private property from theft by criminals. Period. NOTHING MORE. This single-purpose form of governmental protection insures the workability of the 4-step High Standard of Living Formula.

It is important at this stage for you to remember the SELF-EVIDENT principle that GOVERNMENT PRODUCES NOTHING. Government is not a PRODUCER. Government is only a TAKER. Whatever money and property government possesses, it had to first TAKE these things from private citizens who produced and owned them. Understand? That's pretty simple, isn't it? Can you disagree with this?

Now, when the Socialists who believe in potentially unlimited government because rights come from government, when these Socialists are in control of a government, they DO NOT view their primary role as protective of the rights of their citizens, because they feel the citizens only possess the rights which their socialistic government chooses to grant them. So the Socialists always see their primary role as PROTECTING themselves, meaning protecting the very government which they run from its own decent citizens. And the favorite big lie which every socialistic government always tells is this: we are simply doing what the MAJORITY of the people desire.

To accomplish their primary purpose of protecting the government itself from its own decent citizens, the Socialists pass laws which are designed to CONTROL every activity of its citizens, and of course, the police in a socialistic society are used to enforce the laws designed to control the decent people, as well as the criminals.

In the field of economic activity, the Socialists pass laws which tax its citizens to support the Socialist government. Taxes under Socialism are always HIGH for two basic reasons: first, to support the multitude of newly hired bureaucrats placed in charge of administering and enforcing the hundreds of new laws, rules, and regulations designed to control every activity of the citizens; and second, because the Socialists use their police power to forcibly take money from one citizen to give it to another citizen who did not previously own it. This second reason for high taxes under Socialism is known as the DISTRIBUTIVE or REDISTRIBUTIVE function of a Socialist government. There is only one word which can accurately describe this RE-DISTRIBUTIVE process of the Socialists when money is FORCIBLY taken from a decent citizen who owns it, to then be given to a different citizen who does not own it. That word is THEFT, pure and simple. What would this distributive process be called if you as an INDIVIDUAL performed it? The Socialists always use the power of the law to steal money from citizens LEGALLY to re-distribute it to other citizens legally. The Socialists call this LEGAL STEALING simply "supplying WELFARE to our people." Socialists hate to be called what they in absolute reality are, when they pass laws to re-distribute the private property wealth of decent citizens to those citizens who do not own it: BANDITS. Can you think of a more correct word?

Incidentally, a study of history proves that once a government ABANDONS its previous economic passivity, and begins to implement the socialistic re-distributive banditry process, CLASS WARFARE results, and each class of people or special interest group competes with each other to grasp and throw the lever of governmental power IN THEIR FAVOR, or at least to IMMUNIZE themselves from further loss, instead of using their common sense to try to TERMINATE this socialistic re-distributive banditry process EN-TIRELY.

The simple facts are these: if you believe that government SHOULD re-distribute taxpayers' money, you are a Socialist. Specifically, if you believe that state government SHOULD re-distribute taxpayers' money, you are a State Socialist; if you believe that the federal government SHOULD re-distribute taxpayers' money, you are a National Socialist; and if you believe that the federal government SHOULD re-distribute taxpayers' money overseas, you are an International Socialist. If you believe government has NO RIGHT to re-distribute taxpayers' money, you are a real American.

Socialists use this RE-DISTRIBUTIVE power to, in essence, BUY VOTES, or buy the support of different groups of its citizens, who gradually become completely DEPENDENT on these socialistic subsidies for their lifestyles, and sometimes for their very existence. Remember that the primary purpose of the Socialist government is to devise new schemes to protect itself by controlling its people. Can you think of a better way of controlling people than by getting them to become financially dependent on you for their lifestyles, or for their very existence?

Since government is not a producer, but only a taker, the Socialist government uses its power to rob from Peter to pay to Paul. As the Socialist government steals more and more from Peter, to re-distribute to Paul, Peter begins to slow down his productive labor because he realizes that he is only legally allowed to keep LESS and LESS of the fruits of his labor. Peter realizes that his private property is under attack. In fact, Peter begins to realize that he has lost his God-given RIGHT to private property, since he can no longer control it, and use it to his own benefit as he sees fit, because the Socialist government has assumed LEGAL control over it. So Peter slows down his productive labors like the formerly productive people of

Jamestown and Plymouth, and for the EXACT SAME REASON.

In fact, the Socialist government always takes control of ALL of the economic activities within its society, using the excuse of the "need for centralized planning," because the Socialist government always claims that it is responsible for the people's "welfare." This Socialist claim that the Socialist government is responsible for taking care of its people, and that the people are not basically responsible for taking care of themselves, is the socialistic logic the Socialists always use to control the economy, so that they can "more equally distribute the free benefits" to the citizens who supposedly most need them.

No Socialist believes in private property and self-reliance. And remember, private property is that property which YOU control without any governmental interference.

In fact, you may remember the formal definition of Socialism given in every dictionary, as the governmental system which owns and/or controls the means of production and distribution of goods and services. So by dictionary definition, if you believe government should do this, you are a Socialist. In other words, in a Socialist economy, the Socialist government controls and decides who gets what, when, where, how, how much, for how long, and at what price.

You do remember, do you not, that under the American free economic system which our founders gave us, YOU as an individual control and decide for yourself who gets what, when, where, how, how much, for how long, and at what price? Remember?

Americanism and Socialism are direct opposites, and irreconciliably different from each other.

Let's finally come back to the 4-step High Standard of Living Formula which ALWAYS works well to produce abundance.

Wait a minute. Always works well to produce abundance—but only without governmental interference.

Under the Americanism our founders gave us, the humans we allow to run our government for us have NO AUTHORITY to interfere with the 4-step High Standard of Living Formula. It's even defined that way in our Constitution, remember?

Under any form of Socialism, the humans running the socialistic government have FULL AUTHORITY to interfere with the 4-step High Standard of Living Formula. It's not only defined that way in every Socialist Constitution, but it is even defined that way in the dictionary, remember?

For 6,000 years, Socialist governments controlled every one of the 4 blocks of the High Standard of Living Formula. Check it out. What has always been the predictable results for all of the common people? Scarcity, a low standard of living, and in its worst form, famines and starvation. Check it out.

In the 20th century, find out why the people in the city of New Castle, England, who used to be the largest EXPORTERS of coal in the whole world, eventually had to become IMPORTERS of coal; also find out why the people in the Ukraine, which used to be called "the breadbasket of Europe" because they used to be the largest EXPORTERS of wheat in all of Europe, eventually had to become IMPORTERS of wheat; also find out why so many once-beautiful sections of our own major American cities, and why so many once-beautiful sections of the major cities of the rest of the world have become filthy, dirty slums;

and also find out why so many people in once-prosperous rural areas of our own country and in other countries of the world have to NOW live with scarcity and poverty. You will discover that the people's adoption of Socialism caused the main problems in New Castle and the Ukraine. You will also discover that the people's adoption of Socialism caused most of the problems in the major cities and rural areas of the world. Check it out.

You are told that ancient Greece and ancient Rome were destroyed by (are you ready for this?) "progress." Or sometimes you are told that ancient Greece and ancient Rome destroyed themselves because they "just couldn't handle democracy." Check it out. No one will tell you the truth that Socialism was the culprit, that their adoption of Socialism destroyed ancient Greece and ancient Rome. "Bread and circuses" is a perfect synonym for Socialism. And when the people of once freer countries adopt the PROVEN AGE-OLD FAILURE of Socialism, this is not "progress," it is "regress." Only the philosophy and form of government known as Americanism represents "progress."

Even if ancient Greece and ancient Rome founded their earlier civilizations with relative freedom (not needing permission from government), future Greek and Roman generations FORGOT their earlier heritage, and foolishly adopted the Socialism which destroyed themselves.

Legend has it that the EARLY Greeks understood that every single law passed and enforced by any government will always have a direct or indirect effect on every single citizen sooner or later; and that every new law passed could give more and more power to the government, which could eventually make the government the boss of everyone. Legend further has it, that because of this true belief, early Greek legislators who wished to propose a new law, were forced to appear before the population, standing high up on a scaffold with a rope tightly around their neck, and with their hands tied behind their backs, and if the population disapproved of their proposed new law, they could pull the lever which would cause the legislator to hang.

If this legend is true, it no doubt discouraged every citizen and every legislator from casually saying that "we need a new law."

Over a thousand years ago, an ancient Greek historian living in the misery and poverty which Socialism brought to Athens, said this about why the people adopted Socialism: "In the end, more than they wanted freedom, they wanted SECURITY. They wanted a comfortable life. And they LOST it all—security, comfort, and freedom . . . When Athenians finally wanted society to give to them—when the freedom they wished most for was FROM responsibility—then Athens ceased to be free, and was NEVER free again."

It is a curious fact that few humans are born with a strong desire to study their past, and to learn about their heritage. This fact no doubt gave rise to the famous cliché about those who fail to learn from the previous mistakes of history are doomed to repeat those same mistakes. How SHORT is your memory?

The founders of America had LONG memories. They remembered the tragic examples of ancient Greece and ancient Rome. They remembered the lessons of Jamestown and Plymouth. They learned their historical lessons well, analyzed them correctly, and were determined NOT TO REPEAT the same painful-to-humans mistakes ALWAYS PROVEN to be associated with Socialism. This is why they were able to formulate Americanism. This is why they formed a government which was not given the authority to interfere in any destructive way with the 4-step High Standard of Living Formula. This is why our founders chose to operate on the principle so aptly stated by Thomas Jefferson as "that government governs BEST which governs LEAST."

Maybe it was just LUCK that our founders were able to conceive the original idea of Americanism that rights come from God. No other people had ever conceived that idea before in all of recorded history. Maybe it was just LUCK that our founders were able to think up that revolutionary idea.

Forgetting about the BLIND type of luck when you just happen to hit the million dollar lottery, or you just happen to be born to millionaire or very wealthy parents, NORMAL luck is best defined as "where preparation meets opportunity." Have you ever heard of that normal luck definition before? It's so true. Thousands and thousands of people are so well prepared with college degrees and/or excellent training and experience, but they never meet the right opportunity to capitalize on their preparation. Conversely, thousands and thousands of people accidently meet golden opportunities all of the time, but cannot take profitable advantage of these golden opportunities because they are not properly prepared to do so at that time. Both of these types of people are just "unlucky," or "a day late or a dollar short."

You are probably familiar with the interesting cliché

which claims that "everything in life is TIMING," obviously meaning that the degree of your success or failure depends on perfect timing.

Well, doesn't the definition of normal luck as "where preparation meets opportunity" seem to be saying about the same thing as the cliché which claims that "everything is life is timing?" Most people would think so.

In other words, you are considered lucky when your timing is perfect. Consequently, many people do believe in the opinion that our founders were blessed with normal luck and perfect timing. They were "in the right place at the right time." Their preparation met opportunity. That they were brilliant students of past history prepared them for the golden opportunity of self-government. And overcoming their normal fear produced the courage they needed "TO GO FOR IT." So they went for it, and won, and produced the greatest living conditions for the common people ever experienced by them on earth.

America is 200 years old. For the first 150 years, with few exceptions we were the best-fed, best-clothed, best-housed, healthiest, freest, happiest, and proudest people on the face of the earth, because of ONLY THREE REASONS:

1) The majority of our registered voters understood their hertiage; understood our Constitution; understood the definitions of freedom, patriotism, and Americanism; understood the 4-step High Standard of Living Formula and the Real American Syllogism, and understood that the un-American governmental system of Socialism was the ONLY think, repeat, the ONLY

THING, which could possibly destroy our glorious way of life.

2) The majority of our registered voters understood the DIFFERENCE between a POLITICIAN and a STATESMAN, which is that a politician is a candidate who ONLY thinks and worries about the next election, while a statesman is a candidate who ALWAYS thinks and worries about the next generation. Using these wise definitions as their guides, the majority of our registered voters would only vote to elect American statesmen who definitely understood our heritage, our Constitution, the definitions of freedom, patriotism, and Americanism, the 4-step High Standard of Living Formula, the Real American Syllogism, and also the proven dangers of Socialism. And when the majority of our registered voters felt that they had been tricked into making the serious mistake of having elected a politician who cared not for all of these important things, the majority of our registered voters would then vote to defeat that same politician in the next election, and usually did.

3) The majority of our resisted voters PROUDLY ACCEPTED THE RESPONSIBILITY which they felt they had, to PAY THEIR OWN PRICE for the glorious freedom, opportunity, standard of living, and way of life which they realized that they had inherited free from our founders, but which they understood was paid for by our founders, for them, in BLOOD. The majority of these registered voters practiced their belief that they had a PERSONAL RESPONSIBILITY to carefully watch the moves of humans they

allowed to run the government for them, so that these governmental humans would never step out-of-Constitutional-bounds without having to pay the penalty of getting voted out of office. This is why the majority of these registered voters proudly accepted and practiced the American principle that "the price of liberty is eternal vigilance." And the majority of these registered voters for 150 years fulfilled the responsibility they felt they had to protect and to preserve the real American way of life which they had inherited, to protect and to preserve it from Socialism for themselves, their children, and for future generations of Americans.

Summing up simply, for the first 150 years of America's 200 year history, with but few exceptions, Americans remained the best-fed, best-clothed, best-housed, healthiest, freest, happiest, and proudest people on the face of the earth because of only, repeat, only three reasons:

1) The majority of our registered voters understood our heritage, and also understood that the un-American governmental system of Socialism was the only thing, repeat, the only thing which could possibly destroy our glorious way of life.

2) The majority of our registered voters understood the difference between a politician who cares little about defending our heritage because he only worries about the next election, and a statesman who always defends our heritage because he always worries about the next generation, and the majority of our registered voters would always try to elect and re-elect only statesmen.

3) The majority of our registered voters were proud that they felt that they had a personal responsibility to practice their belief that "the price of liberty is eternal vigilance," by carefully watching that their elected representatives stayed within Constitutional bounds to insure that the real American way of life would remain intact from destruction by Socialism, for themselves, their children, and for future generations of Americans.

For the last 50 years of our country's existence, and right up to the present, we STILL have been and are the best-fed, best-clothed, best-housed, healthiest, freest, happiest, and proudest people on the face of the earth — BUT NOT FOR ANY OF THE THREE PREVIOUS REASONS — BUT ONLY FOR THE ONE REASON THAT THE AMERICAN WAY OF LIFE HAS BEEN SO INCREDIBLY DIFFICULT FOR THE SOCIALISTS TO KILL.

Today, and for the last 50 years, the majority of our registered voters DO NOT UNDERSTAND our heritage, DO NOT UNDERSTAND our Constitution; DO NOT UNDERSTAND the definitions of freedom, patriotism, and Americanism; DO NOT UNDERSTAND the 4-step High Standard of Living Formula and the Real-American Syllogism; and DO NOT UNDERSTAND what Socialism is, CANNOT RECOGNIZE who is a Socialist, and DO NOT UNDERSTAND that Socialism has the POTENTIAL to destroy our glorious American way of life. Think about that. Does this statement sound true to you?

Today, and for the last 50 years, the majority of our registered voters DO NOT UNDERSTAND the difference between a politician and a statesman, and therefore they have been primarily electing and keeping politicians i office who DO NOT UNDERSTAND our heritage; who DO NOT UNDERSTAND our Constitution; who DO NOT UNDERSTAND the definitions of freedom, partriotism, and Americanism; who DO NOT UNDERSTAND the 4-step High Standard of Living Formula and the Real American Syllogism; who DO NOT UNDERSTAND what Socialism is CANNOT RECOGNIZE who is a Socialist, and DO NOT UNDERSTAND that Socialism has the POTENTIAL to destroy our glorious American way of life. Think about that. Does this statement sound true to you?

Today, and for the last 50 years, the majority of our registered voters DO NOT FEEL A PERSONAL RESPONSIBILITY TO PAY THEIR OWN PRICE for the glorious freedom, opportunity, standard of living, and way of life which they inherited free from our founders. They DO NOT FEEL A PERSONAL RESPONSIBILITY to carefully watch the moves of the humans they allow to run the government for them. They DO NOT PRACTICE the American principle of "the price of liberty is eternal vigilance." And the majority of our registered voters HAVE BEEN DOING NOTHING AT ALL to protect and to preserve the real American way of life from destruction by Socialism, for themselves, their children, and for future generations of Americans. Think about that. Does this statement sound true to you?

If our 56 founders who unanimously signed our Declaration of Independence, and our 55 founders, including George Washington, who signed our Constitution were all alive here is America today in human form, THEY WOULD ALL TELL YOU THAT EV-

ERY ONE OF THESE LAST STATEMENTS ARE POSITIVELY TRUE.

Because all of these statements are positively true, our American way of life is in deep trouble today, and has been in deep trouble because of being attacked by Socialism for the last 50 years.

Thomas Jefferson made the most fantastically concise comment, which in a perfect nutshell, repeat, perfect nutshell, summarized the wisdom of the purely American governmental attitude regarding the 4-step High Standard of Living Formula. The author of our Declaration of Independence, and the third president of our country said: "Government should no longer waste the labors of the people under the PRETENSE OF TAKING CARE OF THEM. A wise and frugal government—which shall restrain men from injuring one another—shall leave them otherwise free to regulate their own pursuits of industry and improvement, and SHALL NOT TAKE FROM THE MOUTH OF LABOR THE BREAD IT HAS EARNED." No one will ever be able to better summarize the obvious wisdom of preserving the real American economic system for all times, and for all generations of future Americans.

The "bread" labor earns which Tom was referring to, is, of course, "private property." Private property is any material thing you own and should completely control the use of (like money, stocks and bonds, land, insurance policies, buildings, cars, tv sets, guns, businesses, etc.), including your being able to hand down all of these things in their ENTIRETY to whomever you wish, whenever you wish, wherever you wish, however you wish, etc.

True private property is really yours, period, and no other human being has any God-given right to take it away from you, and no God-given right to tell you what you can or cannot do with it, or how you must use it, unless you are using it to hurt someone else. Therefore, acquiring private property is your TRUE INCENTIVE to perform at your maximum labor.

But all Socialists wish to abolish private property, and they therefore use three powerfully destructive governmental weapons against it. These socialistic governmental weapons used against the people's private property are taxation, inflation, and regulation.

Higher and higher taxation takes more and more money away from you, so you have less and less money to use to acquire more and more private property. High taxation in all of its different forms is a socialistic weapon used against the INCENTIVE of private property.

Inflation of the money supply makes your money worth less and less value, so that you need more and more of it to acquire private property. Inflation of the money supply is a socialistic weapon used against the INCENTIVE of private property.

And obnoxious governmental regulation of your private property discourages you from acquiring more and more of it. So governmental regulation in all of its various forms is a socialistic weapon used against the INCENTIVE of private property.

Since a picture is worth a thousand words, this is what the delicately balanced inverted triangle building blocks picture of the American 4-step High Standard of Living Formula looks like today in the 1990s, since the Socialists INSIDE of our government have been attacking it with the socialistic weapons of high taxation, inflation, and governmental regulation for the last 50 years:

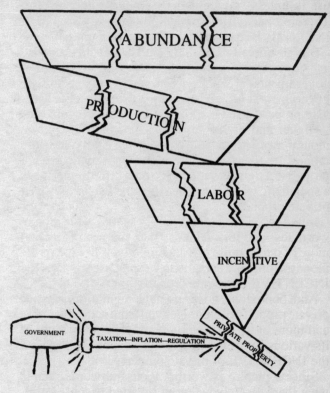

Part III

OUR HERITAGE
BETRAYED

Chapter 10

Identity

> *If a man knows himself and knows his opponent, he need not fear a hundred battles. If a man knows himself and knows not his opponent, for every victory he will suffer a defeat. If a man knows neither himself nor his opponent, he is a fool and will suffer defeat in every battle.*
> —*Sun Tzu, 500 B.C., Chinese philosopher and general*

America used to be the land of the free and the home of the brave. Today, America is the land of the slaves and the home of the cowards. Everyone feels that they need permission from some government agency bureaucrat to do practically anything, and few have the guts to resist. Everything is backwards. Everything is reversed. Instead of our running the bureaucrats' lives, the bureaucrats run our lives. The people are brainwashed. They accept this condition, and think that this is the way things are supposed to be. Those who suspect that this way of life is un-American are scared to do anything about it, and never manage to overcome their fear.

Compared to our country's founding forefathers and mothers, most of today's so-called American men and women are gutless wimps who have betrayed the original American Revolution of 1775 and every govern-

mental principle which those freedom lovers fought
and died for.

In fact, most of today's so-called Americans don't
even know what governmental principles yesteryear's
rebels fought for, and could care less about finding
out. These apathetic ostriches deserve no respect, and
should never be dignified with the stand-alone title
of "American." In fact, the stand-alone title of
"American" should be abolished.

There exists an identity crisis in current day America. Most of today's so-called Americans don't know
who they are, or who and what they want to be, or
who and what they are supposed to be. This almost
universal confusion regarding their true identity as
Americans is the direct cause of their current slavery
and cowardice.

And worst of all, every so-called American is also
unaware that their identity crisis, if left uncorrected,
will be the direct cause of almost every other educational, employment, business, social, and personal
problem that they and their families will ever experience. They have no clue that their confused identity
condition is like a cancer, which foolishly left untreated
with the correct therapy, will be fatal. Because of
their unresolved identity crisis, so-called Americans
are unaware that they have been and still are flirting
with personal and national suicide.

There is only one practical solution to this critical
identity crisis: it is that everyone living in America
today must now search their souls to discover whether
they are Real-Americans, Pseudo-Americans, or Socialist-Americans. No other choices or categories exist
but these three: RA's, PA's, and SA's. And effective
resolution of the identity crisis demands that no one

be allowed the luxury of claiming to be a little bit of all three, or half of two. So-called Americans must understand that the only sure cure lies in being 100% of one of the above. Those who reject this 100% black or 100% white requirement to produce the effective solution will only be practicing the absurd self-deception practiced by a woman claiming to be a little bit pregnant.

Are you a Real-American, a Pseudo-American, or a Socialist-American? Real-Americans are those who understand the definitions of freedom, patriotism, and Americanism, and love the principles behind them all. Pseudo-Americans are those who do not understand these definitions, and therefore they cannot appreciate the principles behind them all. And Socialist-Americans are those who do understand these definitions, but they hate the principles behind them all, which makes them 100% anti-American.

Real-Americans are philosophical descendants of patriotic rebels like George Washington, Thomas Jefferson, Patrick Henry, John Adams, Molly Pitcher, and Tom Paine, who were willing to fight, first as reformers, and then to risk dying as revolutionaries because they loved freedom for the individual so much. RA's.

Pseudo-Americans are philosophical descendants of the colonial neutrals who cowardly refused to join either side, and who chose to do nothing but to go with the flow, because they were afraid to fight for anything, and they would never risk dying for anything. PA's.

And Socialist-Americans are philosophical descendants of the colonial loyalists who conducted business as usual or actively fought for the socialistic status quo; and philosophical descendants of King George, the English big businessmen and their bought Parliamentarians; and philosophical descendants of all of the enforcement bureaucrats; and philosophical descendants of Benedict Arnold; all of whom hated freedom for the individual SA's.

RA's, PA's, and SA's. Who you are depends entirely on your position regarding the issue of freedom for the individual.

The political situation in 1990s America regarding freedom for the individual is strikingly similar, or even closely identical to the political situation in 1775 America regarding freedom for the individual. As it was then, when the early Americans were not free, so it is now, when we are similarly not free, and for exactly the same reasons.

Remember "The Big Business Trick," the standard operating procedure for all big businessmen everywhere for the last 6,000 years, whereby the big businessmen ALWAYS control the governments of their respective countries, no matter how much it may look to the contrary. Big businessmen always love to have power over the people, and always recognize the obvious fact that they need to control their governments to exercise that power.

In 1775, the early Americans were actually living in "occupied" territory. The greedy, bully, power-loving big businessmen who had long ago bought and paid for control of the Parliamentarians to insure their own lucrative profits, had had Parliament pass all of the laws necessary to make early Americans fight wars for big business profit motives, and had had Parliament pass all of the laws to create all of the bureaucracies, which produced all of the jobs for all of the bureaucrats to run the lives of the early Americans, taxing these Americans to pay for their own subjugation, fining them, persecuting, harassing, and imprisoning them when they attempted to live free.

In the 1990s, we are also, like our 1775 brothers and sisters, living in "occupied" territory, territory occupied by Socialist-Americans. The like-minded greedy, bully, power-loving Socialist-American big businessmen have long ago bought and paid for control of our congressmen and senators to insure their own lucrative profits, and these Socialist-American big businessmen who control our Congress, continue to have our Congress pass all of the laws necessary to make us fight foreign wars for big business profit motives, and continue to have our Congress pass all of the laws to create all of the bureaucracies, which produce all of the jobs for all of the bureaucrats to run the lives of the American people, taxing us to pay for our own subjugation, fining us, persecuting, harassing, and imprisoning us when we attempt to live free.

As it was in 1775, so it is in the 1990s. As the colonists in America were not free in 1775, we are similarly not free in the 1990s, and for exactly the same reasons. Not being free means that you are a slave. Remember that slavery is human involuntary servitude, or simply, humans forced by fear of punishment to do something against their will, or humans forced by fear of punishment to ask for permission before they act. As it was then, so it is now.

The nature of government tyranny over the people by eliminating their freedoms is always essentially the same. The principles of government tyranny never change. The only thing that changes is the label or name the tyranny goes by, and the style in which the tyranny is enforced.

The most accurate term you could use to cover every single tyranny of government eliminating the people's freedom from Adam and Eve to the present, is Socialism. Socialism is always the enemy. Socialists are always the enemy. Socialism and Socialists have always been, are now, and always will be the enemy of mankind. Socialism is BIG GOVERNMENT, BAD BROTHER, and LITTLE PEOPLE.

The most accurate term you could use to describe a government's protecting a people's freedom from Adam and Eve to the present, is Americanism. Americanism is the friend. Real-Americans are the friends. Americanism and Real-Americans have always been the friends, are now, and always will be the friends of mankind. Americanism is LITTLE GOVERNMENT, GOOD BROTHER, and BIG PEOPLE.

As it was with the rebels in colonial times, today's Real-Americans recognize their true identity, are conscious of who they are and of what they believe, are proud of who they are, never try to hide their identity, and they represent approximately 5% of our population.

As it was with the loyalists in colonial times, today's Socialist-Americans recognize their true identity, are conscious of who they are and of what they believe, and they represent approximately 5% of our population. But the big difference from colonial times is that today, most Socialist-Americans are NOT proud of who they are, try hard to HIDE their true identity, will NEVER admit to anyone that they are Socialists, and in fact, they strongly DENY to everyone that they are Socialists.

And of course, as it was with the cowardly neutrals in colonial times, today's Pseudo-Americans recognize their true identity, are conscious of who they are and of the fact that they PREFER to remain neutral, strongly try to JUSTIFY that neutrality, have marshmallows where their guts should be, and they represent approximately 90% of our population. They prefer to sit on the fence, or to stay in the middle of the road. Pseudo-Americans need to be reminded that there are only two things in the middle of the road: yellow lines and dead skunks. Middle-of-the-roaders get hit by traffic from both sides, and deserve it for staying in the middle.

It is interesting to note that the RA's recognize who the SA's are; that the SA's recognize who the RA's are; that the RA's recognize who the PA's are; that the SA's recognize who the PA's are; but that the PA's can't recognize who the RA's and SA's are, and sometimes the PA's even find it difficult to recognize their fellow PA's.

As it was with the rebels in colonial times, today the Real-Americans fighting for freedom respect the Socialist-Americans fighting for slavery. Those with a soldier's mentality always respect each other. Both the RA's and the SA's respect each other as ENEMIES fighting against each other. But both the RA's and SA's have NO respect for the cowardly neutral PA's.

The Real-Americans of today understand the true meaning of our original 1775 American Revolution, and LOVE it. The Socialist-Americans of today also understand the true meaning of our original 1775 American Revolution, and HATE it. Lover or hater. Which are you?

But everyone else living in our country today . . .

man, woman, young, old, black, white, brown, red, yellow, rich, middle class, poor, white collar, blue collar, preppie, yuppie, high school or college student who does NOT understand the true meaning of our original 1775 American Revolution should appropriately be referred to as a Pseudo-American.

Pseudo-Americans wishing to remain in this category are a pathetic disgrace. Early American patriotic rebels spilled their blood and guts in vain for these parasites, and have no doubt been tossing in their hallowed graves over these creeps for generations.

Pseudo-Americans wishing to remain in this category have dethroned our magnificently symbolic eagle in favor of worship for the lowly chicken, substituting a wishbone for a backbone. These PA's are stupid and cowardly psychological weaklings who refuse to face the obvious reality that there are only three categories of human beings living in America today: Real-Americans, Pseudo-Americans, and Socialist-Americans. That's it. No more. Every other descriptive definition of our people such as republican, democrat, liberal, conservative, leftwinger, rightwinger, union, non-union, etc. is useless, meaningless, and irrelevant.

Outside of the RA's, PA's, and SA's, every other description of our people should be erased from our mentality, because these other descriptions only serve to hide a citizen's true identity.

Real-American, Pseudo-American, Socialist-American. RA. PA. SA. These three NEW descriptive definitions for the word "American" are needed as the INSTANT cure for the American public's identity problem. AND WE DO MEAN INSTANT! The public's widespread acceptance of this triple definition of the word "American" has about as much potential to CURE a so-called American's identity problem as INSTANTLY as a person's drinking water will CURE a thirst problem.

The public's widespread acceptance of these same three new definitions for the word "American" will also be the EVENTUAL CURE for so-called Americans' slavery and cowardice problems. About as EVENTUAL as penicillin CURES infection.

Remember the definitions of freedom, patriotism and Americanism? Freedom is the condition resulting from never needing permission to act from the humans we allow to run the government for us. Patriotism is loyalty to the Constitution. Americanism is loyalty to limited government because rights come from God.

Real-Americans believe in freedom, patriotism, and Americanism. Socialist-Americans believe in their direct opposites: slavery, treason, and Socialism. And Pseudo-Americans believe in nothing.

What is your true identity? Are you a Real-American, a Pseudo-American, or a Socialist-American? You can't hide anymore. It's time for you to take sides. The Second American REFORMATION is starting. Hopefully, we will not need a Second American REVOLUTION, but like our founding forefathers and mothers, we should never rule out this possibility, however remote.

Original Americans had to shoot the Socialists out of office because the patriots were denied the right to vote. Luckily, we Real-Americans can STILL vote the Socialist-Americans out of office.

As it was in 1775, so it is today. We are living in occupied territory. Socialist-Americans have sneaked back in to rule our lives again. But there is a tremendously big difference today. In 1990s America, this is OUR country, not THEIRS, so the Socialist-Americans are the TRAITORS, not the Real-Americans. Think about that.

In 1776, when America was still THEIR (socialistic) country, Americanism was treason, and the Socialist-Americans declared us Real-Americans to be the traitors. After 1783, when America officially became OUR country, Socialism became treason, and in 1788 we Real-Americans declared IN OUR CONSTITUTION that the Socialist-Americans were the traitors. Remember, it all depends on whose side you choose to be on. Remember?

In the 1990s, America is STILL officially our country, and Socialism is STILL treason, and Socialist-Americans are STILL traitors. Think about that.

Do you understand NOW how important it is that you DECIDE whose side you are on? To choose, or not to choose? That is the question. Do you understand NOW how important it is that you DISCOVER your true identity? To choose, or not to choose? That is the question. Do you understand NOW how important it is that you DECIDE whether you are a Real-American or a Socialist-American? To choose, or not to choose? That is the question. As it was in 1775 and 1776, so it is NOW in the 1990s. Remember? To choose or not to choose? That is the question. Can you feel the madness this question causes? It caused the same madness then, that it causes today. Sorry 'bout that. How's your stomach feel now?

The treason trials are coming back again. And if a fair trial before an impartial jury convicts the Socialist-Americans of the heinous crime of treason, the Real-Americans intend to legally hang them.

In 1776, the Socialist-Americans officially and legally declared all Real-Americans to be enemies of their country and guilty of treason, and they hung many of us, like Nathan Hale. In 1783 when America became our country, the Real-Americans later officially and legally in our Constitution declared all Socialist-Americans to be enemies of their country and guilty of treason, but since then, we haven't hung enough of them.

Our Constitution is 200 years old in 1988. The Constitution IS our country, remember, so the United States of America is 200 years old in 1988.

The Constitution is the rulebook written PRIMARILY for the humans we allow to run the government for us. The Constitution is primarily the rulebook of the game which every government agent MUST play by. The Constitution makes it ILLEGAL for our government agents to FORCE us to seek their permission to do anything, thus insuring our freedom. Our founding fathers primarily wrote our Constitution to keep government agents off of our backs, and out of our pockets, P-E-R-M-A-N-E-N-T-L-Y. That is the pure essence of Americanism, and exactly why Socialist-Americans HATE our Constitution, and exactly why all Socialist-Americans want to CHANGE it. Every secret Socialist-American who is trying to hide their true identity from you, inadvertently exposes themselves, if you have eyes to see and ears to hear, when they tell you that they think our Constitution needs to be changed, usually using the Socialist's favorite deceptive propaganda argument that our Constitution was supposedly written ONLY for a simple, agricultural or agrarian, old-fashioned society.

Do you know if our founding fathers defined any crimes in our Constitution? If they did, do you know how many?

Well, they did. And they specifically defined only ONE, the most dangerous and deadly crime ever known to man throughout all of recorded human history. TREASON.

Treason is the ONLY crime defined in our Constitution. Our founding fathers defined no other crimes therein. Did you realize this?

In our Constitution, Article 3, Section 3 is the treason clause. It reads: "Treason against the United States shall consist only in levying war against them, OR in adhering to their enemies, giving them aid and comfort." The key word here is "OR." Aid and comfort to America's enemies is treason.

In its two distinct parts, this clearly means that any so-called American who fights against the United States, OR any so-called American who helps the enemies of the United States, is guilty of treason.

Since the father of modern Socialism, Karl Marx, published his Manifesto in 1848, Socialists of every different variety OFFICIALLY have been and still are AVOWED ENEMIES of the United States. Therefore, every variety of Socialism (fascism, nazism, communism, syndicalism, etc.) is OFFICIALLY un-American and anti-American, and all Socialist-Americans are OFFICIALLY waging war against the United States. All Socialist-Americans are OFFICIALLY avowed enemies of the United States. And therefore, all Socialist-Americans are GUILTY of the crime of treason against their country.

And according to Article 3, Section 3 of our Constitution, which is the supreme law of the land, any

Pseudo-Americans who help the Socialist-Americans are ALSO guilty of treason.

Obviously then, whenever our federal congressmen, senators, and unelected bureaucrats and judges in the courts or departments pass and enforce socialistic laws, rules, and regulations, they are LITERALLY acting like ENEMIES of the people of the United States, and they are therefore guilty of treason.

Our Constitution not only forbids Socialism on the federal or national level of government, but it wisely also forbids Socialism to be implemented on the state level of government too. Since our national form of government is a republic, and in a true republic NO Socialism can exist, our founding fathers wrote Article 4, Section 4 into our Constitution guaranteeing that each state MUST be a republic also, and can allow NO Socialism to exist against the people within their borders.

In fact, each state has its own written state constitution, and the early founders of most of our states have written treason clauses into their respective state constitutions which are closely similar to the Article 3, Section 3 treason clause in our national Constitution. So each time our state representatives, or unelected state bureaucrats and state judges pass and enforce socialistic laws, rules, and regulations, they are LITERALLY acting like ENEMIES of the people living within the state, and they are therefore guilty of the crime of treason under their own state law.

Traitors do exist, and have existed from the beginning of time, and no one denies this undeniable fact. Do you agree? But very few people ever understand how much easier a population actually makes it for traitors to operate COMFORTABLY in their midst, when a population makes the potentially fatal mistake of considering the unpleasant topic of treason to be unmentionable, and refuses to discuss this treason topic because it is such an unfashionable, radically unpopular subject.

English statesman, Sir John Harrington (1561–1612) expressed this truism best in his cute little rhyme:

> *"Treason doth never prosper, what's the reason?*
> *For if it prosper, NONE DARE CALL IT TREA-*
> *SON."*

But no one has ever made a more profoundly true statement on the distasteful subject of treason than the greatest ancient Roman statesman who ever lived, Marcus Tullius Cicero. Real-Americans are motivated to investigate and discuss the greatest crime known to man because of what Cicero said about treason over 2,000 years ago. Cicero said:

> *"A nation can survive its fools, and even the*
> *ambitious. But it cannot survive treason from*
> *within. An enemy at the gates is less formidable*
> *for he is known and he carries his banner openly.*
> *But the traitor moves among those within the gate*
> *freely, his sly whispers rustling through the alleys,*
> *heard in the very halls of government itself. For*
> *the traitor appears no traitor; he speaks in the*
> *accents familiar to his victims, and he wears their*
> *face and their garments, and he appeals to the*
> *baseness that lies deep in the hearts of all men.*
> *He rots the soul of a nation; he works secretly*
> *and unknown in the night to undermine the pillars*
> *of a city; he infects the body politic so that it*
> *can no longer resist. A murderer is less to be*
> *feared."*

From the time of the founding of our Republic, 200 years ago, there have actually been 40 treason trials on the federal level, and several treason trials on the state level. But almost every person charged with treason has been an outsider, not working for government.

Since the Socialist-American traitors HAVE BEEN RUNNING our federal government for AT LEAST the last 50 years, and illegally and unconstitutionally converting our once free Republic into an unfree socialistic nation; and since the Socialist-American traitors HAVE BEEN RUNNING our state governments for at least the last 25 years and similarly and illegally and unconstitutionally converting our once free states into unfree socialistic states; thus creating the un-American result that government at every level has gradually become everybody's boss; we need to VOTE every Socialist-American out of office to replace them with Real-Americans who will REPEAL EVERY freedom-restricting socialistic law, rule, and regulation on the books, FIRE every Socialist-American bureaucrat and judge, ABOLISH every socialistic government department and agency, INSTITUTE treason trials whenever appropriate, and thus to set the people free again. It's the Real-American way.

There is a musical scale that everyone is familiar with. It goes like this: DO-RE-MI-FA-SO-LA-TI-DO. There is NOW an identity scale which every so-called American MUST become familiar with. It is RA-PA-SA.

RA-PA-SA. Which are you now? Will you remain that way? If not, which will you become? Who goes there?! Did you hear the bolt click? Identify yourself. Your life depends on it.

Chapter 11

Davy Crockett and the Supreme Court

> *Truth will ultimately prevail where there is pains taken to bring it to light.*
> —*George Washington*

In our very early American Republic, our young state legislators and our young national congressmen did make the MISTAKE of passing socialistic legislation occasionally, but these legal errors were definitely the EXCEPTIONS rather than the rule. During the first 150 years of our existence after the ratification of our Constitution in 1788, our American Republic survived relatively free of the evils of Socialism because most of our people, most of our state legislators, most of our national congressmen and national Supreme Court justices ALL clearly understood the principles of freedom, patriotism, and Americanism as defined by our founders. And because at that early time, these three principles were so simple for our people to easily understand, they could easily recognize Socialist-American type legislators and judges, and when they did, they would either vote these elected SA type legislators out of office, or pressure our RA type legislators to impeach the SA type judges. And the story of Davy Crockett PERFECTLY illustrates the truth of this statement regarding our earlier legislators in Congress. And we'll comment on the other subject later, regarding our Supreme Court justices.

Also, after Davy's story has been told, you should understand how EASILY even intelligent people can fall into the errors of Socialism, but also how EASILY sincere people with the virtues of honesty and humility can EASILY correct their ERRONEOUS thinking regarding the fallacious principles of Socialism.

Everyone is familiar with the famous Davy Crockett of Tennessee. He was a legendary American hunter, hostile Indian fighter, frontiersman, pioneer, and hero, who valiantly sacrificed his life fighting at the Alamo for Texas independence from Mexico in 1836. Everyone is familiar with his physical courage, and his mastery over the natural human emotion of fear. But fewer people are familiar with his metaphysical courage, which enabled him to stand up for what he believed in, and to verbally express his convictions, no matter what the cost to himself personally.

This is the story of Davy's metaphysical courage. Davy served 6 years as a member of our national Congress until 1835, one year before he died fighting at the Alamo. Did you remember that? While Davy was a congressman, a bill came up for a vote which proposed to use public money to pay financial benefits to the elderly widow of a highly decorated deceased naval officer veteran of our Revolution and War of 1812. It seemed like a worthy cause, and all of the discussion immediately preceding the vote appeared unanimously in favor of its passage. But Davy got the floor and rose to speak. This is what he said:

> *"Mr. Speaker, I have as much respect for the memory of the deceased, and as much sympathy for the sufferings of the living, if suffering there*

be, as any man in this House, but we must not permit our respect for the dead or our sympathy for a part of the living to lead us into an act of injustice to the balance of the living. I will not go into an argument to prove that Congress has NO POWER to appropriate this money as an act of charity. EVERY MEMBER UPON THIS FLOOR KNOWS IT. We have the right, as individuals, to give away as much of our OWN money as we please in charity; but as members of Congress we have NO RIGHT so to appropriate a dollar of the public money. Some eloquent appeals have been made to us upon the ground that it is a debt due the deceased. Mr. Speaker, the deceased lived long after the close of the war; he was in office to the day of his death, and I have never heard the government was in arrears to him . . .

Every man in this House knows it is not a debt. We cannot, without the grossest corruption, appropriate this money as the payment of a debt. We have not the semblance of authority to appropriate it as a charity. Mr. Speaker, I have said we have the right to give as much money of our own as we please. I am the poorest man on this floor. I cannot vote for this bill, but I will give one week's pay to the object, and if every member of Congress will do the same, it will amount to more than the bill asks."

Remember now, Davy is speaking almost 50 years AFTER the ratification of our Constitution, and boldly claims that EVERY SINGLE CONGRESSMAN knows that they don't even possess the ''semblance'' of power or authority from the Constitution to appropriate the taxpayers' money for government charity, and that if they do, it would be an act of "grossest corruption." Can you believe it? Believe it.

When Davy sat down, no congressman replied, and when the vote was taken, the bill was soundly defeated.

The next day, one of Davy's fellow congressmen challenged him to justify his heartless-appearing position regarding the naval widow's bill, and Davy told the following story by way of explanation.

"Several years ago I was one evening standing on the steps of the Capitol with some other members of Congress, when our attention was attracted by a great light over in Georgetown. It was evidently a large fire. We jumped into a hack and drove over as fast as we could . . . In spite of all that could be done, many houses were burned and many families made houseless, and, besides, some of them had lost all but the clothes they had on. The weather was very cold, and when I saw so many women and children suffering, I felt that something ought to be done for them. The next morning a bill was introduced appropriating $20,000 for their relief. We put aside all other business and rushed it through as soon as it could be done . . .

The next summer, when it began to be time to think about the election, I concluded I would take a scout around among the boys of my district. I had no opposition there, but as the election was some time off, I did not know what might turn up . . . When riding one day in a part of my district in which I was more of a stranger than any other, I saw a man in a field plowing and coming toward the road. I gauged my gait so that we should meet as he came to the fence. As he came up, I spoke to the man. He replied politely, but, as I thought, rather coldly . . .

I began: 'Well, friend, I am one of those unfortunate beings called candidates, and—'

'Yes, I know you; you are Colonel Crockett. I have seen you once before, and voted for you the last time you were elected. I suppose you are out electioneering now, but you had better not waste your time or mine. I shall not vote for you again.'

This was a shock . . . I begged him to tell me what was the matter.

'Well, Colonel, it is hardly worth-while to waste time or words upon it. I do not see how it can be mended, but you gave a vote last winter which shows that either you have not capacity to understand the Constitution, or that you are wanting in the honesty and firmness to be guided by it. In either case you are not the man to represent me. But I beg your pardon for expressing it in that way . . . I intend by it only to say that your understanding of the Constitution is very different from mine; and . . . that I believe you to be honest . . . But an understanding of the Constitution different from mine I cannot overlook, because the Constitution, to be worth anything, must be held sacred, and rigidly observed in all its provisions. The man who wields power and misinterprets it is the more dangerous the more honest he is.'

I admit the truth of all you say, but there must

be some mistake about it, for I do not remember I gave any vote last winter upon any constitutional question.

'No, Colonel, there's no mistake. Though I live here in the backwoods and seldom go from home, I take the papers from Washington and read very carefully all the proceedings of Congress. My papers say that last winter you voted for a bill to appropriate $20,000 to some sufferers by a fire in Georgetown. Is that true?'

Certainly it is, and I thought that was the last vote which anybody in the world would have found fault with.

'Well, Colonel, where do you find in the Constitution any authority to give away the public money for charity?'

Here was another shock; for, when I began to think about it, I could not remember a thing in the Constitution that authorized it. I found I must take another tack, so I said:

Well, my friend; I may as well own up. You have got me there. But certainly nobody will complain that a great and rich country like ours should give the insignificant sum of $20,000 to relieve its suffering women and children, particularly with a full and overflowing Treasury, and I am sure, if you had been there, you would have done just as I did.

'It is not the amount, Colonel, that I complain of; it is the principle. In the first place, the government ought to have in the Treasury no more than enough for its legitimate purposes. But that has nothing to do with the question. The power of collecting and disbursing money at pleasure is *the most dangerous power that can be entrusted to man, particularly under our system of collecting revenue by a tariff, which reaches every man in the country, no matter how poor he may be, and the poorer he is the more he pays in proportion to his means. What is worse, it presses upon him without his knowledge where the weight centers, for there is not a man in the United States who can ever guess how much he pays to the government. So you see, that while you are contributing to relieve one, you are drawing it from thousands who are even worse off than he. If you had the right to give anything, the amount was simply a matter of discretion with you, and you had as much right to give $20,000,000 as $20,000. If you have the right to give to one, you have the right to give to all; and, as the Constitution neither defines charity nor stipulates the amount, you are at liberty to give to any and everything which you may believe, or profess to believe is a charity, and to any amount you may think proper. You will very easily perceive what a wide door this would open for fraud and corruption and favoritism, on the one hand, and for robbing the people on the other.' "*

The farmer continued:

'Individual members may give as much of their OWN money as they please, but they have NO RIGHT to touch a dollar of the public money for that purpose. If twice as many houses had been burned in this county as in Georgetown, neither you nor any other member of Congress would have thought of appropriating a dollar for

our relief. There are about two hundred and forty members of Congress. If they had shown their sympathy for the sufferers by contributing each, one week's pay, it would have made over $13,000 . . . The congressmen chose to keep their own money, which, if reports be true, some of them spend not very creditably; and the people about Washington, no doubt, applauded you for relieving them from the necessity of giving by giving what was not yours to give. The people have delegated to Congress, by the Constitution, the power to do certain things. To do these, it is authorized to collect and pay moneys, and for nothing else. Everything beyond this is USURPATION, and a VIOLATION of the Constitution.

'So you see, Colonel, you have violated the Constitution in what I consider a vital point. It is a precedent fraught with danger to the country, for when Congress once begins to stretch its power beyond the limits of the Constitution, there is no limit to it, and no security for the people. I have no doubt you acted honestly, but that does not make it any better, except as far as you are personally concerned, and you see that I cannot vote for you.'

This farmer was truly a Real-American if ever there was one.

When the farmer finished his lecture, Davy humbly admitted that he had been wrong in this matter, and that his vote to appropriate public money for the victims of the Georgetown disaster had been UNCONSTITUTIONAL. But this farmer was not satisfied with Davy's apologies, and not satisfied with Davy's solemn oath

not to vote for another unconstitutional law. The farmer
continued:

> *'You have sworn to that once before, (obviously
> referring to the oath of office each congressman
> must STILL TAKE TODAY to uphold and defend
> the Constitution from all enemies, domestic and
> foreign) but I will trust you again upon one condi-
> tion. You say that you are convinced that your
> vote was wrong. Your acknowledgment of it will
> do more good than beating you for it. If, as you
> go around the district, you will tell people about
> this vote, and that you are satisfied it was wrong,
> I will not only vote for you, but will do what I
> can to keep down opposition, and, perhaps, I
> may exert some little influence in that way.'*

It is interesting that the farmer would agree to trust
Davy just one more time, even though Davy admitted
to violating his original oath of office to uphold and
defend our Constitution. The quality of mercy is not
strained . . . to err is human . . . to forgive is divine.

Davy agreed to publicize his mistake as widely as
possible, and kept his promise to the farmer to do
just that. Because he did, the farmer gave Davy his
full support for re-election, and the two men became
close friends. Right before the election, Davy visited
his former critic, and later reported:

> *"Though I was considerably fatigued when I
> reached his house, and, under ordinary circum-
> stances, should have gone early to bed, I kept
> him up until midnight, talking about the principles
> and affairs of government, and got more real,
> true knowledge of them than I had got all my
> life before . . .*

> *I have known and seen much of him since,
> for I respect him—no, that is not the word—I
> reverence and love him more than any living man,
> and I go to see him two or three times every
> year; and I will tell you, sir, if every one who
> professes to be a Christian lived and acted and
> enjoyed it as he does, the religion of Christ would
> take the world by storm . . . Now, sir, you know
> why I made that speech yesterday.''*

Davy Crockett was a congressman who had the
courage of his convictions in the principles of freedom,
patriotism, and Americanism. He was not afraid to
admit his socialistic mistake, and because he loved
the country which our founders gave us, he would
never again vote for Socialism, no matter how worthy
a cause appeared, or how emotional was its appeal.
Davy realized that he was not elected by the people
of Tennessee to give away their tax dollars for so-
called welfare or government charity. His farmer friend
made Davy realize the American principle that he
could donate his own money in true charity, but that
the public's money was not his to TAKE TO GIVE
AWAY.

And it is interesting that Davy did not consider
Christ to be a Socialist by any stretch of the imagination. In fact, Davy knew that Christ never lobbied
the Roman government to tax one to give to another.
That would be legal theft, pure and simple. And Socialism.

But there was a well-known Christian minister living
in America who apparently believed that Christ was
a Socialist. His name was Norman Thomas.

Norman Thomas entered the political arena and ran

for the office of President of the United States, but not on the Democratic Party ticket, nor on the Republican Party ticket, but as the official presidential candidate of the Socialist Party, U.S.A.

He was the official Socialist Party presidential candidate on 6 consecutive occasions, for the first time in the presidential election of 1928, then in the consecutive presidential elections of 1932, 1936, 1940, 1944, and for the 6th and final time in 1948, and all on the Socialist Party ticket.

Interestingly enough, in 1932, Norman Thomas received 900,000 votes. That vote count could mean that 900,000 of our registered voters in 1932 considered themselves to be Socialist-Americans. After all, this 900,000 consciously voted for a candidate who OFFICIALLY and PUBLICLY identified himself as a Socialist-American. It simply has to be a curious coincidence, no doubt, that after our Revolution had won our freedom for us from Socialist England, an estimated 900,000 loyalists disappeared into our midst. Remember? But it would probably be insane to seriously entertain the thought that these 900,000 Socialist-Americans in 1932 could possibly be direct descendants of the 900,000 loyalists who became invisible in 1783. That thought would be much too unbelievable, wouldn't it? Interesting though.

But there is a more interesting point to contemplate about officially-admitted Socialist-American Norman Thomas, which is extremely significant and phenomenally REVEALING. This point concerns the MAIN reason why he finally decided to stop running for President.

After he again lost the 1948 presidential election, Norman Thomas announced that he would NEVER again run for political office of any kind on the Socialist Party ticket, because, as this 20 year promoter of Socialism said, there was no need to run as a Socialist third-party candidate since the Democrats and Republicans BY THIS TIME had adopted into both of their official platforms EVERY SINGLE OFFICIAL SOCIALIST PARTY POSITION on EVERY MAJOR ISSUE of the day. Want to read that again? Because his statement was definitely true. Think about that. And also think about the fact that the Socialist Party USA advocated and was always announcing in their official party platform, that if elected, they would essentially abolish private property.

And you might also want to think about the sad fact that what Socialist-American Norman Thomas said about the Democrats and Republicans in 1948 is STILL TRUE TODAY.

But back to our Supreme Courts.

Now, during the first 150 years of our existence after the ratification of our Constitution in 1788, the individuals on our state Supreme Courts and our national Supreme Court fulfilled their true legal obligation of striking down as unconstitutional, null and void, almost every socialistic law which the members of our State Houses and national Congress made the mistake of passing. These personal freedom-protecting actions on the part of the patriotic judges of our land helped to keep the country which our founders gave us, free of un-American, unconstitutional Socialism. But of course, Supreme Court action was seldom necessary.

Our patriotic justices on our states' and national Supreme Court for 150 years correctly viewed their function as the LAST-RESORT protectors of their respective Constitutions, and that their proper function was to INTERPRET THE LAWS passed by state and national congressmen TO MAKE SURE THAT THOSE LAWS WERE CONSTITUTIONAL.

These patriotic justices on our states' and national Supreme Court for 150 years paid attention to George Washington's Farewell Address, warning that unconstitutional, socialistic law-passing is a "usurpation" of power, which appears that it "in one instance may be the instrument of good, it is the CUSTOMARY weapon by which free governments are destroyed." Remember? These patriotic justices for 150 years lived by our fearless spirit's warning to NEVER allow a change to occur in our state or national Constitutions through the simple House-Senate type law-passing procedure, but only through the more cumbersome, slow, cautious, time-consuming, everybody paying attention, widespread publicity causing, debate generating, AMENDMENT PROCESS. And for your information, our founders did their job of writing our national Constitution so well that it has been amended only 26 times in the last 200 years, with the 26th amendment ratified in 1971, recognizing the right of all citizens 18 years old and older to vote in every political election, at every level of government within the United States.

So Supreme Court justices did their patriotic jobs for 150 years after our national Constitution was ratified, and after their state constitutions were ratified, striking down as null and void almost every socialistic law our state and federal legislators made the mistake of passing. And our people were able to maintain glorious freedom because of these Supreme Court actions.

But the last time our national Supreme Court COR-RECTLY struck down as socialistic and unconstitutional a law passed by our national Congress was in 1935. Since that time, the Socialist-American justices on our formerly patriotic national Supreme Court HAVE BEEN DECLARING SOCIALISTIC LAWS CONSTITUTIONAL, and CONSTITUTIONAL LAWS AS UNCONSTITUTIONAL. What a tragedy. What a tragic reversal of their true function.

Today, and for the last 50 years, our Socialist-American national Supreme Court has been the CHIEF PRO-TECTOR of socialistic legislation, and these socialistic justices on our national Supreme Court view it as their proper function to INTERPRET OUR CONSTI-TUTION to justify as constitutional almost every socialistic law our Socialist-American Congress passes, and which our Congress has been passing for the last 50 years. What an absolute and complete reversal of the judicial system for which our founders fought and died to give us.

Chapter 12

Blame

> *A people may want a free government, but
> if, from insolence, or carelessness, or cow-
> ardice, or want of public spirit, they are
> unequal to the exertions necessary for pre-
> serving it; if they will not fight for it when
> it is directly attacked; if they can be delud-
> ed by the artifices used to cheat them out of
> it; if by momentary discouragement or
> temporary panic, or a fit of enthusiasm for
> an individual, they can be induced to lay
> their liberties at the feet of even a great
> man, or trust him with powers which en-
> able him to subvert their institutions; in all
> these cases they are more or less unfit for
> liberty; and though it may be for their good
> to have had it even for a short time, they are
> unlikely long to enjoy it. –John Stuart Mill*

A Frenchman named Francois Guizot who was visiting our young country asked his American friend, James
Russell Lowell, "How long do you think the American
Republic will endure?" Lowell replied, "So long as the
ideas of its founders continue to be dominant. ''Guizot
commented back, ''I agree with you."

In 1990s America, the ideas of our founders are not
dominant. They are LOST.

Two hundred years ago, on September 17, 1787,
at our Constitutional Convention in Philadelphia at

Independence Hall, with George Washington presiding, our founders signed and delivered the final draft of the Constitution of the United States, which would be submitted to each colony for consideration of ratification.

The Father of our Country, for nearly FOUR MONTHS OF DEBATE during the writing of that glorious document, had been sitting on a massive chair, on the back of which had been carved a glowing sun.

As each delegate came forward to sign the Constitution, 81 year old Benjamin Franklin, who had done so much to win our liberty, was heard to remark with tears in his eyes: "I have often and often in the course of the session, and the vicissitudes of my hopes and fears as to its issue, looked at the sun behind the President without being able to tell whether it was rising or setting. But now at length I have the happiness to know that it is a rising and not a setting sun."

For almost the last 50 years, at least since the ending of World War II in 1945, the sun has been SETTING on the United States of America. And the night is almost here.

We have LOST the country which our founders gave us. It was STOLEN from most of us before we were even born. So it's not our fault. But we still have a chance to get it back NOW if we want to, for ourselves, our children, and for future generations, but the price will be high.

Some of our fathers and mothers, grandfathers and grandmothers, tried to stop the socialistic theft, but failed. Some of our relatives did nothing but watch this socialistic takeover and hope that it wouldn't hurt them. And some of our relatives helped the socialistic thieves.

Ask your relatives today what they tried to do to stop the Socialist-Americans from stealing away the personal freedom that our founders handed all of us on a silver platter. Their answers will tell you who they are, their identities as RA's, PA's, or SA's, and you will sadly understand HOW and WHY we lost our freedom.

5% of your blood relatives fought the socialistic reformers. 90% of your blood relatives did nothing. And 5% of your blood relatives WERE the socialistic reformers. The 90% were the PA's who let us down, and betrayed us with their silent cowardice. As Abraham Lincoln explained, "Silence, when we should speak, makes cowards of us all." Remember Abe's statement the next time you experience a bully or a jerk, and what you say and do will surely tell you WHO you are.

No one held a gun to your father's and mother's and grandfather's and grandmother's heads to force them into the socialistic CAGE we are in today. They gradually walked into the cage voluntarily because they all fell for the socialistic con job that they could get something for nothing inside.

Your blood relatives kept voting for SA politicians who promised to put more bait inside the cage. The SA politician's increasing the amount and variety of the bait gradually brought more and more of your blood relative suckers into the cage.

Soon the socialistic cage was full with your father, mother, grandfather, and grandmother inside. But the escape door was still opened, but nobody seemed to know how to walk out.

The reality that government is not a producer, but only a taker, that government produces nothing, but takes everything, the reality that government has nothing to distribute until it first takes something from the producing people, this reality was DELIBERATELY ignored by most of the cagemates. Most of the cagemates preferred the delusion of abracadabra—something for nothing.

None of your blood relatives wanted to think about WHERE all of the "free-to-them" goodies were coming from. When Real-Americans tried to remind them that the "free" goodies provided for them by the now socialistic government were first being stolen from their neighbors, or even from themselves, these RA's were told to shut up, lest the truth burst the bubble of the DELUSION of security that they wanted to keep feeling. No one likes to hear bad news, and historically, the bearers of the bad news have always been CONDEMNED for the news which they bore, as if the bearers were responsible for it.

Your blood relatives didn't want to hear the REALITY that what the Socialist-Americans were actually doing to them inside of the cage was similar to a dog's master whacking off his loyal dog's tail, and then feeding that SAME tail back to the dog, and after eating his own tail, the dog would lick his master's hand in gratitude.

This reality was too insulting to their senses of pride and intelligence, and your blood relatives didn't want to accept the possibility that they might be STUPID FOOLS who may have been conned. Heaven forbid.

So your blood relatives just kept on voting for more and more SA cage-master politicians, who kept passing more and more socialistic dog-tail-whacking laws to take from one to give to another, practicing the noble-sounding socialistic principle of "from each according to his ability, to each according to his needs," without focusing the cagemates' attention on the ignoble fact that the SA politicians would first have to STEAL whatever goodies they could provide.

Each unconstitutional, socialistic law which your blood relatives were encouraging the SA politicians to pass was closing the cage's escape door, bit by bit. The SA politicians didn't want your blood relatives to think that there was a price that your relatives had to pay for all of the "free" goodies, much less that that price was that your blood relatives had to gradually give up the freedom which our founders had won for them, and that they had to gradually turn over more and more of their inherited power to the SA cage-master politicians who were stealing from everyone to feed, clothe, house, educate, care for, and entertain them.

So to distract your blood relatives' attention away from the CLOSING socialistic cage door, and away from the fact that they were trading the freedom which our founders had won for them, for what looked to them to be comfortable SECURITY, the SA's in the school system inside of the cage, and also the SA's in the news media inside of the cage, began to bombard your relatives' minds with the supposedly glorious benefits of Socialism, but the SA's in the schools and news media CLEVERLY preached that all of the goodies that the government was providing were coming from the glorious benefits of DEMOCRACY, not from the age-old CATASTROPHE called Socialism.

Soon your blood relatives FORGOT that our founders gave us a Republic, not a Democracy. But by then, the SA's "teaching" in the schools, and "preaching" in the news media, had convinced your blood relatives of the LIE that there wasn't really any difference between the two forms of government anyway, so why worry about it?

Commenting on this same subject of the GREAT differences between a republic and a democracy, the great Roman Cicero said regarding ancient Rome's conversion into a socialistic democracy: "Our age, however, inherited the REPUBLIC . . . but we have failed to PRESERVE its form and outlines. For what remains to us nowadays, of the ancient ways on which the commonwealth, we were told, was founded? We see them so LOST in oblivion that they are not merely neglected BUT QUITE FORGOT. Our customs have PERISHED for want of men to STAND BY THEM . . . Through our VICES, rather than from FATE, we retain the word 'Republic' long after WE HAVE LOST THE REALITY."

So our Real-American founders, who shed their warm, bubbling, red-running blood to make your relatives the free bosses of a slave government, watched from the other side of eternity as your blood relatives, the free bosses of a slave government, VOLUNTARILY walked into the cage of socialistic boss government slavery.

When your blood relatives finally realized that they had been TRICKED into giving up their inherited freedom, meaning that when they had finally realized that they were no longer the free bosses of a slave government, and that the government was now THEIR BOSS, and that they needed permission from government to do practically everything, they watched the escape door close, and they finally realized that they were CAUGHT, and that they had indeed become slaves.

So, why didn't your blood relatives then try to get out of the socialistic cage? Good question. Your small percentage of Real-American relatives, who had resisted the whole socialistic process, DID try to get out, but failed. The largest majority, your Pseudo-American relatives, went with the flow, and never tried to escape, because they were cowards, or lazy, or stupid, or too proud to admit to themselves what they had done, or were addicted to bennies like a drug addict, or were insecure about their ability to make it on their OWN after so many years of DEPENDENCE on the SA politicians for their survival, or were riddled with a death-wish guilt complex for what they had allowed to happen to themselves, or a COMBINATION of all of the above.

And, of course, your Socialist-American relatives just rejoiced that it was a cage of their own construction, so why would they want to escape from something which THEY controlled, or in which they hoped to land a good-paying, secure bureaucratic, administrative, or enforcement job on the inside for privileged management and income purposes.

Realizing that they were trapped inside of a socialistic cage NEVER deterred your Real-American blood relatives (with the Socialist progression pattern always fresh in their minds) from not only attempting to escape themselves, but also attempting to knock down the socialistic cage door for any Pseudo-Americans who might still come to their senses, and desire freedom back again. You should still be proud of these Real-American relatives of yours, with the blood of the founders in their veins, because they didn't know how to QUIT fighting for freedom.

But the ninety percenters, your Pseudo-American blood relatives, realizing that they were trapped inside of a socialistic cage, decided MEEKLY to stay and to ADJUST to their slavery by convincing themselves that it wasn't so bad, that their SA bosses weren't killing anybody, that they were still RELATIVELY FREE, and that they still could vote their favorite SA politicians into office, so that those SA's could keep sending more and better goodies their way, or at least to make sure that they would get their fair share of the pie, without allowing SA politicians from other districts to vote to take too much away from THEIR district.

Your PA dummy blood relatives never understood what the RA's understood regarding the 6,000 year UNBROKEN record of the EVOLUTIONARY socialistic PROGRESSION PATTERN which always moved from an initial MINOR loss of freedom into the concentration camps and firing squads. So your PA relatives offered NO resistance, adjusted, and became docile conformists.

Adjustment and conformity for your blood relatives meant that they had to FORGET our founders' definitions of freedom as never needing government's permission to act, and forgetting patriotism as loyalty to our Constitution, and forgetting Americanism as loyalty to limited government because rights come from God. And if any of your Real-American relatives tried to remind the PA's of our founders' definitions of these concepts, your PA relatives would RELAX THEIR MINDS with the thought that these definitions may have been O.K. for that old-fashioned, out-dated, earlier generation, but that these SIMPLE concepts were NOW considered RADICAL, and that they were UN-ACCEPTABLE for our modern, complex, progressive society living every day with the threat of a nuclear holocaust.

And the Socialist-Americans in our midst even had the NERVE in 1935 to place their centuries-old international symbol of Socialism on our one dollar bill, the all-seeing eye of big government inside of a triangle, along with their international slogan in Latin, "NOVUS ORDO SECLORUM," which translates into the words , "NEW WORLD ORDER," which all Socialists hope to establish in every country. And if anyone ever wrote the government asking then for the significance of that all-seeing eye, they were told that the all-seeing eye was a symbol for God.

So America became a Socialist country, run by Socialist-Americans, at least 50 years ago.

How old are you now? When were you born? When did you grow up? What is the identity of your blood relatives? Can you understand NOW why the true principles of freedom, patriotism, and Americanism have seemed so MYSTERIOUS to you? Can you understand NOW why you have lived in a state of constant CONFUSION from the time that you were born?

You were born into, grew up in, and have been living in a Socialist America. You entered the theater during the third act. How could you possibly appreciate what the play is REALLY all about? You arrived at the baseball game in the 9th inning. How could you possibly appreciate WHY your team has really been losing?

Your blood relatives forgot the truth that the government's power to TAX you represents the government's power to DESTROY you. Your grandparents and great-grandparents forgot about the true significance of Isaac Barre's freedom-loving, anti-socialistic advice to the big-business-controlled Parliament in 1765 regarding the subject of taxation. Barre said, ". . . keep your hands OUT of the pockets of the Americans and they will be obedient subjects." Remember? Parliament ignored Barre's advice and a revolution in America was the result.

An indirect tax is a tax on a product or service which is ONLY paid by end-users of that product or service. Only smokers pay the taxes built into each pack of cigarettes. Non-smokers don't. A direct tax, promoted by Karl Marx in 1848, is a tax on personal income and paid by everyone making an income.

Our taxation-sensitive founders forbid the government they created from instituting direct taxation of our people, and wrote that prohibition into our Constitution. Our founders' wise and just taxation policy lasted for 124 years after our Constitution was ratified, and our government was financed through INDIRECT TAXATION for 124 years. And everyone survived in decent shape with freedom and dignity.

But the big-business-controlled Socialist-American politicians TRICKED your relatives and their fellow congressmen into supporting the passage of the un-American personal Income Tax (the 16th Amendment) in 1913. It was the FIRST socialistic direct taxation by Frankenstein in America which required only a one page form to be filled out, and the tax was never supposed to exceed taking more than 1% of your income like Marx's heavy progressive type. But this socialistic tax law put the government's hand DIRECTLY into our pockets for first time.

But guess what? This un-American, socialistic, direct income tax law DID NOT put the government's hands directly into the big-businessmen's pockets. Want to read that again? Big-businessmen millionaires are not stupid. They get laws passed to tax YOU, not THEMSELVES.

Remember the double-barreled Big Business Trick (control the government legislators and use them to pass laws which HURT big business COMPETITION, and also to have laws passed to tax the people to pay for their own SUBJUGATION). Well, at the exact same time that we got the socialistic income tax in 1913, their bought legislators also passed special legislation creating for the super-rich big-businessmen the TAX-ESCAPE LOOPHOLE called the private tax-exempt foundation. This special legal creation meant that the super-rich big-businessmen could hide and SHELTER from taxation most of their profit millions by putting these millions into their tax-exempt foundations, but they could spend this sheltered tax-free money in practically the same way you spend the money in your private checking account. Clever, no? The documented facts prove that the super-rich, greedy, bully big-businessmen have paid practically NO INCOME TAXES every year since 1913 because of their use of the tax-exempt foundation loophole. Check it out. Millionaires are not stupid, and NEVER allow their bought-legislators to pass laws which would actually hurt themselves, no matter how it APPEARS to the contrary.

Our country's senior citizens survived in decent shape with freedom and dignity, with savings, private investments, insurance, and FAMILY SUPPORT for 146 years after our Constitution was ratified, but your blood relatives allowed the Socialist-Americans in Congress to go deeper into our pockets by directly taxing us for so-called Social Security starting in 1935, although NOT one documented case of misery or starvation could be produced in the previous 147 years of our country's existence WITHOUT this socialistic program.

The socialistic direct income taxation Frankenstein was nearing adolescence when the big-business-controlled Socialist-Americans in Congress wanted to make sure that government's hands in our pockets would be PERMANENT, and could go deeper and deeper whenever it wanted to. So we lived in our country for 153 years with the freedom and dignity of NOT having the Withholding Tax, which was passed in 1942, and allows the government to collect taxes from you automatically, BEFORE you get your own hands on your own money.

After the federal withholding tax of 1942, our blood relatives became CONDITIONED to living with the never-before-experienced situation of adjusting their lives to "take-home pay."

In the 1990s, the socialistic direct income taxation BABY Frankenstein which gradually evolved into the socialistic direct income taxation ADOLESCENT Frankenstein, has finally grown up into the socialistic direct income taxation ADULT Frankenstein monster which can legally confiscate in personal federal income tax alone, over 50% of your gross yearly income. You are FORCED into paying this federal direct per-sonal income tax because you know that if you don't our socialistic gestapo-type IRS will FREEZE your bank account, REPOSSESS your car, THROW you and your family out of your house or off of your farm, and SELL all of your property, or put you in JAIL for a year. All this oppression WITHOUT a jury trial. How free do you feel, and how much dignity as a human being do you feel living under this un-American, no-choice, Marxian socialistic system of direct in-come taxation? Our founders revolted over taxation-slavery at a tremendously LOWER rate than what we are experiencing today.

If you sat down today with your calculator, and added up the money you must pay in direct income taxes to the federal, state and local governments for all of the services you like and want, and for all of the services that you DON'T like and DON'T want but have NO CHOICE about; and after adding up all of these direct income taxes which you can SEE and FEEL, you then added to this sum all of the money you MUST pay in INDIRECT taxes to the federal, state, and local governments which are hidden within, and which mandatory taxes the businessmen must build into the selling price of every product and service that you buy, but which taxes you are paying but CANNOT see and feel because they are HIDDEN; you will be shocked when you realize that every American must work EVERY DAY, from January 1 to May 1, just to pay for ALL of their federal, state, and local taxes. You read that right. You only make money for yourself during 8 months of the year. You work in essence for NO PAY FOR YOURSELF for 4 months of every year.

If this fact does not convince you that NOTHING IS FREE, especially that SOCIALISM IS NOT FREE, then you are a definite candidate for a lobotomy.

In fact, try to figure out why the very second every newborn baby comes out of his or her mother's womb in America, this baby owes the federal government over $5,000 dollars before this baby is even a minute old. Seriously, no kidding.

When our Constitution was ratified 200 years ago in 1788, our founders were operating on the legitimate logical principle that YOU CAN'T GIVE WHAT YOU DO NOT HAVE, and that if you as an individual cannot FORCE your neighbor to pay for something, then you cannot use the government to FORCE your neighbor to pay for that SAME something either. This is why our founders authorized only 18 functions in our Constitution which the government could perform and tax you to pay for, and this fundamentally American principle SURVIVED INTACT FOR ALMOST 150 YEARS.

But for the last 50 years, the big-business-controlled Socialist-American politicians we allow to run our federal government have illegitimately and unconstitutionally authorized the federal government to perform over 500 NEW and different functions which you as an individual could NEVER FORCE your neighbor to help you to pay for, but which our socialistic federal government illegitimately and unconstitutionally FORCES you and all of your neighbors to pay for in direct income taxes. And this damned taxation tyranny is purely un-American.

Most of these 500 un-American, unconstitutional, socialistic endeavors which the Socialist-Americans we allow to run our federal government have illegitimately set up, and illegitimately force you to pay for in direct income taxation whether you want to or not, are in DIRECT COMPETITION with PRIVATE enterprise companies, pay NO taxes, and LOSE money every year, but NEVER go out of business.

If 500 tax-paying private enterprise companies LOST money every year, it would mean that they are delivering products or services that not enough customers really want or need; or if a real customer demand exists, the companies are delivering inferior products and services; or lastly, the companies might be grossly mismanaged; and consequently, these inferior 500 tax-paying private enterprise companies would go OUT OF BUSINESS.

But government-created companies DO NOT experience the market risks experienced by private enterprise companies. When government-created companies lose money every year, they DO NOT go out of business. The government simply RAISES your taxes to support them for the next year.

In fact, these 500 un-American, unconstitutional, illegitimate, socialistic FEDERAL companies lose MORE money each year than the TOTAL amount of money the federal government collects from the people in personal income taxes. Do you understand what has just been written? You better read it again, and think about it.

The bottom line is this: if the socialistic Federal Government GRADUALLY PHASED OUT of these 500 un-American activities over a THREE YEAR period, the direct federal personal income tax could also be ABOLISHED at the end of that same three year period, and socialistic direct income taxation could DIE a natural death in America.

And you probably thought that your personal income tax money was going to pay for our Army, Navy, Air Force, and Marine Corps. How does it make you feel to know now that NOT ONE SINGLE PENNY of the personal income tax which you pay every year, goes to pay for even ONE of the 18 legitimate functions of the government our founders set up with our magnificent Constitution, which insured our glorious freedom and prosperity for our first 150 years of existence?

Our American Constitution, which is the supreme law of the land, does not authorize, but it rather FORBIDS our federal government to manufacture and sell helium gas and fertilizer, and this same Constitution does NOT authorize, but specifically FORBIDS our federal government to own and operate motion picture studios, magazine publishing companies, real estate companies, construction and building companies, electric power companies, airports, railroads, shipping companies, banks, insurance companies, mortgage companies, etc. But our socialistic federal government ILLEGITIMATELY does all of these things, and CHARGES YOU FOR DOING THEM. And almost every one of these government companies (agencies) LOSE tons of money every year.

Following is a partial and incomplete list of these 500 un-American, unconstitutional, illegitimate, socialistic federal companies as of 1970, and in alphabetical order, which you are paying for:

A

ABACA PRODUCTION AND SALES PROGRAM
ADMINISTRATION ON AGING
ADMINISTRATIVE CONFERENCE OF THE
   UNITED STATES
ADVANCED RESEARCH PROJECTS AGENCY
ADVISORY COMMITTEE ON THE ARTS
ADVISORY COMMITTEE ON VOLUNTARY
   FOREIGN AID

ADVISORY COUNCIL ON HISTORIC
  PRESERVATION
AERONAUTICAL EXHIBITION,
  INTERNATIONAL
AGENCY FOR INTERNATIONAL
  DEVELOPMENT
AGRICULTURAL CONSERVATION PROGRAM
  SERVICE
AGRICULTURAL CREDIT INSURANCE
  FUND
AGRICULTURE, DEPARTMENT OF
AGRICULTURAL EXTENSION SERVICE
AGRICULTURAL LIBRARY, NATIONAL
AGRICULTURAL MARKETING SERVICE
AGRICULTURAL RESEARCH CENTER
AGRICULTURAL RESEARCH SERVICE
AGRICULTURAL STABILIZATION &
  CONSERVATION SERVICE
AIR FORCE INDUSTRIAL FUND
AIR FORCE STOCK FUND
AIR NAVIGATION COMMISSION
AIR NAVIGATION FACILITIES
AIR POLLUTION CONTROL ADMINISTRATION,
  NATIONAL
AIR TRANSPORT BUREAU
AIR TRANSPORT COMMITTEE
AIRWAYS MODERNIZATION BOARD
AIRWAYS SYSTEM INVESTMENT &
  DEVELOPMENT
ALASKA COMMUNICATIONS SYSTEM
ALASKA DEVELOPMENT PLANNING,
  FEDERAL FIELD COMMITTEE FOR
ALASKA HOUSING AUTHORITY
ALASKA HOUSING PROGRAM

ALASKA INTERNATIONAL RAIL & HIGHWAY
  COMMISSION
ALASKA PIPELINE
ALASKA POWER ADMINISTRATION
ALASKA RAILROAD
ALASKA RAILROAD REVOLVING FUND
ALASKA ROAD COMMISSION
ALIEN PROPERTY OFFICE
ALLIANCE FOR PROGRESS
AMERICAN BATTLE MONUMENTS
  COMMISSION
AMERICAN PRINTING HOUSE FOR THE BLIND
AMES RESEARCH CENTER
ANIMAL QUARANTINE STATION
APOLLO SPACE PROGRAM
APPALACHIAN REGIONAL COMMISSION
APPALACHIAN REGIONAL DEVELOPMENT
  PROGRAMS
APPRENTICESHIP TRAINING, BUREAU OF
AREA DEVELOPMENT ADMINISTRATION
ARMY CORPS OF ENGINEERS, CIVIL
ARMY INDUSTRIAL FUND
ARMY STOCK FUND
ASIAN DEVELOPMENT BANK
ASSISTANCE PAYMENTS ADMINISTRATION
ATLANTIC-PACIFIC INTEROCEANIC CANAL
  STUDY COMMISSION
ATOMIC ENERGY COMMISSION
AVIATION WAR-RISK INSURANCE
  REVOLVING FUND

B

BANKS FOR COOPERATIVES
BOARD OF FOREIGN SCHOLARSHIPS

BOARD ON GEOGRAPHIC NAMES
BONNEVILLE POWER ADMINISTRATION
BOULDER CANYON PROJECT
BUILDINGS MANAGEMENT DIVISION
BUILDING SERVICE, PUBLIC
BUREAU OF ADULT, VOCATIONAL &
  TECHNICAL EDUCATION
BUREAU OF APPRENTICESHIP & TRAINING
BUREAU OF THE CENSUS
BUREAU OF COMMERCIAL FISHERIES
BUREAU OF DATA PROCESSING & ACCOUNTS
BUREAU OF DISABILITY INSURANCE
BUREAU OF DISTRICT OFFICE OPERATIONS
BUREAU OF EDUCATION FOR THE
  HANDICAPPED
BUREAU OF EDUCATIONAL & CULTURAL
  AFFAIRS
BUREAU OF EDUCATIONAL PERSONNEL
  DEVELOPMENT
BUREAU OF ELEMENTARY & SECONDARY
  EDUCATION
BUREAU OF FACILITIES
BUREAU OF FEDERAL CREDIT UNIONS
BUREAU OF HEALTH INSURANCE
BUREAU OF HEALTH PROFESSIONS
  EDUCATION & MANPOWER TRAINING
BUREAU OF HEARINGS & APPEALS
BUREAU OF HIGHER EDUCATION
BUREAU OF INDIAN AFFAIRS
BUREAU OF INDIAN AFFAIRS, REVOLVING
  FUND FOR LOANS
BUREAU OF INTERNATIONAL COMMERCE
BUREAU OF INTERNATIONAL ORGANIZATION
  AFFAIRS

BUREAU OF INTERNATIONAL SCIENTIFIC &
  TECHNOLOGICAL AFFAIRS
BUREAU OF LABOR STANDARDS
BUREAU OF LABOR STATISTICS
BUREAU OF LAND MANAGEMENT
BUREAU OF LIBRARIES & EDUCATIONAL
  TECHNOLOGY
BUREAU OF MINES
BUREAU OF MOTOR CARRIER SAFETY
BUREAU OF OUTDOOR RECREATION
BUREAU OF POWER
BUREAU OF PUBLIC ASSISTANCE
BUREAU OF PUBLIC ROADS
BUREAU OF RAILROAD SAFETY
BUREAU OF RECLAMATION
BUREAU OF RETIREMENT & SURVIVORS
  INSURANCE
BUREAU OF UNEMPLOYMENT & SICKNESS
  INSURANCE
BUSINESS AND DEFENSE SERVICES
  ADMINISTRATION

C

CABINET COMMITTEE ON OPPORTUNITIES
  FOR SPANISH SPEAKING PEOPLE
CANAL ZONE COMPANY
CANAL ZONE GOVERNMENT
CAPITAL ASSISTANCE GRANTS & LOANS
CARIBBEAN COMMISSION
CENTRAL BANK FOR COOPERATIVES
CHECK FORGERY INSURANCE FUND
CITIZENS' ADVISORY COMMITTEE ON
  ENVIRONMENTAL QUALITY

CITIZENS' ADVISORY COUNCIL ON THE STATUS OF WOMEN
CIVIL AERONAUTICS BOARD
CLINICAL CENTER
COASTAL PLAINS REGIONAL COMMISSION
COLLEGE HOUSING
COLLEGE HOUSING LOANS
COLORADO RIVER BASIN PROJECT
COMMISSION OF FINE ARTS
COMMISSION ON CIVIL RIGHTS
COMMISSION ON PRESIDENTIAL SCHOLARS
COMMITTEE FOR THE PRESERVATION OF THE WHITE HOUSE
COMMITTEE ON JOINT SUPPORT OF AIR NAVIGATION SERVICES
COMMITTEE ON PURCHASES OF BLIND MADE PRODUCTS
COMMODITY CREDIT CORPORATION
COMMODITY EXCHANGE AUTHORITY
COMMODITY EXCHANGE COMMISSION
COMMUNITY FACILITIES ADMINISTRATION
COMMUNITY RELATIONS SERVICE
COMMUNITY SERVICES ADMINISTRATION
CONSUMER ADVISORY COUNCIL
COOPERATIVE STATE RESEARCH SERVICE
CORPS OF ENGINEERS (CIVIL FUNCTIONS-ARMY)
COUNCIL ON ENVIRONMENTAL EQUALITY
COUNCIL ON FOREIGN ECONOMY POLICY
CUBA NICKEL COMPANY

D

DARIEN GAP HIGHWAY
DEFENSE ELECTRIC POWER
  ADMINISTRATION
DEFENSE HOUSING
DEFENSE MATERIALS SYSTEM
DEFENSE PRODUCTION ACT
DELAWARE RIVER BASIN COMMISSION
DEPARTMENT OF DEFENSE (CIVIL
  FUNCTIONS)
DEPARTMENT OF HEALTH, EDUCATION &
  WELFARE (CHANGED TO HEALTH & HUMAN
  SERVICES)
DEPARTMENT OF TRANSPORTATION
DEPARTMENT OF INSURANCE
DISTINGUISHED CIVILIAN SERVICE AWARDS
  BOARD
DISTRICT OF COLUMBIA REDEVELOPMENT
  LAND AGENCY
DIVISION OF BANK OPERATIONS
DIVISION OF BIOLOGICAL & MEDICAL
  SCIENCES
DIVISION OF BIOLOGICS STANDARDS
DIVISION OF COMPUTER RESEARCH &
  TECHNOLOGY
DIVISION OF INTERNATIONAL FINANCE
DULLES INTERNATIONAL AIRPORT

E

ECONOMIC DEVELOPMENT ADMINISTRATION
EISENHOWER COLLEGE GRANTS
ENVIRONMENTAL HEALTH SERVICE

ENVIRONMENTAL SCIENCE SERVICES
  ADMINISTRATION
EQUAL EMPLOYMENT OPPORTUNITY
  COMMISSION
ESKIMO DWELLINGS
EXCHANGE STABILIZATION FUND
EXPORT ADMINISTRATION REVIEW BOARD
EXPORT-IMPORT BANK OF WASHINGTON
EXPORT MARKETING SERVICE

F

FARM LABOR & RURAL MANPOWER SERVICE
FARMER COOPERATIVE SERVICE
FARMERS HOME ADMINISTRATION
FARMERS HOME ADMINISTRATION-DISASTER
  LOANS
FARMERS HOME ADMINISTRATION-
  REVOLVING FUND
FEDERAL ADVISORY COUNCIL ON REGIONAL
  ECONOMIC DEVELOPMENT
FEDERAL AVIATION ADMINISTRATION
FEDERAL COMMUNICATIONS COMMISSION
FEDERAL COUNCIL FOR SCIENCE &
  TECHNOLOGY
FEDERAL CROP INSURANCE CORPORATION
FEDERAL DEPOSIT INSURANCE
  CORPORATION
FEDERAL EXTENSION SERVICE
FEDERAL FARM CREDIT BOARD
FEDERAL FARM MORTGAGE CORPORATION
  FUND
FEDERAL FIELD COMMITTEE FOR
  DEVELOPMENT PLANNING IN ALASKA
FEDERAL FIRE COUNCIL

FEDERAL HIGHWAY ADMINISTRATION
FEDERAL HOME LOAN BANK BOARD
FEDERAL HOME LOAN BANK OPERATIONS
FEDERAL HOUSING ADMINISTRATION
FEDERAL INSURANCE ADMINISTRATION
FEDERAL INTERMEDIATE CREDIT BANKS
FEDERAL LAND BANKS
FEDERAL MEDIATION & CONCILIATION
  SERVICE
FEDERAL NATIONAL MORTGAGE
  ASSOCIATION
FEDERAL OPEN MARKET COMMITTEE
FEDERAL POWER COMMISSION
FEDERAL PRISON INDUSTRIES, INC
FEDERAL RADIATION COUNCIL
FEDERAL RAILROAD ADMINISTRATION
FEDERAL RESERVE BANKS
FEDERAL RESERVE SYSTEM
FEDERAL SAVING & LOAN ASSOCIATIONS
FEDERAL SAVINGS & LOAN INSURANCE
  CORPORATION
FEDERAL SHIP MORTGAGE INSURANCE FUND
FEDERAL SUPPLY SERVICE
FEDERAL WATER QUALITY ADMINISTRATION
FLIGHT RESEARCH CENTER
FOOD & NUTRITION SERVICE
FOOD FOR PEACE
FOREIGN AGRICULTURAL SERVICE
FOREIGN CLAIMS SETTLEMENT COMMISSION
FOREIGN ECONOMIC DEVELOPMENT STAFF
FOREIGN SERVICE OF THE UNITED STATES
FOREIGN TRADE ZONES BOARD
FOREST SERVICE
FOUR CORNERS REGIONAL COMMISSION

INSTITUTE OF INTERNATIONAL STUDIES
INTERAGENCY COUNCIL ON INTERNATIONAL
  EDUCATION & CULTURAL AFFAIRS
INTER-AMERICAN DEFENSE BOARD
INTER-AMERICAN DEVELOPMENT BANK
INTERDEPARTMENTAL COMMITTEE ON THE
  STATUS OF WOMEN
INTERDEPARTMENTAL SAVINGS BONDS
  COMMITTEE
INTERGOVERNMENT COMMITTEE FOR
  EUROPEAN MIGRATION
INTERNATIONAL ATOMIC ENERGY AGENCY
INTERNATIONAL BANK FOR
  RECONSTRUCTION & DEVELOPMENT (Name
  changed to AGENCY FOR INTERNATIONAL
  DEVELOPMENT)
INTERNATIONAL CRIMINAL POLICE
  COMMISSION
INTERNATIONAL DEVELOPMENT
  ASSOCIATION
INTERNATIONAL FINANCE CORPORATION
INTERNATIONAL FISHERIES COMMISSION
INTERNATIONAL LABOR CONFERENCE
INTERNATIONAL LABOR OFFICE
INTERNATIONAL LABOR ORGANIZATION
INTERNATIONAL MONETARY FUND
INTERNATIONAL SECRETARIAT FOR
  VOLUNTEER SERVICE
INTERNATIONAL TECHNICAL ASSISTANCE
  CORPS
INTERNATIONAL TELECOMMUNICATION
  UNION
INTERSTATE COMMERCE COMMISSION
ISLAND TRADING COMPANY OF MICRO-NESAI

J

JAMES MADISON MEMORIAL COMMISSION
JET PROPULSION LABORATORY
JOHN E. FOGARTY INTERNATIONAL CENTER
  FOR ADVANCED STUDY IN THE HEALTH
  SCIENCES
JOHN F. KENNEDY SPACE CENTER
JOINT AEC-NASA SPACE NUCLEAR
  PROPULSION OFFICE
JOINT COMMISSION ON COINAGE
JOINT COMMITTEE ON ATOMIC ENERGY
JOB CORPS

L

LABOR-MANAGEMENT SERVICES
  ADMINISTRATION
LANDS DIVISION (JUSTICE DEPT.)
LANGLEY RESEARCH CENTER
LAW ENFORCEMENT ASSISTANCE
  ADMINISTRATION
LEWIS RESEARCH CENTER
LISTER HILL NATIONAL CENTER FOR BIO-
  MEDICAL COMMUNICATIONS
LOAN GUARANTIES
LONGSHOREMENS & HARBOR WORKERS
  COMPENSATION

M

MANNED SPACECRAFT CENTER
MANPOWER SKILL CENTERS
MARINE CORPS MEMORIAL COMMISSION
MARINE CORPS STOCK FUND

MARITIME ADMINISTRATION
MEDICAL SERVICES ADMINISTRATION
MENTAL HEALTH (PROGRAMS)
MENTAL HEALTH ADMINISTRATION
MIGRATORY BIRD CONSERVATION
  COMMISSION
MILITARY AIR TRANSPORT SERVICE (Name
  changed to MILITARY SEALIFT COMMAND)
MILITARY SEA TRANSPORT SERVICE (Name
  changed to MILITARY SEALIFT COMMAND)
MISSISSIPPI RIVER COMMISSION
MODEL CITIES PROGRAM
MORTGAGE INSURANCE FUND
MUTUAL MORTGAGE INSURANCE FUND

N

NATIONAL ACADEMY OF ENGINEERING
NATIONAL ACADEMY OF SCIENCES
NATIONAL ADVISORY COUNCIL ON THE
  EDUCATION OF DISADVANTAGED
  CHILDREN
NATIONAL ADVISORY COUNCIL ON
  INTERNATIONAL MONETARY & FINANCIAL
  POLICIES
NATIONAL ADVISORY COUNCIL ON
  VOCATIONAL EDUCATION
NATIONAL ADVISORY HEALTH COUNCIL
NATIONAL AERONAUTICS & SPACE
  ADMINISTRATION
NATIONAL BANKING SYSTEM
NATIONAL CANCER INSTITUTE
NATIONAL CAPITAL HOUSING AUTHORITY
NATIONAL CAPITAL PLANNING COMMISSION

NATIONAL CAPITAL VISITOR CENTER
NATIONAL CENTER FOR EDUCATIONAL
  COMMUNICATIONS
NATIONAL CENTER FOR EDUCATIONAL
  RESEARCH & DEVELOPMENT
NATIONAL CENTER FOR EDUCATIONAL
  STATISTICS
NATIONAL COUNCIL ON INDIAN
  OPPORTUNITY
NATIONAL COUNCIL OF MARINE RESOURCES
  & ENGINEERING DEVELOPMENT
NATIONAL CREDIT UNION ADMINISTRATION
NATIONAL DEFENSE RESERVE FLEET
NATIONAL EYE INSTITUTE
NATIONAL FOREST RESERVATION
  COMMISSION
NATIONAL FOUNDATION ON THE ARTS AND
  THE HUMANITIES
NATIONAL HEART & LUNG INSTITUTE
NATIONAL HIGHWAY SAFETY ADVISORY
  COMMITTEE
NATIONAL HIGHWAY SAFETY BUREAU
NATIONAL HISTORICAL PUBLICATIONS
  COMMISSION
NATIONAL INDUSTRIAL RESERVE DIVISION
NATIONAL INSTITUTE OF ALLERGY &
  INFECTIOUS DISEASES
NATIONAL INSTITUTE OF ARTHRITIS &
  METABOLIC DISEASES
NATIONAL INSTITUTE OF CHILD HEALTH &
  HUMAN DEVELOPMENT
NATIONAL INSTITUTE OF DENTAL RESEARCH
NATIONAL INSTITUTE OF ENVIRONMENTAL
  HEALTH SERVICES

NATIONAL INSTITUTE OF GENERAL MEDICAL SCIENCES
NATIONAL INSTITUTE OF HEALTH
NATIONAL INSTITUTE OF MENTAL HEALTH
NATIONAL INSTITUTE OF NEUROLOGICAL DISEASES
NATIONAL LABOR RELATIONS BOARD
NATIONAL LIBRARY OF HEALTH
NATIONAL LIBRARY OF MEDICINE
NATIONAL MEDIATION BOARD
NATIONAL MEDICAL AUDIOVISUAL CENTER
NATIONAL PARK FOUNDATION
NATIONAL PARK SERVICE
NATIONAL PETROLEUM COUNCIL
NATIONAL RESEARCH COUNCIL
NATIONAL REVIEW BOARD FOR THE CENTER FOR CULTURAL & TECHNICAL INTERCHANGE BETWEEN EAST & WEST
NATIONAL SCHOOL LUNCH PROGRAM
NATIONAL SCIENCE FOUNDATION
NATIONAL SERVICE LIFE INSURANCE
NATIONAL TRANSPORTATION SAFETY BOARD
NATIONAL VISITOR FACILITIES ADVISORY COMMISSION
NATIONAL WATER COMMISSION
NATIONAL WOOL ACT (OPERATIONS)
NAVAL INDUSTRIAL FUND
NAVAL MANAGEMENT FUND
NAVAL PETROLEUM RESERVES
NAVAL STOCK FUND
NEW ENGLAND REGIONAL COMMISSION

O

OFFICE OF ADVANCED RESEARCH &
  TECHNOLOGY
OFFICE OF BUSINESS ECONOMICS
OFFICE OF CHILD DEVELOPMENT
OFFICE OF CIVIL FUNCTIONS (ARMY)
OFFICE FOR CIVIL RIGHTS
OFFICE OF COAL RESEARCH
OFFICE OF CONTRACT COMPLIANCE &
  EMPLOYMENT OPPORTUNITY
OFFICE OF ECONOMIC AFFAIRS
OFFICE OF ECONOMIC OPPORTUNITY
OFFICE OF EDUCATION
OFFICE OF EMERGENCY PREPAREDNESS
OFFICE OF FIELD SERVICES
OFFICE OF FOREIGN BUILDING
OFFICE OF FOREIGN COMMERCIAL SERVICES
OFFICE OF FOREIGN DIRECT INVESTMENTS
OFFICE OF HIGH SPEED GROUND
  TRANSPORTATION
OFFICE OF HOUSING MANAGEMENT
OFFICE OF HOUSING OPPORTUNITY
OFFICE OF INDIAN AFFAIRS
OFFICE OF INTERNATIONAL
  ADMINISTRATION
OFFICE OF INTERNATIONAL CONFERENCES
OFFICE OF INTERNATIONAL ECONOMIC &
  SOCIAL AFFAIRS
OFFICE OF INTERNATIONAL LABOR AFFAIRS
OFFICE OF LABOR AFFAIRS
OFFICE OF LEGAL SERVICES (OEO)
OFFICE OF MANNED SPACE FLIGHT
OFFICE OF MANPOWER ADMINISTRATION

OFFICE OF MARINE AFFAIRS
OFFICE OF MINERALS AND SOLID FUELS
OFFICE OF MINORITY BUSINESS
 ENTERPRISE
OFFICE OF NAVAL PETROLEUM & OIL SHALE
 RESERVES
OFFICE OF NEW COMMUNITIES
 DEVELOPMENT
OFFICE OF OIL AND GAS
OFFICE OF PLANNING ASSISTANCE &
 STANDARDS
OFFICE OF POLICY & PROGRAM ANALYSIS
OFFICE OF PROGRAM PLANNING AND
 EVALUATION
OFFICE OF RENEWAL ASSISTANCE
OFFICE OF RESOURCES DEVELOPMENT
OFFICE OF SALINE WATER
OFFICE OF SCIENCE & TECHNOLOGY
OFFICE OF SMALL TOWN SERVICES & INTER-
 GOVERNMENTAL RELATIONS
OFFICE OF SPACE SCIENCE & APPLICATIONS
OFFICE OF THE SPECIAL REPRESENTATIVE
 FOR TRADE NEGOTIATIONS
OFFICE OF SUPERSONIC TRANSPORT
 DEVELOPMENT
OFFICE OF TERRITORIES
OFFICE OF TRACKING & DATA
OFFICE OF TRANSPORTATION
OFFICE OF WATER RESOURCES RESEARCH
OLIVER WENDELL HOLMES DEVISE FUND
OPERATION MAINSTREAM
ORGANIZATION OF AMERICAN STATES
ORGANIZATION FOR ECONOMIC
 COOPERATION & DEVELOPMENT

OVERSEAS TRADE CENTERS
OZARKS REGIONAL COMMISSION

P

PANAMA CANAL COMPANY
PAN AMERICAN HEALTH ORGANIZATION
PAN AMERICAN RAILWAY CONGRESS
  ASSOCIATION
PAN AMERICAN SANITARY ORGANIZATION
PASSAMAQUODDY TIDAL POWER PROJECT
PEACE CORPS
PERMANENT COMMITTEE FOR THE OLIVER
  WENDELL HOLMES DEVISE
POSTAL SAVINGS SYSTEM
PRESIDENT'S ADVISORY COMMITTEE ON
  LABOR-MANAGEMENT POLICY
PRESIDENT'S COMMISSION ON PERSONNEL
  INTERCHANGE
PRESIDENT'S COMMISSION ON WHITE HOUSE
  FELLOWSHIPS
PRESIDENT'S COMMITTEE ON CONSUMER
  INTERESTS
PRESIDENT'S COMMITTEE ON THE
  EMPLOYMENT OF THE HANDICAPPED
PRESIDENT'S COMMITTEE ON MENTAL
  RETARDATION
PRESIDENT'S COUNCIL ON AGING
PRESIDENT'S COUNCIL ON PHYSICAL FITNESS
  AND SPORTS
PRESIDENT'S COUNCIL ON YOUTH
  OPPORTUNITY
PRESIDENT'S FOREIGN INTELLIGENCE
  ADVISORY BOARD

PRESIDENT'S SCIENCE ADVISORY
  COMMITTEE
PRIBILOF ISLANDS FUR SEAL INDUSTRY
PRODUCTION CREDIT ASSOCIATIONS
PROPERTY DISPOSAL PROGRAMS
PROPERTY MANAGEMENT & DISPOSAL
  SERVICE
PROVISIONAL INTERGOVERNMENT
  COMMITTEE FOR THE MOVEMENT OF
  MIGRANTS FROM EUROPE
PUBLIC BUILDINGS SERVICE
PUBLIC HEALTH SERVICE
PUBLIC SERVICE CAREERS PROGRAM

R

RAILROAD RETIREMENT BOARD
RAMA ROAD, NICARAGUA, BUREAU OF
  PUBLIC ROADS
RECONSTRUCTION FINANCE CORPORATION
REHABILITATION SERVICES
  ADMINISTRATION
RENEGOTIATION BOARD
RESEARCH DEVELOPMENT &
  DEMONSTRATION (URBAN MASS TRANS.)
RIVER BASIN SURVEYS
ROADS & TRAILS FOR STATES, NATIONAL
  FOREST FUND
ROOSEVELT CAMPOBELLO INTERNATIONAL
  PARK COMMISSION
RURAL COMMUNITY DEVELOPMENT SERVICE
RURAL ELECTRIFICATION ADMINISTRATION
RURAL LOAN PROGRAM

RURAL TELEPHONE BANKS
RURAL TELEPHONE LOAN PROGRAM

S

SAINT ELIZABETH'S HOSPITAL
SALINE WATER CONVERSION PROGRAM
SCHOOL BREAKFAST PROGRAM
SCHOOL LUNCH
SLUM CLEARANCE PROGRAM
SMALL BUSINESS ADMINISTRATION
SMALL DEFENSE PLANTS ADMINISTRATION
SMITHSONIAN INSTITUTION
SMITHSONIAN TROPICAL RESEARCH
  INSTITUTE
SOCIAL & REHABILITATION SERVICE
SOCIAL SECURITY ADMINISTRATION
SOIL CONSERVATION SERVICE
SOUTH AMERICAN RAILROAD CONGRESS
SOUTH PACIFIC COMMISSION
SOUTHEASTERN POWER ADMINISTRATION
SPECIAL MILK PROGRAM FOR CHILDREN
ST. LAWRENCE SEAWAY DEVELOPMENT
  CORPORATION
SUGAR ACT PROGRAM

T

TENNESSEE VALLEY AUTHORITY
TENNESSEE VALLEY AUTHORITY,
  FERTILIZER PROGRAM
TENNESSEE VALLEY AUTHORITY FUND
TEXAS CITY TIN SMELTER
TRADE EXPANSION ACT ADVISORY
  COMMITTEE

TRADE STAFF COMMITTEE
TRANSPORTATION SYSTEMS CENTER

U

UNEMPLOYMENT INSURANCE PROGRAM
UNITED NATIONS
UNITED NATIONS CONFERENCE ON
 INTERNATIONAL ORGANIZATIONS
UNITED NATIONS FOOD & AGRICULTURAL
 ORGANIZATION
UNITED STATES ADVISORY COMMISSION ON
 INFORMATION
UNITED STATES ADVISORY COMMISSION ON
 INTERNATIONAL EDUCATIONAL AND
 CULTURAL AFFAIRS
UNITED STATES BOTANIC GARDENS
UNITED STATES DEPARTMENT OF
 AGRICULTURE GRADUATE SCHOOL
UNITED STATES GOVERNMENT LIFE
 INSURANCE
UNITED STATES INFORMATION AGENCY
UNITED STATES NATIONAL COMMISSION FOR
 UNESCO
UNITED STATES SAVINGS BONDS
 DIVISION
UNITED STATES TERRITORIAL EXPANSION
 MEMORIAL COMMISSION
UNITED STATES TRAINING & EMPLOYMENT
 SERVICE
UNITED STATES TRAVEL SERVICE
UNIVERSAL PARCEL POST
UPPER GREAT LAKES REGIONAL
 COMMISSION

URBAN MASS TRANSPORTATION
  ADMINISTRATION
URBAN RENEWAL ADMINISTRATION

V

VIRGIN ISLANDS CORPORATION
VIRGIN ISLANDS SOIL CONSERVATION
VOLUNTEERS IN SERVICE TO AMERICA

W

WAGE & HOUR & PUBLIC CONTRACT DIVISION
WAGE & LABOR STANDARDS
  ADMINISTRATION
WALLOPS STATION
WAR RISK INSURANCE
WASHINGTON NATIONAL AIRPORT
WATER FACILITIES LOANS
WATER RESOURCES COUNCIL
WOMEN'S BUREAU (LABOR)
WORLD CONGRESS
WORLD HEALTH ORGANIZATION
WORLD METEOROLOGICAL ORGANIZATION

Y

YOUTH CONSERVATION CORPS

Under Americanism, anyone desiring and using
these products or services would pay for them ALL
themselves, PRIVATELY, and not have an un-American method of forcing YOU to pay for them too. If
you can't afford to buy a hamburger at McDonald's,
only a Socialist-American would feel that he has a
right to use the government to force his neighbors to
pay for one.

If customers really desired all of these products and services, the American way of PRIVATE enterprise would DELIVER them all with HIGHER quality, BETTER efficiency, and at a LOWER price because of our competitive market environment which ALWAYS keeps the customer, king or queen.

Your blood relatives USED TO UNDERSTAND this truism about the free, private enterprise system, but something DRAMATIC happened to CHANGE their minds. The greedy, bully big-businessmen in our midst DELIBERATELY ENGINEERED the stock market crash of 1929 to wipe out their legitimate competition, and while this crash made these rich bullies RICHER and MORE POWERFUL, it destroyed their competition, and drove the entire country into a great depression, which caused the joblessness and hardships which TRICKED your blood relatives into LOSING SO MUCH FAITH in the free enterprise system.

And the Socialist-American politicians in our Congress (which the greedy big-businessmen had bought and paid for) passed dozens of socialistic laws which actually KEPT America in a depression for 10 consecutive years, when we could have NATURALLY gotten out of the artificially created mess in about 3 years if NO laws were passed at all.

Check the facts, and you will discover that 9 million Americans were out of work and unemployed in 1932, and that 9 million Americans were STILL out of work and unemployed in 1939.

And do you realize that our socialistic federal government actually unconstitutionally HOLDS AND OWNS almost 50% of ALL of the land in the United States? Almost 1 billion acres, which is even larger than the entire land mass of Europe. Can you believe it? Well, it's true. Check the percentage of land our socialistic federal government OWNS in Arizona, Colorado, Montana, Wyoming and several other states, and your mind will be blown. Try 50% of California, 70% of Utah, and 90% of Nevada. Check it out.

If this unconstitutionally held land WERE GIVEN BACK to each state, or SOLD to private Americans within each state, our National Debt could be TOTALLY eliminated, and our government treasury could acquire billions of dollars in SURPLUS. If our government invested that GUARANTEED surplus, every American and every future American might FOREVER be able to live in our country income tax-free.

In fact, can you imagine the PHENOMENAL financial shape America would achieve if the Real-American Syllogism were thoughtfully applied, and caused a GREAT DIVESTITURE of all illegitimately owned government real estate, cars, machines, and all other tangible material assets and properties of the 500 federal government socialistic operations, hundreds of state government socialistic operations, and dozens of local government socialistic operations? This socialistic government operations PHASE-OUT and gradual GREAT SELL-OFF of illegitimately government-owned properties to private citizens would practically ABOLISH taxation and unemployment.

The millions of socialistic government employees (1 out of every 5 so-called Americans) whose salaries are now funded through socialistic direct taxation would automatically be given a tremendous OPPORTUNITY to happily restore their LOST dignity and self-respect by being productively re-employed by private industry.

But because today's Real-Americans remember well that almost everyone whose income was dependent on the government back during our original Revolution remained loyalists, no RA's are holding their breath waiting for current government employees to convert to becoming Real-Americans.

Well, enough for now.

No one has ever before told you the truth about America UNTIL NOW, so it's not your fault that we are STILL living in a socialistic cage on a conveyor belt moving into hell.

But NOW you've been told the sad truth about our country, and you can have no more excuses, or anyone else to blame but yourself if you choose to do nothing to change our country in the immediate future.

And there is one date which you should always remember. It is May 1st.

George Washington, as our first president, warned all early Americans that the actual international Socialist Movement was born as a secret conspiracy on May 1st, 1776, in Germany, calling itself the Illuminati, (check under "I" in any encyclopedia), meaning "enlightened ones" (why historians call the 18th century the Age of Enlightenment); and George warned his countrymen that the members of this secret international socialist group were VERY ACTIVE in our young country, working hard to secretly CONVERT our free republic into a socialistic nation.

In fact, an Englishman named John Robison, and a Frenchman named Barruel, each wrote a book, with each book published in 1798, exposing how this secret socialist group operating under various names, actually

PLANNED, CAUSED, FINANCED and DIRECTED the French Revolution of 1789.

Robison's book is entitled PROOFS OF A CONSPIRACY, and Barruel's is entitled MEMOIRS AND HISTORY OF JACOBINISM.

It is only fitting that the Americanism Movement, which represents the exact opposite of the Socialism Movement, was born and established on May 1st, 1987, calling ourselves the Real American Movement. Humans are so sentimental about memorable dates. They love to celebrate on them. Think about that.

Chapter 13

Opposites

*The beginning of wisdom is calling things
by their right names.* —Chinese proverb

The philosophy of Americanism is the EXACT OP-POSITE of the philosophy of Socialism.

The principles of Americanism are the EXACT OP-POSITE of the principles of Socialism.

The economic results of Americanism are the EX-ACT OPPOSITE of the economic results of Socialism.

The political results of Americanism are the EXACT OPPOSITE of the political results of Socialism.

The social results of Americanism are the EXACT OPPOSITE of the social results of Socialism.

The domestic results of Americanism are the EX-ACT OPPOSITE of the domestic results of Socialism.

The foreign results of Americanism are the EXACT OPPOSITE of the foreign results of Socialism.

The personal results of Americanism are the EXACT OPPOSITE of the personal results of Socialism.

The thinking of a Real-American is the EXACT OPPOSITE of the thinking of a Socialist-American.

The attitudes of a Real-American are the EXACT OPPOSITE of the attitudes of a Socialist-American.

The abusive, monopolistic power of big business CONTROL of our government would not exist under Americanism. It can ONLY exist under Socialism.

Big business aid and comfort to and trade (practically free give-a-ways) with our sworn Socialist foreign enemy governments like the U.S.S.R. and mainland China would not exist under Americanism. This TREASON can ONLY exist under Socialism.

The abusive, MONOPOLISTIC POWER of big labor unions would not exist under Americanism. It can ONLY exist under Socialism.

Strikes by workers would NEVER be necessary under Americanism. They are ONLY necessary under Socialism.

The insanity of murderous big business-inspired foreign wars would not exist under Americanism. They can ONLY exist under Socialism.

The forced, involuntary servitude, slavery of the military draft to fight the phony wars would not exist under Americanism. It can ONLY exist under Socialism.

The tyrannical I.R.S. and the obnoxious income tax would not exist under Americanism. They can ONLY exist under Socialism.

The problem of inflation would not exist under Americanism. It can ONLY exist under Socialism.

The farm problem would not exist under Americanism. It can ONLY exist under Socialism.

The out-of-control crime situation would not exist under Americanism. It can ONLY exist under Socialism.

Every major problem in our schools would not exist under Americanism. They can ONLY exist under Socialism.

The number of good-paying jobs available would dramatically INCREASE under Americanism. They will dramatically DECREASE under Socialism.

A dramatic increase in the standard of living for

most people is POSSIBLE under Americanism. It is IMPOSSIBLE under Socialism.

The problem of poverty would substantially DE-CREASE under Americanism. It will substantially IN-CREASE under Socialism.

For the amount of money they have paid in, and for the amount of money you will have to pay in, our retired senior citizens would receive at least 4 times their current yearly incomes under Americanism. They will always receive one-fourth of what they are entitled to, under Socialism.

You would be able to keep MORE of your hard-earned money in your own pockets under Americanism. You can only keep LESS money in your pockets under Socialism.

Charity, or your voluntarily giving of your own money to whomever YOU please, ONLY exists under Americanism. You may not do this exclusively, under Socialism, but you are FORCED to pay the tab for government charity given to whomever the humans we allow to run the government pleases, either at home or abroad, and this is the legalized theft under Socialism.

You will never again be forced to pay 40% of your gross yearly income in taxes to the local, state, and federal governments under Americanism. You must pay this much NOW under Socialism, and it can only increase.

You are free to STOP PAYING in taxes for a vicious criminal's legal defense fees under Americanism. You are not free and cannot get permission from the humans we allow to run the government to do this under Social-ism.

You are free to STOP PAYING in taxes for someone else's birth control pills and abortions under Americanism. You are not free and cannot get permission from the humans we allow to run the government to do this under Socialism.

You are free to STOP PAYING in taxes for scientific research into subjects like the interesting mating habits of frogs under Americanism. You are not free and cannot get permission from the humans we allow to run the government to do this under Socialism.

You are free to STOP PAYING in taxes for someone else's medical care under Americanism. You are not free and cannot get permission from the humans we allow to run the government to do this under Socialism.

Enough, enough already! The repetition is driving me crazy!

You are now being FORCED to pay in taxes for all of the items listed above, and the list could go on for hundreds of more pages. Under Socialism, you are FORCED to pay for all of these things whether you would like to or not. How free do you feel? Talk about un-American.

Just a few more examples to make sure you get the point.

Under Americanism, if you wanted to, you would be free to STOP PAYING for guns, ammunition, ships, planes, and helicopters for foreign socialistic governments to better enslave their peoples.

Under Americanism, if you wanted to, you would be free to STOP PAYING to support concentration camps and Gulag Archipelagos where foreign socialistic governments imprison, torture, and brutally murder their people.

Under Americanism, if you wanted to, you would

be free to STOP PAYING for building roads in other states outside of your own, or roads in the jungles of foreign socialistic countries.

The list is endless, but the point is made. You'd be a lot RICHER, and a lot FREER under Americanism than you could ever be under Socialism.

Homes would be MORE affordable under Americanism. They are DIFFICULT to afford under Socialism.

Prices across-the-board would be LOWER under Americanism. Prices are HIGHER under Socialism.

The quality of medical care would IMPROVE under Americanism, and the cost would DROP. It will DETERIORATE under Socialism, with cost INCREASES.

Murderers, rapists, child molesters, kidnappers, criminally insane, and traitors, after a fair trial before an impartial jury, and if convicted, all would be QUICKLY sent back to their maker under Americanism, for the protection of decent citizens. Under Socialism, you are forced to pay for supplying these ANIMALS with free food, free clothing, free housing, free medical and dental care, and free recreation and entertainment, FOR LIFE, or until they are released to prey on innocent citizens again, and AGAIN.

What about thieves? Theft is practically a NONEXISTENT crime in Arab countries. Why? For a minor theft, authorities amputate one of the thief's FINGERS. For a major theft, they amputate one of the thief's HANDS. For repeated thefts, authorities amputate the thief's HEAD. Who ever claimed that severe punishment is not a DETERRENT to crime? Only the intellectuals. Do you think this type of severe punishment would deter you from pursuing a life of crime?

Under Americanism, the convicted thief must RE-

TURN the stolen property, or its EQUIVALENT to the victim. Under Socialism, you must forfeit and lose your property, and also, to add insult to injury, you must then PAY for the thief's rehabilitation in prison.

Thieves who repeatedly rob and rob are treated like murderers under Americanism. They are PAMPERED some more under Socialism.

Regarding repetition of crimes, repeated juvenile offenders would NOT grow up to full maturity under Americanism. Repeated juvenile offenders grow up into HARDENED CRIMINALS under Socialism.

Lenient judges are FIRED QUICKLY under Americanism. They are PROMOTED under Socialism.

The prison system would SHRINK and practically DISAPPEAR under Americanism. The prison system PROLIFERATES under Socialism.

Regarding drug usage of marijuana and cocaine, ONE of TWO possibilities would happen under Americanism. Either their purchase, sale, and usage would be made legal, or convicted drug dealers would be sent back to their maker. Neither option exists under Socialism.

Church leaders would again be free to tell the truth under Americanism. This does not happen under Socialism.

City, county, state, and federal bureaucratic, administrative, and enforcement officials would have to get HONEST jobs again to contribute beneficially to society under Americanism. This does not happen under Socialism.

Under Americanism, the major newspapers, major national magazines, and major TV networks would LOSE their advertisers, and go out of business if they were lying and hiding the truth from the public. This does not happen under Socialism.

Under Americanism, every citizen who has never been arrested, nor convicted of a crime, would be free to buy and own firearms, preferably safely stored in locked areas of their homes, so that they would be free to defend and protect themselves and their families from criminal intruders BEFORE the police arrived. This situation is similar to conditions existing in Switzerland, but it is impossible to bring about under Socialism.

Under Americanism, every man and woman who has never been arrested, nor convicted of a crime, would be free to carry a CONCEALED weapon on their person for self-defense purposes if they need it to make themselves feel MORE COMFORTABLY SECURE, all in accordance with the 2nd Amendment to our Constitution which states that . . . ". . . the right of the people to keep and bear arms, shall NOT be infringed.'' This is not allowed under Socialism.

This list is INCOMPLETE because it is practically ENDLESS. But you get the picture. The bottom line is that the physical, psychological, emotional, and financial security of the people would INCREASE under Americanism. They all DECREASE under Socialism.

And this is why 40 million Europeans left their SOCIALISTIC HOMELANDS between 1790 and 1921 to come to America. Unlike our Pseudo-Americans of today, these 40 million immigrants of yesterday FULLY understood the growth and natural PROGRESSION PATTERN of Socialism, when once the people make the mistake of allowing it to be born, because these 40 million immigrants were VICTIMS of that

Socialist progression pattern in their original homelands. That's WHY they fled when the last straw broke the camel's back. And this is STILL why immigration into our country CONTINUES today, but with the sadly unforeseen results that the modern immigrants EVENTUALLY come to the TRAGIC realization that they have jumped out of the socialistic FIRE and into the socialistic FRYING PAN.

At birth, Socialism is a harmless, cute-looking baby Frankenstein. As an adolescent, Socialism is an annoying nuisance. As a fully grown adult, Socialism is an ugly, frightening Frankenstein monster looking for blood. This evolutionary pattern of Socialism has NEVER been broken for 6,000 years.

Real-Americans understand and believe in evolution—the evolution of the evils of Socialism. Pseudo-Americans don't understand, and consequently don't believe that this is the way it ALWAYS happens.

It is easier for freedom-lovers to kill the baby Socialist-Frankenstein soon after its birth. It is harder for freedom-lovers to kill the adolescent Socialist-Frankenstein. The odds of successfully killing the Socialist-Frankenstein monster approaching adulthood are about the SAME as the odds faced by our founders in 1775.

So Real-Americans understanding these truths about the evils of Socialism believe in and really prefer abortion—the abortion of Socialism in the womb before its actual birth.

Pseudo-Americans MUST learn the lesson that our founders taught us so long ago: NOTHING IS FREE. If you receive it for free, somebody else had to pay the price for it.

And freedom isn't free. Everyone wishing to keep

their pride, self-respect, and dignity MUST pay their OWN price to restore their OWN freedom.

To finish up with more tangible information, you need to be aware of ONE important historical fact: that the Socialist-American millionaire big businessmen formed a prestigious membership type organization over 50 years ago, whose primary purpose was to first convert our country's Americanism system into a Socialism system, which could then be more easily merged into a one world socialistic system.

To achieve their treasonous, subversive, un-American, socialistic objective, this organization recruited, and still recruits members into it who come from the HIGHEST LEVELS of government, labor, education, religion, military, and the news, information, and communication medias.

In the last 50 years, and even today, guess which individuals have joined this prestigious, socialistic, un-American organization, and have been, or still are active members. Presidents of the United States have been members; Secretaries of State have been members; Secretaries of Commerce have been members; Secretaries of Agriculture have been members; Secretaries of the Treasury have been members; Chairmen of the Federal Reserve System have been members; Secretaries of Labor have been members; Chairmen of the Military Joint Chiefs of Staff have been members; Secretaries of the Army, Navy, and Air Force have been members; U.S. Representatives to the United Nations have been members; Ambassadors to foreign countries have been members; Directors of the CIA have been members; U.S. Senators and Congressmen have been members; Chief Justices and associate justices of the U.S. Supreme Court have been members; Governors of our states have been members; Chairmen and presidents of major newspapers, magazines, radio, and TV stations have been members; Presidents of major universities have been members; Presidents of tax-exempt foundations have been members; important religious figures have been members; Presidents of hundreds of major business corporations have been members; and many prominent attorneys have been members.

Currently, this 3,000 member prestigious socialistic organization publishes a highly intellectual quarterly magazine called FOREIGN AFFAIRS, available for reading in most major libraries. This prestigious socialistic organization also conducts SECRET meetings periodically in every major region of our country.

The existence of this private, socialistic, membership-by-invitation-only organization, composed of the most wealthy, powerful, and influential people in America for the last 50 years, and still today, LOGICALLY explains how our country has been converted into a completely Socialist nation.

The name of this treasonous, un-American, socialistic organization is the Council on Foreign Relations (CFR), headquartered in the Harold Pratt House at 58 E. 68th St. in New York City. The listed telephone number is 212-734-0400. Check it out.

And a man we all know, by the name of George Bush, rose within this organization to the rank of a Director of the CFR. Think about that.

Chapter 14

A Love Story

*Where there is no vision of the future, the
people perish.*   —*From the Bible*

This is a love story. Love. You've heard of it?
Believe it or not, love is what this thing is all about.
Being in love with our country, beautiful America.
In love with America, forever and ever. For what
she is. For what you are. Both the same. Free spirits.
It's in your blood.

Love for our country. In love with our country.

Love like the kind you feel for a sweetheart, a
lover, a person outside of yourself. Love like the kind
you feel for only one person living on planet earth.
Love. Like the feelings you get when you talk to
each other, write to each other, see each other, walk
with each other, dine with each other, drink cocktails
with each other, dance with each other. Love. Like
the feelings you get when your fingers touch, when
you hug each other, when you smell each other, and
when you kiss each other's lips. Emotional. Romantic.
Unselfish. Glamorous. Altruistic. Idealistic. Real people. Givers, not takers. Love. Like cramps in your
stomach. Losing your breath. When separation makes
you feel sick and empty, and like a piece of you is
missing. Love. Like not ever being able to get the
other person out of your mind. Love. Like staring
into the other person's eyes. Love which gives you
the shakes from head to toe. Love which makes you

scream at each other, and then feel so sorry that you'd almost like to die if you can't make up. Love for another person who seems like an unexplainable, unbelievable carbon copy of yourself. Clones. Like for the only soulmate you know you will ever meet this side of eternity. Love like heart-to-heart, body-to-body, mind-to-mind, soul-to-soul. Love like being possessed. Irrational madness. Crazy for someone. Like never being able to get enough of each other. Never being able to do enough for each other. Love. Undying loyalty. Unconditional trust. Faithfulness. Out-of-the-market love. And lastly, love, true love, the real test if it's true love. The bottom line test of true love. You would risk your life for this person. You would give up your life willingly if you think that this act could save this person's life. Willingly. Greater love hath no one than this.

Real-Americans love America this way.

Love. For your one and only. Like what you would do if some bastard tricked your lover. Like what you would do if some bastard cheated your lover. Like what you would do if some bastard threatened your lover. Like what you would do if some bastard hurt your lover. Like what you would do if some bastard raped your lover. Like what you would do if some bastard killed your lover. True love.

Like what you want to do to the Socialist-Americans, who did ALL of the above things to the Real America, the real country which our founders gave us, your country, which you love.

We're talking about true love, but talk is cheap. True love means ACTIONS speak louder than WORDS. Always. Actions are the bottom line, the real test of true love. Real-Americans have always passed this test. Pseudo-Americans say that they love America, but how can you really love something with true love if you don't understand it?

You know what a counterfeit is. A counterfeit is an imitation of the genuine. A counterfeit is an imitation of the real thing. A counterfeit may seem like the real thing, but it's not. Words are the counterfeit of love. Actions are the real love.

Counterfeit lovers exist. There are plenty of them. They use WORDS to tell you they love you, but they love themselves MORE. I love you. Fakers. Phonies. Hypocrites. Selfish. Takers, not givers. I love you. Users. Abusers. Desperate thrill seekers. Narcissists. Libertines. I love you. Sexual gluttons. Gigolos. Nymphomaniacs. Warm-body-swappers. Girls using good guys like boytoys. Guys using good girls like whores. I love you. Guys acting like male prostitutes for the drinks, dinners, presents, and the fun of it. Girls acting like part-time hookers for the drinks, dinners, presents, and the fun of it. Girls and guys playing at love like the people in the songs, Easy Lover and Maneater. Guys having sex with guys, girls having sex with girls, and menage a trois. I love you. Proud. Arrogant. Liars. Manipulators. Fast and loose. Excitement freaks. Self-destructives. Heartbreakers. I love you. Bi-sexuals. Prostitutes. Lusters, not lovers. Counterfeit lovers really mean I lust you, and I assume you lust me, so let's get it on. Why not? Takes one to know one. Let's take advantage of each other as long as it lasts. Why not? I love you. No strings attached. No commitments. No trust. No faithfulness. Infidelity. Always in the market. Chow! Arrivederci. Sayonara. Later-baby specialists. But sometimes lusters fool around and really do fall in love, but only by mistake.

I love you. And lastly, counterfeit lovers would NEVER risk losing their own lives to save yours.

Pseudo-Americans love America with words like counterfeit lovers.

Real-Americans do not hate Pseudo-Americans, but have no respect for them. Real lovers do not hate counterfeit lovers, but have no respect for them. Judge not, lest ye be judged, even if you've walked in the same shoes before. True love does conquer all. And we're all sinners. Hate the sin, not the sinner.

A counterfeit lover or luster has an out-of-control appetite for sex, similar to an obese person who has an out-of-control appetite for food, or an alcoholic or drug addict's out-of-control desire for alcohol or drugs. This doesn't mean that they are bad people. On the contrary, they could even be better people personally than true lovers in many different respects. They may be kinder, more generous, more charitable, more loving, more understanding, more tolerant, and more loyal in friendships than others.

Lust and obesity problems may originate from deep-seated emotional problems of insecurity and fear of rejection, like from a broken-up former real love affair, or a divorce, or a death or serious illness in the family, or a lack of friends, or a lack of religion, or failure in business, or lack of love and understanding, or too much stress and tension, or from many other disappointments, which expresses itself openly in the self-gratification of sex or food for sanity preservation through indulgence in these pleasures. Some people like to come and copulate more than sucking up lobster tail with drawn butter, and vice versa. Some like equally to do both. It's tough being a human being, isn't it? That's life.

Most people with a psychological reason (whether they understand it themselves or not) for an out-of-control appetite for food, with an obesity problem, are basically good, decent people when they really have no desire to hurt anyone else by forcing food down their throats. Similarly, people with a psychological reason (whether they understand it or not) for an out-of-control appetite for sex, with a lust problem, are basically good, decent people when they really have no desire to hurt anyone else by forcing them to participate in sex with them.

Fatsoes who shove food down people's throats are bad people who will be arrested and tried for assault, and suitably punished. Lusters who rape and child molest are bad people who will be arrested and tried for their crimes, and, if proven guilty will be executed as an act of mercy-killing love. We may JUDGE criminally bad people to protect good people. No sweat. Kool, no? And thoroughly American. And of course, all of the rationale above applies equally to the alcoholics and drug addicts.

All of our founders, meaning George Washington, all of the brave souls at Lexington and Concord, all of the members of the Continental Congress, all of the signers of our Declaration of Independence, every man who carried and shot his musket at the Redcoats, every woman and young person who somehow supported our Revolution, all the framers of our Constitution, all of our founders were SINNERS. So what? And they all disagreed on many, many subjects. So what? But they all had one important thing IN COMMON: their true love of liberty, their true love of freedom, their true desire TO LIVE FREE, or die trying. None of them had to be SAINTS headed for heaven in order to truly love and fight for their country. As it was THEN, so it is NOW.

Thus, all of our founders loved freedom so truly, that they were willing to risk giving up their lives if that was what was needed to secure freedom for themselves and their loved ones. As it was THEN, so it is NOW.

Being willing to risk giving up your life is the real test of true love. True love for a PERSON, or true love for your COUNTRY.

Which girl or boy, man or woman do you truly love? The real, loyal, faithful, out-of-the-market, one-on-one, dedicated soulmate; or the gigolo or nymphomaniac counterfeit? There are TWO different kinds of people you know. Which kind do you truly love?

Do you truly love our country? Our real country which our founders gave us, or the counterfeit country which our Socialist-Americans have given us? Which country do you love with true love? There are TWO different kinds of countries you know. Which kind do you truly love?

Which girl or boy, man or woman would you really miss if you lost one of them? The real soulmate, or the counterfeit gigolo or nymphomaniac?

Which country would you really miss if you lost one of them? The real country which our founders gave us, or the counterfeit country which our Socialist-Americans gave us?

Which girl or boy, man or woman would you fight to protect and defend if you had to choose just ONE of them? The real soulmate, or the counterfeit gigolo or nymphomaniac?

Which country would you fight to protect and defend if you had to choose just ONE of them? The real country which our founders gave us, or the counterfeit country which our Socialist-Americans gave us?

Which girl or boy, man or woman would you risk losing your life for to save just ONE of them? The real soulmate, or the counterfeit gigolo or nymphomaniac?

Which country would you risk losing your life for to save just ONE of them? The real country which our founders gave us, or the counterfeit country which our Socialist-Americans gave us?

Real-Americans LOVE their real country, and hate their counterfeit country. Pseudo-Americans LOVE their counterfeit country because they don't understand their real country. And Socialist-Americans hate their real country, and LOVE the counterfeit country which they themselves created.

So the next time someone asks you if you LOVE our country, be careful how you answer. In fact, before you answer their question, maybe you should ask them which country they mean: our real country, or our counterfeit country? The Real America or the Counterfeit America? The Real America which our founders gave us, or the Counterfeit America which our Socialist-Americans gave us? The difference between the TWO countries is like day and night, good and evil, right and wrong.

Maybe an understanding, however conscious or subconscious, of this RADICAL DIFFERENCE between our real country and our counterfeit country could be the MAIN reason why so many of our young men decided to go to Canada rather than to fight in Vietnam, and also, maybe this exact same understanding, also however conscious or sub-conscious, of this radical difference between our real country and our counterfeit country could be the main reason why so many of our young men who served in Vietnam are still confused about the REAL meaning of this disturbing personal experience.

In fact, many of our young men later admitted that the proverbial straw which broke their camel's back, and caused them to make the unpopular, emotionally disturbing, and personally traumatic decision to run to Canada as a "draft-dodger" occurred as soon as they discovered the BEST-KEPT SECRET of the Vietnam War. That unbelievably shocking, little-known fact was this: during the entire Vietnam War, greedy big-American-businessmen, with the full approval and support of our Counterfeit American government, were supplying the enemy with almost ALL of the war material that the enemy needed to fight the war. Maybe you should re-read that statement to make sure you understood it.

Socialist North Vietnam was, and still is, a primitive agricultural farming community without the industrial, technical, and manufacturing capability to fight a modern war. The only war which Socialist North Vietnam could ever have an even chance of fighting and winning would be a war in which they and their enemy abided by the following rule regarding the use of weapons: only bow-and-arrows, knives, spears, and sling-shots can be used. That is NO exaggeration.

So how could primitive North Vietnam and their primitive South Vietnam Vietcong allies possibly fight a modern war using modern weapons? They were ONLY able to do so because during the entire war, the Socialist Soviet Union and all of the Socialist Soviet Union's Eastern European satellites (like Socialist Hungary, Socialist Yugoslavia, Socialist Poland, Socialist East Germany, etc.) were supplying over 85% of the modern war material used by the North Vietnamese and Vietcong to kill and maim American soldiers.

That fact was more widely known, and is not a big secret. The big secret was the fact that during the entire Vietnam War, our own big-business-controlled Commerce Department allowed our greedy big-American-businessmen to export and ship to the Soviets and their bloc such strategic modern war materials as JET ENGINES, DIESEL ENGINES, HELICOPTERS, FUEL for these engines, CHEMICALS for the production of GUNPOWDER and EXPLOSIVES, RIFLE-CLEANING COMPOUNDS, STEEL, BOAT PARTS, BRIDGES, ALUMINUM, RUBBER, ELECTRONIC RADAR DEVICES, COMPUTERS, and hundreds more. The Soviets would then simply TRANSFER and RE-SHIP all of these strategic items in FINISHED FORM to the North Vietnamese and Vietcong.

Our boys were LITERALLY being killed and maimed by products "MADE IN THE U.S.A." For proof, see if you can get your hands on copies of the same document which CONVINCED many of our young men to dodge the draft. It is Current Export Bulletin Number 941, Supplement to the Comprehensive Export Schedule, published by the U.S. Department of Commerce, Bureau of International Commerce, Office of Export Control, dated October 12, 1966, and you will see listed for unrestricted export to the Soviets and their bloc, all of the strategic items listed above, plus many, many more. If you cannot obtain Bulletin 1941, just ask a Vietnam vet about all of the captured enemy war material that he saw with the "MADE IN THE USA" stamped right on it.

In fact, if you believe that an army travels on its stomach, it might make you sick to learn that during the entire Vietnam War, American wheat was being shipped DIRECTLY to Socialist Poland. The American ships loaded with American wheat would dock in Polish harbors, and unload the wheat DIRECTLY on to the waiting Polish ships. Then the Polish ships loaded with American wheat would DIRECTLY sail non-stop to, and dock in the North Vietnamese harbor of Haiphong, where the AMERICAN wheat would be unloaded to feed the North Vietnamese and Viet-cong soldiers so that they could have full bellies when they killed, captured, and maimed American soldiers.

So, essentially because of this treasonous foreign aid and trade policy, Counterfeit America was supplying the war material and food supply for both sides of the Vietnam War, ours and theirs.

A Real-American-controlled Congress could have stopped this (aid and comfort to our enemies) treason, but we had back then, and still have now a big-businessmen-controlled-Socialist-American Congress. After checking the 1966 Export Bulletin, check the current 1990s export Commerce Department Bulletin, and you will be shocked to discover that the SAME treasonous foreign aid and trade policies exist today, which means that we ourselves, or our sons and daughters, or grandsons and granddaughters may have to fight potential foreign wars in the Middle East, Central America, or Southern Africa under the SAME treasonous (but profitable to the big businessmen) foreign aid and trade conditions as we fought the Vietnam War.

Besides, why should Real-Americans risk dying in foreign wars to ENRICH the pocketbooks and bank accounts of the owners, executives, employees, and stockholders of over 300 big businesses in Counterfeit America, which sell or try to sell military equipment, warfare hardware, and military technology to the Socialist Soviet Union, its Eastern European Socialist satellites, and Socialist China, which are the Socialist nations which foment, finance, and supply the men and war material for practically every war since 1945, including the dozens of shooting wars going on right this minute, all around the world? Real-Americans are not willing to foolishly risk their lives to support this un-American hypocrisy.

As it was in 1775, so it is again in the 1990s. The so-called American big-business corporations of the 1990s are SIMILAR in their greedy philosophy and bully methods of operation to the English big-business trading companies of 1775. As the English big-business trading companies of yesterday BOUGHT the Parliament and used it as an instrument or enemy of freedom everywhere in the world, so also has the so-called American big-business corporations BOUGHT our Congress, and similarly use it as an instrument or enemy of freedom everywhere in the world.

Your expecting the owners, executives, employees, and stockholders of the more than 300 major so-called American corporations, who have a vested interest in the financial success of these corporations, to join the side of the Real-American Movement, is analagous

to our original Americans in 1775 and 1776 expecting
the owners, executives, employees, and stockholders
of the English big-business trading companies to join
the side of the American rebels. Don't bet on it.

Some of these big business so-called American corporations involved in this treasonous aid and trade
with our Socialist enemies are:

Abbott Laboratories
Allen-Bradley
Allis Chalmers
American Cyanamid
American Express
Archer Daniels Midland
Armco
Chase Manhattan Bank
Chemical Bank
Caterpillar
Cargill
Control Data
Deere & Company
Dow Chemical
Dresser
Dupont
FMC
General Electric
Gleason
Ingersoll-Rand
International Harvester
Kodak
Litton Industries
Minnesota Mining
Monsanto
Occidental Petroleum

Stauffer Chemical
Tenneco
Union Carbide
Worthington Pump
Xerox

And interestingly enough, Chase Manhattan Bank opened up a branch office in Moscow at the prestigious Number One Karl Marx Square.

If you work for any one of these corporations, or own the stock of these corporations (in your personal or company pension portfolio), or of 300 others, how does it make you feel knowing that you personally are helping the Soviets to kill Afghanistani babies, and also helping the Soviets and Socialist Chinese to kill millions of human beings in brutal slavery? Sleep tight. Pleasant dreams.

Foreigners have good, valid reasons for hating our Counterfeit America, which is helping their socialist slavemasters. These same foreigners would love the Real America that our founders created, just like Lafayette, DeKalb, Steuben, Pulaski, and Kosciuszko did. Foreigners love freedom too.

Also, do you own any Counterfeit American savings bonds, or any mortgage-backed securities in Counterfeit America? Like Ginny Mae's, Fanny Mae's, or Freddy Mac's? Sleep tight, and pleasant dreams.

As an interesting aside regarding the so-called American socialistic big businessmen's treasonous greed and bullyism, remember the fact that big-business millionaires are NOT stupid, and that they hate to lose their OWN money. They'd much rather see you lose YOUR money. So the socialistic big-businessmen are ALWAYS thinking up new and innovative tricks to protect their millions. For instance, from 1917 to 1922, the Russian Socialists brutally murdered over 10 million of their OWN people, but in the late 20's, General Electric and Ford Motor Company still went to Russia to set up their electrical, automotive, and truck industries. But GE and Ford were worried about the possibility of NOT being paid by their murderous Socialist customers. So in the early 1930's, the so-called American socialistic big-businessmen had their bought-socialistic-congressmen pass a law setting up what is called the Export-Import Bank. Now get this. The Export-Import Bank is funded with taxpayers' money. The EX-IM loans this taxpayer money to foreign socialistic governments so that they can be able to buy and pay for the products and services of our so-called American socialistic big-businessmen, OR the EX-IM guarantees the loans which our so-called American socialistic big-businessmen make to their foreign socialistic government customers buying on credit. This means that when GE and the other so-called American socialistic big-businesses allow the Socialist Russians, or the Socialist Chinese to buy on credit, and these Socialists governments renege on payment, or refuse to pay outright, the EX-IM will use your tax money to pay our so-called American socialistic big-businessmen in full. How does it make you feel knowing that you are being FORCED to financially back this so-called American socialistic big-businessmen's treasonous aid and trade with all of our foreign socialistic enemies? And that this RISKLESS policy for the so-called American big-businessmen is still in existence today, and has been in existence for the last 50 years? What a tragedy.

World War II veterans have really been shocked

and saddened to learn from recently declassified information, that our government had actually broken the secret Japanese code called PURPLE in October of 1941, and consequently discovered at least 5 weeks IN ADVANCE that the Japanese would sneak-attack Pearl Harbor at dawn on December 7th. But General George Marshall, our military Chairman of the Joint Chiefs of Staff, NEVER communicated this decisive information to our Pacific commanders, Admirals Kimmel and Short, and therefore, 5,000 American boys were slaughtered at Pearl Harbor by SURPRISE like sitting ducks. What a tragedy.

And in 1945, as the war was ending, and when we were the most powerful nation on the face of the earth, and the ONLY nation in possession of THE BOMB, this same de-classified information reveals how our Counterfeit American government gradually turned over all of the millions and millions of innocent Eastern Europeans, Chinese, and other Asians to Socialist dictators, Russian Stalin and Chinese Mao-Tse-Tung, for torture, starvation, extermination, and imprisonment. And our soldiers and sailors thought that they were fighting to ensure freedom for everyone around the world. What a tragedy.

And the biggest mind-blower of them all is how this de-classified information reveals how our Counterfeit American government OFFICIALLY shipped to the Russian Socialist Soviets from our air base at Great Falls, Montana, ALL of the uranium and special materials and technology necessary to manufacture THE BOMB, thus starting the Socialist Soviets off into the nuclear arms race, even after our Counterfeit American government knew that German Socialist dictator Hitler AND Russian Socialist dictator Stalin BOTH invaded Poland TOGETHER to start World War II. What a tragedy.

In fact, while mentioning THE BOMB, further de-classified information reveals that the Japanese were trying to SURRENDER to us to end the war at least SIX MONTHS before our Counterfeit America dropped THE BOMB on Hiroshima and Nagasaki in August of 1945, thus incinerating over 200,000 Japanese men, women, and children. Want to read that over again? Talk about a mind-blower. What a tragedy.

Who was responsible for this horrifying and completely unnecessary murder of innocent Japanese civilians? Counterfeit American President Harry "Give 'em Hell" Truman. He sure gave those innocent civilians hell. This is the same Harry Truman who was endorsed for the presidency by the Communist Party U.S.A.'s official daily newspaper, "The Daily Worker," when Truman was running for re-election as President of the United States in 1948. Want to read that over again? And in 1950, Truman was the same Counterfeit American President who fired our heroic General Douglas MacArthur after Doug won the Korean War with his famous Inchon Landing. What a tragedy.

Also, de-classified information has recently exposed the United Nations organization, headquartered in New York City, as an entity which was conceived by the Socialists and communists, created by the Socialists and communists, and which is now and has always been completely controlled by the Socialists and communists. This explains why this so-called "peace organization" established to prevent future wars has been such a miserable failure in achieving its supposedly avowed purpose, and why almost 100 wars have broken out since the UN's formation in 1945, and why at least a dozen wars are being waged right now as you read this statement.

In fact, de-classified information further reveals some interesting facts regarding the UN's power structure. The UN positions comparable to our President's and Vice President's (numbers 1 and 2) are the Secretary-General and Under or Assistant Secretary-General for Political and Security Council Affairs. The first Secretary-General of the UN during its formation in 1945, who was the most influential American in setting it up, was the right hand man of President Franklin Delano Roosevelt. His name is Alger Hiss, a member of the Council on Foreign Relations (CFR), who in 1948 was exposed as a communist agent. This explains why the number two position of Under or Assistant Secretary-General for Political and Security Affairs HAS ALWAYS BEEN HELD by a Russian communist. Want to read that over again?

And it shouldn't be surprising that F.D.R. loved communist agent, Alger Hiss, especially since this President F.D.R. once said, ". . . there is nothing wrong with the communists in this country; several of the best friends I have got are communists."

The Under or Assistant Secretary-General for Political and Security Council Affairs of the UN is, by the way, in complete charge of all NUCLEAR DISARMAMENT proceedings. This means that if the United States agrees to disarm itself, the U.S. must turn over ALL of our nuclear weapons to the Russian communist occupying the number two position at the UN. How does this fact make you feel about the controversial subject of disarmament? Think about it.

But back to the subject of war.

Real Americans, who love the real country which our founders gave us, will never be tricked or forced into risking our lives on foreign soil in any war supposedly designed to protect and defend the counterfeit country which our Socialist-Americans gave us, especially since RA's know that our Counterfeit American government fights foreign wars to make big businessmen RICHER. And our position just happens to coincide with the exact same position in foreign wars which George Washington expressed in his Farewell Address to his countrymen.

Real-Americans, who love our real country which our founders gave us, will only risk our lives on DOMESTIC SOIL fighting to get back our real country from the Socialist-Americans who stole it from us.

Remember that our real country's founders believed that the only legitimate justification for fighting a shooting war is to avoid becoming a slave, OR to break out of existing slavery (needing permission from government to act), which they themselves broke out of. As it was in 1775 America, so it is in 1990s America. The real battle is HERE AGAIN on our own soil, and NOT OVER THERE on foreign soil .

And there is no Constitutional justification anyway for the socialistic practice of using our soldiers and resources to supposedly defend the entire world. NONE. And this practice is completely un-American. It is one of the major tricks of Counterfeit America, and we need to bring all of our boys and girls back home NOW.

Also the last piece of recently declassified information which you should never forget is this: Socialist-Americans long ago have purged all Real-American type individuals out of the policy-making position levels of the FBI and the CIA. All critically important strategic and tactical policy-making positions in the FBI and the CIA are unfortunately held NOW, and unfortunately have been held for a long time, by Socialist-Americans. Think about that.

There is a mysterious disease running rampant throughout America which has infected 90% of our population. Only 10% of our population has remained immune. This terrible disease has struck every age, race, sex, and socio-economic-political category in the United States, except the immune 10%. The cause of this disease has remained unknown. The cure for this disease naturally has also remained unknown. Like the disease of AIDS so far, this terrible disease is also fatal. But long before it kills, this horrible disease is extremely PAINFUL to its victims.

Pain affects different people differently. Some tolerate pain better or worse than others. Assuming that you are not a masochist, pain makes you feel very unhappy, sad, depressed, and in rare cases of extreme pain, mentally erratic, unstable, and irrational; and all of this to varying degrees.

Because researchers for so long have been unable to discover a logical, provable, understandable, believable, and explainable cause for the contraction of this disease, most victims suffering from it have gone deeply into despair, lost all hope of a real cure, and have resigned themselves to the tragic fact that only temporary relief is possible from the pain which it causes.

For TEMPORARY RELIEF from the suffering caused by this disease, and in their desperate attempts to forget or kill the pain which it causes, many victims get themselves into marijuana, cocaine, and booze. Similarly, for DISTRACTION PURPOSES, many victims get themselves into sex, food, cars, music, parties, gambling, physical fitness, travel, games, sports, hobbies, local politics, and the whole gamut of outside extracurricular activities, including but not necessarily limited to, throwing themselves into and become heavily involved with their work, religion, or with the lives of their families and friends, and curiously enough, their TV soap opera favorites.

These panaceas, these placebos, certainly work well most of the time to KILL the pain, or make the victim FORGET the pain, and do provide the welcomed temporary relief, thank God. But soon after the victims cease participating in these therapeutic activities, the pain from the mysterious disease returns almost immediately to haunt them again.

Real-Americans have finally identified this mysterious disease for what it really is. Real-Americans have also discovered its definite cause. And Real-Americans have also isolated its only sure cure.

This killer disease has been identified as BOREDOM.

The mysterious disease of boredom which produces in its victims the painful feelings of frustration, anguish, loneliness, and emptiness, which requires the therapy of drugs, booze, or busy diversionary activities to alleviate, is caused by A LACK OF UNDERSTANDING OF THE FUNDAMENTAL PURPOSE OF LIFE.

Test yourself. What is your REAL purpose in life? Why were you born? What do you want to be when you grow up? (And kool 45 year olds, who grew up with Elvis and are charter members of the rock 'n roll generation, should answer that question with their own question of what the hell does "growing up" mean anyway? When I think I've "grown up" I'll let you know what I think I want to be). And even if you are an adult, holding a job or working in a profession, are you happy, and is this what you really want to be doing? What do you REALLY want to be doing? Rare indeed is the individual who can answer all of these fundamental questions positively.

"Coins have always fascinated me, so since I was a kid, I've always wanted to become a toll booth collector on the thruway." Uh huh. "I love food, so since I was a kid, I just couldn't wait to get a job as a check-out clerk at the local supermarket." Uh huh. "Leftovers and junk have always intrigued me, so I couldn't wait to become a garbage collector." Uh huh. "Everyone loves good-looking waitresses, and I just couldn't wait to become one." Uh huh. "Once I realized that the wheel was man's greatest invention, I just couldn't wait to become a truck driver." Uh huh. "Since I've always hated to stay in one place for very long, I deliberately made up my mind to hold 25 different jobs before I died." Uh huh. "Since knowing secret inside information always turned me on, I just knew I'd become a secretary." Uh huh. "Since my childhood psychiatrist told me that my two strongest desires in life were for me to be secure, but for me to scare everyone else I could (which really surfaced on Halloween), I just knew I'd be working for the government, or a bank, or be a cop." Uh huh.

With the single exception of lobotomy patients, you

have had ONE question on your mind for a long time: WHAT THE HELL IS LIFE ALL ABOUT ANY-WAY?

If you honestly answer this question with confusion and say "I don't know," then you have to be afflicted with the painful disease of boredom, caused by a lack of understanding of the real purpose and meaning of life.

90% of our population has contracted this disease of boredom. 10% of our population are immune. Real-Americans and Socialist-Americans do not have this disease of boredom, but every Pseudo-American does.

Real-Americans feel today, exactly like our founders felt yesterday, that the fundamental purpose of life is TO LIVE FREE. This is, and always has been from the very beginning of time, the fundamental REASON for our existence. This is WHY we are here. This is HOW we are born. Let freedom ring throughout all of the land!

The proof of this fundamental purpose in life is self-evident. Every human was born with this desire for freedom built-in INSIDE of them. And so were the animals in the wild kingdom.

A captured wild horse must be caged and broken to become tame. A little child must be taught to become civilized. In other words, learning to accept being "unfree" is a mental conditioning process, which must be IMPOSED on animals and humans from the OUT-SIDE, to control their natural desire for total freedom, coming from their INSIDE.

Actions speak louder than words. Real-Americans of today speak AND act like our founders of yester-day. Like our founders of yesterday, RA's of today are on a MISSION to live free. They have a definite purpose in life. They know their assignment. They have a definite goal in life. They know the direction they are headed. They have a map, a plan, and are trying to follow it. They have a built-in radar. RA's don't just pay LIP-SERVICE to freedom. They know that the essence of freedom is the limitation of government control. They know how to obtain it. They're working to obtain it. They're exercising their purpose in life. SO THEY ARE NOT BORED.

When Real-Americans engage in all of the boredom-killing therapeutic activities previously listed above, they enjoy the SAME fun, thrills, and excitement which the Pseudo-Americans enjoy, but only as a RE-WARD to themselves for working so hard on their MISSION to restore the Real America which our founders gave us, so that we can really live free again IN OUR LIFETIME. RA's live up to their true responsibilities in life, responsibilities to themselves, and to their present or future children, to PASS ON the freedom which they inherited. Because Real-Americans live up to this important MISSION in life, they experience little shame, and little guilt, and usually feel real good about themselves. In fact, because they know that they are living up to their MISSION in life to FIGHT for freedom, they are very proud of themselves. And it is axiomatic that if you are not proud of yourself, nobody else will be proud of you either.

Actions speak louder than WORDS. Pseudo-Americans of today, like the neutrals of yesterday, SPEAK like they want to live free, but without having to pay any price but empty LIP-SERVICE to freedom, followed by NO ACTIONS designed to bring about the limitation of government which would insure that freedom. PA's understand NO PURPOSE in life, understand NO MISSION in life, and consequently PA's are BORED.

When Pseudo-Americans engage in all of the boredom-killing therapeutic activities previously listed above, they enjoy fun, thrills, and excitement as an ESCAPE from their feelings of boredom associated with their purposeless lives. PA's believe in mentally running away, and sometimes, even literally running away, from their real purpose in life to fight for freedom, which they do NOT understand, or even worse, will NOT accept. PA's do NOT live up to their true responsibilities in life, responsibilities to themselves, and to their present or future children, to pass on the freedom which they inherited. Consequently, Pseudo-Americans have MUCH to be ashamed of, MUCH to feel guilty about, and NOTHING to be proud about in this critical regard.

Actions speak louder than words. Socialist-Americans of today RARELY speak, but ALWAYS ACT, like the loyalists, King George, big businessmen, Parliamentarians, bureaucrats, Redcoats, and Benedict Arnold of yesterday. Like the bullies of yesterday, SA's are on a MISSION to use the POWER of government to FORCE their WILL on everybody, to take ADVANTAGE of everybody, to PUSH everybody around, as far and as fast as they can, to HERD everybody into a cage, to ELIMINATE their freedom, and to CONVERT everybody into a slave. SA's have a DEFINITE purpose in life. They know their assignment. They have a DEFINITE goal in life. They know the direction they are headed. They have a map, a plan, and are trying to follow it. They have a built-in radar. SA's pay LIP-SERVICE to freedom, but

DO NOT pay lip-service to bullyism and slavery. They know that the essence of slavery is the unlimitation of government control. They know HOW to obtain it. They're WORKING to obtain it. They're EXERCISING their purpose in life. SO THEY ARE ALSO NOT BORED.

When Socialist-Americans engage in all of the boredom-killing therapeutic activities previously listed above, they also enjoy the SAME fun, thrills, and excitement which the RA's and PA's enjoy, but unlike the Pseudo-Americans' motivation of ESCAPE, but like the Real-Americans' motivation of REWARD, the Socialist-Americans enjoy these pleasures as a REWARD to themselves for working SO HARD on their MISSION to increase, to expand, to enforce, and to consolidate the government's POWER over the lives of the people living in the Counterfeit America which they have created, and which they INTEND TO MAINTAIN, so that NOBODY will really ever be able to live free in America, in the true sense of the definition of free, ever again, LIKE BEFORE.

So now the next time you WONDER why you got yourself so high on pot or coke, or so drunk and sick on booze, or why you had so much fun, so many thrills, or so much excitement and enjoyment from whatever it was you were doing, you might be able to determine that it was a satisfying ESCAPE from your BOREDOM, or a glorious REWARD for your working towards the eventual fulfillment of your MISSION. The answer you give yourself should establish in your mind and heart whether your IDENTITY is that of a RA, PA, or SA.

It is an OBVIOUS FACT that people can and sometimes do become addicted to pain-killers, because pain-killers make them feel so good. Their physical and/ or psychological addiction to these pain-killers sometimes make them DEPENDENT on these things as their very PURPOSE for life itself.

If you have become so addicted to these pain-killers, and if the pain-killers you are using to ease the pain of your BOREDOM have gotten so out-of-control that they have practically become your REAL REASON for living, it is highly UNLIKELY that you will RESPOND to the truth of what our founders tried to teach us, that the fundamental purpose of life is TO LIVE FREE. Without your knowledge or understanding, these boredom-killing pain-killers have actually become the GREATEST ENEMY to your individual freedom, and the GREATEST ENEMY to your chances of your ever being able to live free in the promised land of the Real America which our founders gave us.

Old habits die hard. Trying to BREAK old habits hurts real bad. Sometimes old habits NEVER die, and wind up killing you. If you cannot BREAK the old habit of spending ALL of your spare time addicted to the boredom pain-killers, so that you can devote at least SOME of your spare time towards attempts to RESTORE the Real America which our founders gave us, you and your loved ones will live the rest of your lives, and die in the progressively alien Counterfeit America which our Socialist-Americans tricked us into by using the appealing, but FALSE, concept of GUARANTEED SECURITY.

Before the formation of the Real American Movement (RAM) on May 1, 1987, you have had the GREATEST FRIEND which you could possibly have had, but without your even realizing who or what it is.

Just as boredom, and what that boredom makes you do, has been your GREATEST ENEMY, you have had the GREATEST FRIEND for the last 50 years, which the Socialist-Americans have not been able to kill, even though the SA's have been trying hard to do so for so long.

This GREATEST FRIEND of yours has kept the TRUE SPIRIT of the Real America alive and well in your soul, when nobody else could. This GREATEST FRIEND has kept the fire of Real Americanism lit in your brain, when nobody else could. This GREATEST FRIEND has reminded you over and over again of the true definition of freedom, when nobody else could. This GREATEST FRIEND has reminded you over and over again of who our founders were, how they thought, what type of government they gave us, and what you have to do to get it back, when nobody else could. This GREATEST FRIEND would never let you forget your real identity, who you really are, or who you really wish to become, when nobody else could. This GREATEST FRIEND would never allow you to forget the true definition of courage as not being the absence of fear, but the mastery over it, when nobody else could. This GREATEST FRIEND would never let the thought die in your being that the fundamental purpose of your life is TO LIVE FREE, or DIE TRYING TO.

This GREATEST FRIEND has been HOLLY-WOOD.

Without Hollywood, the Real-American soul in you, which you inherited from our founders, would have

DIED a long time ago, and unbreakable concrete rigor mortis would have set in by now.

Real-Americans whose RA souls have not died yet, love (really love) movies like: Tom Cruise in TOP GUN; Eddie Murphy in BEVERLY HILLS COP; Sylvester Stallone in ROCKY, FIRST BLOOD, and RAMBO; Clint Eastwood in DIRTY HARRY and cowboy movies; Jo Don Baker in WALKING TALL; Sean Connery in JAMES BOND movies; Charles Bronson in DEATH WISH; Sally Fields in NORMA RAE; the actresses in NINE TO FIVE; Harrison Ford in STAR WARS; Ralph Macchio in THE KARATE KID; Lou Gosset and the young man in IRON EAGLE; Christopher Reeves and Margot Kidder in SUPERMAN; and hundreds more.

Older Real-American souls were inspired by Hollywood actresses and actors like the Duke, John Wayne, Steve McQueen, Paul Newman, Yul Brynner, Jimmy Stewart, James Cagney, Gregory Peck, Burt Lancaster, Kirk Douglas, Charleton Heston, Katharine Hepburn, Spencer Tracy, Lauren Bacall, Humphrey Bogart, Bette Davis, and many others.

These great actors and actresses in their great movies INSPIRED THE SOULS of all Real-Americans, because all RA's never lost the built-in desire to be heroes and heroines, and free-spirits, and to fight against all odds, to fight for right against an oppressive, freedom-stifling bullyism system, to risk their lives as UNDERDOGS, to say and DO whatever it took to WIN, and to NEVER QUIT. Go for it!

In every Real-American's mind, heart, and soul, Hollywood also reinforced, and continues to reinforce the feelings about who and what a Real-American NEVER WANTS TO BECOME: namely, a weak, tame, docile, dependent, controversy-avoiding, go-along-with-the-flow, cowardly Pseudo-American, or a no-good, freedom-restricting, bully bastard Socialist-American bureaucratic tyrant.

Hollywood is the GREATEST FRIEND of all Real-Americans, and another way of saying Hollywood is SHOW BUSINESS. Hollywood and SHOW-BIZ are the GREATEST FRIENDS of all Real-Americans. SHOW-BIZ includes TV, famous singers, and rock-n-roll music stars and groups.

This element of SHOW-Biz has inspired all Real-Americans with the RA free spirit of Magnum, Moonlighting, and many other shows down through the years; and with the free spirit singing greats like Frank, Elvis, Neil, and Bruce; and with the outrageous, revolutionary rock groups which light the fire of RA's fighting spirit.

Without HOLLYWOOD and SHOW-BIZ, the true spirit of Real America which we inherited from our founders would probably never be able to rise again. Because of HOLLYWOOD and SHOW-BIZ, we RA's shall overcome. WE SHALL OVERCOME.

All truth is simple. All error is complex. All truth is light. All error is darkness. All truth is tranquility. All error is chaos. All truth is acceptance. All error is confusion. It is easy to understand that $1 + 1 = 2$. It is hard to understand that $1 + 1 = 3$. All truth is simple. All error is complex.

The simple truth is that we have VOTED ourselves INTO Socialism. The simple solution is that we can VOTE ourselves OUT of Socialism, and back again into Americanism. It is a simple process of REVERSAL.

The simple truth is that we have voted to make

the government our boss. The simple solution is that we can vote to make ourselves the boss again. It is a simple process of reversal.

The simple truth is that we have been voting ourselves INTO slavery. The simple solution is that we can vote ourselves OUT of slavery, and BACK into freedom. It is a simple process of reversal.

The simple truth is that we have voted Real-Americans out of office, and REPLACED them with Socialist-Americans. The simple solution is that we can vote the Socialist-Americans out of office, and REPLACE them with Real-Americans again. It is a simple process of reversal.

The simple truth is that we have VOTED our Real America out, and REPLACED her with the Counterfeit America. The simple solution is that we can VOTE the Counterfeit America out, and REPLACE it with our Real America again. It is a simple process of reversal.

But guess what? The truth is simple. The solution is simple. But the successful implementation of the solution is NOT EASY. In fact, it will be very difficult to accomplish.

It is analogous to your doctor telling you that the truth is very simple: your heart is defective. Also the solution is very simple: you need a heart transplant. But the successful implementation of the simple solution is not easy to accomplish.

Or the situation we now find ourselves in is also analogous to your doctor telling you that the truth is very simple: you have a malignant cancer. Also the solution is very simple: it must be cut out. But the successful implementation of the simple solution is not easy.

Or the situation we now find ourself in is also analagous to your doctor telling you that the truth is very simple: you have amnesia. Also the solution is very simple: you need shock treatments. But the successful implementation of the simple solution is not easy.

Simple but not easy. The simple solution to all of our major problems in these United States is for you to have a RA heart transplant, for you to cut the cancer of socialistic thinking out of your head, and for you to shock the PA and SA induced amnesia out of your brain by REMEMBERING that you are SUPPOSED TO BE a Real-American. Simple, but not easy.

Recognizing, accepting, and admitting TO OTHERS that you have discovered your true identity as a Real-American is STEP ONE. Recognizing the identity of everyone around you, but ESPECIALLY of the politicians REPRESENTING YOU in your federal, state, and local districts is STEP TWO .

If you recognize the politicians representing you as Socialist-Americans, voting them OUT of office and REPLACING them with Real-Americans is STEP THREE.

This is the simple Real American Movement (RAM) 1-2-3 Freedom Plan. One, identify yourself. Two, identify the enemy. Three, vote accordingly. RAM's 1-2-3 Freedom Plan. Simple, but not easy.

Step One (identify yourself) can be accomplished by studying UNCOMMON SENSE, particularly Part I, Chapter 8 and Part III, Chapter 10 .

Step Two (identify the enemy) can be accomplished with citizens OUTSIDE of government by asking them WHERE they think rights come from, and then asking them for their DEFINITIONS of freedom, patriotism, and Americanism; and with citizens INSIDE of government, you can simply APPLY the Real American Syllogism on EVERYTHING they say and do; and lastly, you can read RAM's Voting Record Scorecard (VRS), which will be mailed to every registered voter in the country, as soon as possible.

Politicians can CONFUSE YOU all they want on where they stand on all the issues, but how they ACTUALLY vote on those issues will tell you where they REALLY stand. And politicians CANNOT HIDE from their voting record.

RAM's VRS will POSITIVELY IDENTIFY which politicians are voting like Real-Americans, and which are voting like Socialist-Americans. Actions speak louder than words.

Step Three (vote accordingly) is up to you.

Sounds simple, right? It is simple. But easy to accomplish it is not. Every Socialist-American in Counterfeit America whom you speak to personally about this subject will scream bloody murder, telling you that RAM is crazy, and also telling you that YOU are crazy if you believe RAM. And every Pseudo-American in Counterfeit America whom you speak to personally about this subject will say, "What the hell are you talking about, and why?"

And when RAM soon reaches the stage where the mass media can no longer IGNORE us, they will flood the ink and air waves with SOPHISTICATED PROPAGANDA regarding super-patriotism, chauvinistic nationalism, anachronistic jingoism, and the argument that "these RAMROD people think that they are better Americans than me and you, HA—HA—

HA—HA—HA—HA—HA—HA—HA—HA—HA
—HA—HA—HA—HA—HA—HA—HA—HA—
HA—HA—HA—HA—HA—HA—HA—HA—HA
—HA—HA—HA—HA—HA—HA—HA—HA—
HA—HA—HA—HA—HA—HA—HA—HA—HA
—HA—HA—HA—HA—HA—HA—HA—HA—
HA—HA—HA—HA—HA—HA—HA—HA—HA
—HA—HA—HA—HA—HA—HA—HA—HA—
HA—HA—HA—HA—HA—HA—HA—HA—HA
—HA—HA—HA—HA—HA—HA—HA—HA—
HA—HA—HA—HA—HA—HA—HA—HA—HA
—HA—HA—HA—HA—HA—HA—HA—HA—
HA—HA—HA—HA—HA—HA—HA—HA—HA
—HA—HA—HA—HA—HA—HA—HA—HA—
HA—HA—HA—HA—HA—HA—HA—HA—HA
—HA—HA—HA—HA!" Glory, glory, hallelujah, the
fun is coming. We just can't wait!

As it was back in 1775, so it is again in the 1990s: the
battle for men's minds. You're all alone. Trust yourself. The truth will set you free. When it does, just act
on it. Remember, courage is not the absence of fear, but
the mastery over it. Practice your mastery over fear.
Practice your courage. Practice your guts. Practice
makes perfect. Be your own person. Go for it! You can
do it.

After you elect ENOUGH Real-Americans to the
Congress, State Houses, and local government bodies,
these Real-Americans of EITHER political party will
vote out of existence, in the least harmful manner (a
gradual phase-out), every local socialistic program,
every state socialistic program, every national socialistic program, and every international socialistic program which exists in Counterfeit America, and hope-

fully, by the year 2000, we will have RETURNED
to the freedom of our Real America which our founders
gave us.

And in the year 2000, your author of UNCOMMON
SENSE, writing now under the pen name of a Real-
American, will reveal him or herself to the public,
because by that date, your author will have reached
an age old enough to legally run for the office of
President of the United States, which he or she intends
to do.

This is a love story, and a conversion experience.
Converts are a SPECIAL people who have the courage
of their convictions to leave their old false beliefs
and practices to embrace their newly-found true beliefs. As a SIGN of their conversion to and love for
the Real America, and also as an ACT OF DEFIANCE
to the socialistic Counterfeit America, Real-American
converts are starting to wear RAM dogtags, RAM
wrist bands, RAM T-shirts, and RAM baseball caps.
These RAM converts are also displaying RAM posters
in their rooms, and RAM bumper stickers on their
cars. These RAM converts are also singing and dancing
to RAM theme songs, and greeting and saying good-
byes to each other using the RAM-adopted, but centuries-old, clenched-fist salute, popularized by hundreds
of our greatest athletes.

The Real-Americans are coming.

This is a love story. A love which demonstrates
itself in ACTIONS as well as words. Real-Americans
understand that rights come from God, and that government is created by them to protect those God-given
rights. RA's understand that one person's rights cannot
tread on another person's rights. RA's understand the
logical principle that you cannot give what you do

not have. RA's believe that if you as an individual have no right to do something, then the government can have no right to do that same thing either. RA's believe in a Republic, not a Democracy. RA's do not believe that the majority has the right to force their will on the minority. RA's understand and believe in the concepts of private property and free enterprise, but RA's are more cause-oriented than money-motivated. RA's believe in the Constitution our founders gave us. RA's believe they are literally the boss of government. RA's understand that government is simply legalized force. RA's do not appreciate being threatened by government. RA's have memorized the true definitions of freedom, patriotism, and Americanism. RA's believe in the Real-American Syllogism and apply the Real-American Syllogism to every governmental action at every governmental level. RA's believe that all gun laws against non-criminal citizens are un-American. In dealing with non-criminal citizens, RA's believe that the only legitimate tool to use is the principle of persuasion, not the un-American principle of government force. RA's understand the irreconcilable difference between a political reformer/revolutionary and a social reformer/revolutionary. RA's feel about SA's like a mongoose feels about a cobra. RA's understand that results count more than intentions. RA's believe in living their lives, not wasting their lives. RA's understand that taxation WITH representation can be just as evil as taxation without it. RA's believe in using fashionable, instinctive patriotic feelings for more important purposes than just selling beer and cars. RA's hate slavery as a concept, as well as an institution. RA's believe that eternal vigilance and courage is the price to maintain freedom.

RA's are willing to pay the price for freedom. RA's believe that war is hell, but that slavery is worse. RA's believe SA's are traitors. RA's love their children and other loved ones enough to realize that NOTHING is more important to leave them than a free country. RA's love freedom more than they love life. RA's believe in resistance to domestic tyranny, even unto death. RA's believe in courage. RA's refuse to be treated like mushrooms. RA's understand that man's greatest enemy has always been his own government. RA's love Mary Ball. RA's love George Washington. RA's love Tom Paine. RA's believe in reality, not technicality. RA's do not believe that "illegal" and "immoral" are the same thing. RA's believe in motivation, not manipulation. RA's do not need authority to act. They are the authority. RA's do not need permission to act. They just act. RA's love our Real America and hate our Counterfeit America. RA's believe that our Counterfeit America is like the hidden portrait of Dorian Gray. RA's do not believe in fighting foreign wars. RA's believe only in fighting on our own soil to defend our Real America. RA's love Robin Hood and Zorro. RA's love Hollywood. RA's love the New Hampshire motto on their automobile license plates. RA's have no respect for anyone, in business or in government, in uniform or not, who bullies people around using the cowardly excuse that they are "just doing their job." RA's are prouder for their having memorized their national joining-sequence number on their RAM dogtags and wrist-bands, than their having memorized the number on their Social Security card which the Counterfeit American government forced them to acquire before they were allowed to hold a job. RA's believe in the principle of NO NEUTRAL-

ITY. RA's know who and what they are. RA's know who and what the enemy is. RA's believe exactly what our founders believed. RA's take all negative criticism of our founders personally, as if that smear was directed towards an actual blood relative of theirs who died while saving their lives. And finally, Real-Americans believe in their slogan: WHATEVER IT TAKES.

There are just TWO more subjects we need to cover before we rest our case to you, the jury. They're called life and death.

Life. The quality of your daily personal existence depends on the ways boys and girls, and men and women get along with each other. The Equal Rights (for women) Movement has been extremely successful in the last 10 years in destroying the major opportunity barriers which had kept women down as second-class citizens for way too long. Women now have available to themselves about the same opportunities available to men.

Life. The success of the Equal Rights Movement has created a whole new generation of intelligently assertive women. Women are now as confident as men have always been, that their opinions count, and most women now are as vocal in expressing those personal opinions as men have always been. Women realize now that they no longer have to "take a back seat" to men.

Life. After some naturally confusing soul searching, and a normal period of adjustment, most men now have accepted the facts that women are now, and always should have been treated in as equal a fashion as men had always been treated.

Life. The bottom line regarding this new relationship

which now exists between men and women is this: they are more HONEST and FAIR with each other today than they have ever been before, and more AP-PRECIATIVE with each other for that honesty and fairness. It's safe to say that this open, honest, fair relationship which now exists between men and women is the HEALTHIEST thing that has happened between the sexes in the last 6,000 years. The traditional battle of the sexes has been disappearing.

So why discuss this subject now? For a very important reason. Today, the battle of the sexes will be RE-APPEARING on the same level which existed in 1775. Think about that.

Real life. Real-American women will have no respect for Pseudo-American men. Real-American men will have no respect for Pseudo-American women. RA women will not date PA men. RA men will not date PA women. RA wives will lose respect for their PA husbands. RA husbands will lose respect for their PA wives. Only Real-American soulmates will stick together from now on. The war against the Socialist-Americans has begun. The war to restore our Real America has begun.

RA—PA—SA identities will become the new criteria for loving relationships between the sexes, and you will realize this fact when someone you feel romantic about asks you the question, "Are you wearing your RAM dogtags tonight? Show me." Or, "Where is your RAM wrist band? Show me."

Remember. All's fair in love and war. And we ARE talking about both.

Concerning death. We are all terminal. Everyone must die. Some day, some how. So what. Would you prefer dying from a lingering heart condition, or an instant heart attack? Would you prefer dying of a lingering cancer? Would you prefer living the last few years of your life in a rest home, and dying peacefully in your sleep of old age? Or shot in bed by a jealous . . . etc. Do you really have a preference? Do you really determine the way you live by the feelings you have about the way you prefer to die?

Life is short. Here today, gone tomorrow. When your time is up, it's up. TS. We all have to go sometime. Why worry about it? You could get hit by lightning, or hit by a car. You could die in a car wreck, or a plane crash. So what.

Does it really matter to you so much about the way you will die? Who cares?

Sane people accept death as an inevitable fact of life, and more often than not, intelligently fear pain and suffering more than eventual death. Sane people realize that the QUALITY of life is more important than the QUANTITY of life. And sane people don't see a hell of a lot of sense in having to physically and mentally suffer terribly before dying. Do you?

Your personal attitude regarding death will determine how you live your life. All Real-Americans have the same personal attitude regarding eventual, inevitable death. This RA attitude regarding death can be expressed this way, very simply: the later the better, but quickly. If you instantly saw through the surface contradiction, and understood the true meaning of this concept instantly, you are probably a Real-American. If you can't understand that statement regarding the RA attitude towards death, it makes no sense trying to explain it to you.

Real-Americans feel about death the same way George felt about it. " 'Tis well."

RA's attempts to destroy the Counterfeit America which the Socialist-American traitors have given us, in order to RESTORE the Real America which our founders gave us, is risky business.

Real-Americans, like our founders before us, are willing to face every possible consequence of our actions on the national and international scenes. And Real-Americans are fully aware of EVERY possible consequence, and have OVERCOME their fear of every one of them. Just like our founders. Because we love freedom EXACTLY the way they did. And we REFUSE to live like slaves. Just like our founders refused to live like slaves.

Remember what John Adams said: "We may die . . . die slaves . . . die, it may be, ignominiously and on the scaffold. Be it so. Be it so. If it be the pleasure of Heaven that my country shall require the poor offering of my life, the victim shall be ready . . . But while I do live, let me have a country, or at least the hope of a country, and that a free country . . . Independence now, and Independence forever."

At least the hope of a country, and that a free country.

Notice John did not say "Interdependence" with foreign countries because of nuclear blackmail. Every one of our founders were NATIONALISTS. NONE WERE INTERNATIONALISTS.

Remember what Patrick Henry said: "Is life so dear, or PEACE so sweet, as to be purchased at the price of chains and slavery? Forbid it, Almighty God! I know not what course others may take; but as for me, give me liberty or give me death!"

Even if it might mean a possible nuclear holocaust? You're damn right! Pat would say "yes," even at that risk, because NO FORM OF BLACKMAIL by the enemy, however terrible sounding, could cause our founders to give up their fight for freedom, and to VOLUNTARILY live as slaves. Remember the story of Declaration signer Abraham Clark when the English used the blackmail of his two cherished sons imprisoned aboard the Jersey in New York Harbor.

Our founders were warriors, and in the warrior's code, there is no surrender, FOR ANY REASON. Besides, our founders were astute students of history, and were intimately familiar with what ancient Rome did to ancient Carthage, so they understood well that surrender to foreign enemies for any reason meant certain SLAUGHTER before the inevitable SLAVERY anyway, with the enemy using the rationale that they need to kill every POTENTIAL resister, in order to break everyone else's will to resist, so that the enemy can govern easily after the takeover.

History and our founders' own personal experience with the Redcoats had taught them the lesson of war called TERRORISM. Our founders understood that those who fail to learn from history are doomed to repeat it. And our founders were not SUICIDAL FOOLS like the ancient Carthaginians and our Pseudo-Americans of today.

Terrorism BEFORE an internal or external enemy takeover of a country means the enemy's use of violence on the target population to intimidate the eventual victims into submissive silence, and actual non-resistance to the takeover artists. Terrorism on the victims of a country immediately AFTER their surrender to an internal or external enemy means mass murder, torture, and imprisonment of large segments of the victim population, in order to break the takeover victims' POTENTIAL will to resist the enemy any longer, since that resistance looks so futilely suicidal, and with no resistance left, the enemy has an easier time ruling PEACEFULLY.

Can you now understand why the Russian Socialists murdered 10 million of their OWN innocent people AFTER their takeover, and why they still keep 10 million of their OWN innocent people as slaves, guarded by dogs and machine guns, in the concentration camps and forced-labor camps of the Gulag Archipelago? And why the Chinese Socialists murdered 30 million of their OWN innocent people AFTER their takeover, and why they still keep millions of their OWN innocent people in their concentration and slave-labor camps? Terrorism after a takeover WORKS. It destroys all the people's POTENTIAL resistance to their conquerors.

The proof that terrorism works is the reason so-called Americans return from the U.S.S.R. (the Union of Soviet Socialist Republics which are NOT true republics) and from the People's Socialist Republic of China (which is also NOT a true republic) with glowing reports of how happy, content, and peaceable all of the natives living there behave. The natives realize that if they refuse to behave that docile way, they will be imprisoned or shot.

Smart Socialists running any government prefer confiscating all of the people's firearms BEFORE building the murderous concentration camps. Socialists don't like the thought of getting shot at while attempting to progress to total government enslavement of the people.

Our Socialist-American politicians running our government are smart. This explains why in recent years they have introduced hundreds of bills in Congress to register and confiscate guns which are in the hands of the targeted victims, we the people. Disarmament of a targeted population is one of the standard tactics of the Socialists. Remember Lexington and Concord?

Remembering the Real-American attitude regarding a preference for death (the later the better, but quickly) rather than slavery, if nuclear war is ever in the cards (and we say: who cares?), if it happens here on our soil, every Real-American prays that the BOMB WILL LAND RIGHT ON THEIR HEAD! REALLY! NO FOOLING!

When Teddy Roosevelt was our President, while our country was still the Real America, Barbary pirates off the coast of Tripoli, led by some jerk named Raisuli, had kidnapped an American citizen named Perdicaris, and were holding him for financial ransom. "Not one penny for tribute" was a RA slogan then. Teddy sent an American warship loaded with Marines to anchor off the coast of Tripoli, and had the American captain deliver a written message to Raisuli which simply said, "Perdicaris alive, or Raisuli dead." Within a matter of hours, Perdicaris was aboard the ship, alive and well, and very proud of his country.

When the Real-Americans we elect to Congress RESTORE our Real America, we will be sending a similar message to every tyrant still holding even one of our POW's from the Vietnam War. And we will mean it, just like Teddy Roosevelt meant it.

2500 American POW's and MIA's never came back from Vietnam. Many are still alive and living in hell as you are reading this. What if one were your grandfather, or your father, or your brother, or your son, or your best friend? What would you do? If this were the case, what would you want your government to do? Hell, what if you yourself were the POW? What would you want your government to do? What if the POW was your boyfriend, or your girlfriend, or your husband, or your wife?

In the last few years alone, there have been more than 900 eye witness accounts of live sightings of American POW's in Southeast Asia by escaped oriental refugees. And all of these Asian escapee witnesses, testifying before a U.S. Senate Subcommittee have passed multiple lie-detector tests.

Real-Americans feel: whatever it takes to get our POW's back. And we are NOT talking about buying them back!

As soon as we vote the Socialist-American traitors out of the Congress, and replace them with Real-Americans, volunteers are going over there to get our boys back. Pseudo-Americans try real hard to FORGET that our boys are still over there. Real-Americans will NEVER FORGET!

When Real-Americans in Congress restore the Real America, we will stop ALL aid to and trade with the Socialist slavemasters in control of every foreign Socialist government. When we do this, EVERY Socialist government in the world will collapse, and glorious freedom will be restored to ALL the people of the world. Remember Estonia, Latvia, and Lithuania.

Viva Cuba libre, viva Mexico libre, etc., etc., etc.

And by the year 2,000 A.D., the treason trials of ALL the Socialist-American businessmen and their stooges in every level of government, and in every other area of our national life, will begin.

This has been, and still is, a love story. Love. You've heard of it? Believe it or not, love is what this thing is all about. Being in love with our real country, beautiful Real America. In love with Real America, forever and ever. For what she is. For what we are. Both the same. Free spirits. It's in our blood.

Like George Washington, don't be afraid of anything, don't be afraid of anyone. Don't ask anyone for permission. Live free, and just act to do what you think is right.

Frederick Douglass made a prophetic statement regarding freedom on August 4, 1857, because he foresaw what was then coming. It is the PERFECT message to all Pseudo-Americans. He said: "Those who profess to favor freedom, and yet deprecate agitation, are men who want crops without plowing up the ground. They want rain without thunder and lightning. They want the ocean without the awful roar of its waters. This struggle may be a moral one; or it may be a physical one; or it may be both moral and physical; but it must be a struggle. Power concedes nothing without a demand. It never did and it never will. Find out just what people will submit to, and you have found out the exact amount of injustice and wrong which will be imposed upon them; and these will continue until they are resisted with either words or blows, or with both. THE LIMITS OF TYRANTS ARE PRESCRIBED BY THE ENDURANCE OF THOSE WHOM THEY OPPRESS."

And Tom Paine, the Father of Real America's Independence, who not only wrote about freedom, but also actually took up arms and marched and fought along side of George Washington in many shooting battles, was asked by George to write something additional to his COMMON SENSE pamphlet, which would inspire his Continental Army soldiers to continue the fight in the darkest hours of the Revolution, when defeat was staring them all in the face, because desertions were so numerous, and re-enlistments were so few, because the rebel soldiers and militiamen continued to go back home to plant and/or harvest crops to feed their families, and so many of them never returned to fight.

It was months after our Continental Congress proclaimed our Declaration of Independence from England, and acquiescing to George's request, Tom wrote the PERFECT message which slowed up the desertions, and increased the number of re-enlistments. Tom's new message, called CRISIS, saved our Revolution. Here is part of what he said in his CRISIS pamphlet, and it is a PERFECT message to all Real-Americans of today: "These are the times that try men's souls; the summer soldier and sunshine patriot will, in this crisis, shrink from the service of his country; but he that stands it now, deserves the love and thanks of man and woman. Tyranny, like hell, is not easily conquered; yet we have this consolation with us, that the harder the conflict, the more glorious the triumph. What we obtain too cheap, we ESTEEM too lightly: 'Tis dearness only that gives every thing its value. Heaven knows how to put a proper price upon its goods; and it would be strange indeed, if so celestial an article as freedom should not be highly rated."

Have you ESTEEMED freedom too lightly, because you obtained it for nothing?

Where is your imagination? If someone literally risked their life to save yours, and did save yours, but they died in the process, wouldn't you love, remember and cherish that savior for the rest of your life? This is EXACTLY what our founders did for you. They bought your freedom at the expense of their lives. They gave up their lives willingly so that they and YOU could live free.

And remember: freedom is the condition resulting from never needing permission to act from the humans we allow to run the government for us.

Real-Americans appreciate so much the gift of freedom which they inherited from our founders that RA's are willing to fight to restore and preserve it for future generations, and Real-Americans take the Socialist-American RAPE of the Real America personally. Because Tom Paine had such tremendous insight into human nature, he prefaced his COMMON SENSE pamphlet with a very perceptive statement concerning the reaction he anticipated from his audience regarding his logical analysis, and daring suggested course of action. What Tom said to his 1776 audience of his COMMON SENSE, applies equally to the reaction RAM anticipates from our 1990s audience of our UNCOMMON SENSE, regarding our similar type of analysis, and suggested course of action. Here it is: "Perhaps the sentiments contained in the following pages, are not YET sufficiently FASHIONABLE to procure them general favor; a long habit of NOT thinking a thing WRONG, gives it a superficial appearance of being RIGHT, and raises at first a formidable outcry in defense of CUSTOM. " Speaking in modern lingo, Tom seemed to be saying something like this: a handful of people always make everything happen, while everybody else watch things happen, or don't know what happened.

Look out for this reaction in yourself and in others,

and by the way, welcome to the BATTLE for men and women's minds.

What is your IDENTITY? Are you a Real-American, a Pseudo-American, or a Socialist-American? There are no other categories. There are no other options. You cannot be a little bit of all three, or some of two. You can only be all of one.

Now look at yourself in a mirror, straight into your eyes, the windows of your soul. If you can't hold that glance for more than a second or two, and you automatically look away, maybe you don't like what you see. Maybe you see a gutless faker, and a Pseudo-American. Every time you shave, or comb your hair, or put on your face, the mirror mirror on the wall, will tell you whether you are the bravest of them all. Know thyself, and to thine own self be true. Every mirror will now become your newest friend, or your newest enemy. And remember, breaking them is bad luck. And TS, you can't break 'em all.

Real-Americans look into the mirror, defiant and proud, and right into everyone else's eyes, and ask them for their identity. If the people look away, they are PA's or SA's. The eyes have it, and tell ALL as they always have, and always will.

This has been, and still is, a love story. Love for freedom. Love for our Real America. If the political reformer Real-Americans find in the 1990s what our founders found back in 1775, that they cannot VOTE themselves into freedom, and if after trying so hard and failing, the Socialist-Americans decide to come to take our guns as the final step to total tyranny and slavery, it will be Lexington and Concord all over again. As it was back then, so will it be again.

Whatever it takes.

Oh, you who dare oppose, not only the tyranny, but the tyrant, not only the Socialism, but the Socialist-American, STAND FORTH!

P. S. to our Real America: We love you. You'll see. Whatever it takes.

FREE!
CATALOG

OF OTHER TITLES

CALL

(800) 729-4131

OR

WRITE

AMERICA WEST
P. O. BOX 3300
BOZEMAN, MT 59772

QUANTITY DISCOUNTS AVAILABLE

THE TRUTH WILL SET YOU FREE!